VIDEO COMPRESSION

Edited by **Amal Punchihewa**

Video Compression
Edited by Amal Punchihewa

Published by InTech

Janeza Trdine 9, 51000 Rijeka, Croatia

Publishing Process Manager Vedran Greblo

Technical Editor Teodora Smiljanic

Cover Designer InTech Design Team

Additional hard copies can be obtained from orders@intechopen.com

Video Compression, Edited by Amal Punchihewa
p. cm.
ISBN 978-953-51-0422-3

For EU product safety concerns:
IN TECH d.o.o., Prolaz Marije Krucifikse Kozulić 3, 51000 Rijeka, Croatia, info@intechopen.com or visit our website at intechopen.com.

Meet the editor

Dr. Amal gained his BE, specializing in Electronics and Telecommunication with honours in 1986, ME from the Technical University of Eindhoven, The Netherlands in digital video signal processing. Amal has worked in both academia and industry over the past twenty-seven years, including as a research engineer at the national television in Sri Lanka. In 1994 he became a senior lecturer at the University of Moratuwa, and then joined Massey University. His Ph.D was on framework for rapid evaluation of image and video compression artefacts objectively. His current research interests are objective assessment of compression artefacts and image processing for surveillance, distributed video coding, routing algorithms, cooperative communication for next generation networks, IPTV and its Quality of experience, implementation of signal processing algorithms in FPGA, signal processing for precision agriculture, multimedia communication and care of the elderly. Amal is a registered, chartered professional engineer, ITU-Expert, Senior Broadcast Consultant, fellow-IET, a professional member of IPENZ and a life member of the Sri Lanka Association for Advancement of Science. In 2000 he was awarded the Wimalasurendra award in recognition of the contribution he made to the broadcasting development by the Institution of Engineers Sri Lanka.

Contents

Preface

Visual compression has been a very active field of research and development for over 20 years, leading to many different compression systems and to the definition of international standards. There is likely to be a continued need for better compression efficiency, as video content becomes increasingly ubiquitous and places unprecedented pressure on upcoming new applications in the future. At the same time, the challenge of handling ever more diverse content coded in a wide variety of formats makes reconfigurable coding a potentially useful prospect.

This book aims to bring together selected recent advances, applications and some original results in the area of image and video compression. They can be useful for researchers, engineers, graduate and postgraduate students, experts in this area and hopefully also for people interested generally in computer science, video coding and video quality.

Regarding the organization of the book, it is divided into three parts having seven chapters in total. Chapters are clustered into compression, motion estimation and quality.

The first chapter presents a review of techniques proposed compressed sensing. Compressive Sensing is a new field and its application to video systems is even more recent. There are many avenues for further research and thorough quantitative analyses are still lacking. Number of encoding strategies that has been adopted is described.

Chapter two analyses the transcoding framework for video communications between mobile devices. In addition, it is proposed a WZ to H.264/AVC transcoder designed to support mobile-to-mobile video communications. Since the transcoder device accumulates the highest complexity from both video coders, reducing the time spent in this process is an important goal. This chapter also presents two approaches to speed-up WZ decoding and H.264/AVC encoding.

Chapter three presents a few evaluations and analysis that characterize the loss in perceived interpretability of motion imagery arising from various compression methods and compression rates. Evaluation of image compression for motion imagery illustrates how interpretability-based methods can be applied to the analysis of the image chain. The chapter also presents both objective image metrics and analysts' assessments of various compressed products.

Chapter four presents an overview of H.264 motion estimation and its types and also the various estimation criterions that decides the complexity of the chosen algorithm.

Chapter five is a systematic review of the pixel domain based global motion estimation approaches. The chapter discusses shortcomings in noise filtering and computational cost, the improvement approaches including hierarchical global motion estimation, partial pixel set based global motion estimation and compressed domain based global motion estimation are provided. Four global motion based applications including GMC/LMC in MPEG-4 video coding standard, global motion based sport video shot classification, GM/LM based error concealment and text occluded region recovery are described in this chapter.

Chapter six argues that exploiting saliency-based video compression is a challenging and exciting area of research and especially nowadays when saliency models include more and more top-down information and manages to better and better predict real human gaze. Multimedia applications are a continuously evolving domain and compression algorithms must also evolve and adapt to new applications. The explosion of portable devices with less bandwidth and smaller screens, but also the future semantic TV/web and its object-based description will lead in the future to a higher importance of saliency-based algorithms for multimedia data repurposing and compression.

The large amount of studies developed for this purpose related to quality assessment gives a general idea about the importance of this theme in video compression. The evolution of metrics and techniques is constant, finding the best ways of evaluating the quality of video sequences.

Chapter seven describes a state of the art in quality assessment and techniques of subjective and objective assessment, with the most common artefacts and impairments derived from compression and transmission.

I wish to thank all the authors who have contributed to this book. I hope that by reading this book you will get many useful ideas for your own research, which will help to bridge the gap between video compression technology and applications.

I also hope this book is enjoyable to read and will further contribute to video compression, which requires a further interest and attention in both research and application fields.

Dr Amal Punchihewa
PhD, MEEng, BSC(Eng)Hons, CEng, FIET, MIPENZ,
MIEEE, MSLAAS , MCS, Leader - Multi-Media Research Group,
The School of Engineering and Advanced Technology, Massey University (Turitea),
New Zealand

Part 1

Compression

1

Compressive Video Coding: A Review of the State-Of-The-Art

Muhammad Yousuf Baig, Edmund M-K. Lai and Amal Punchihewa
Massey University
School of Engineering and Advanced Technology
Palmerston North
New Zealand

1. Introduction

Video coding and its related applications have advanced quite substantially in recent years. Major coding standards such as MPEG [1] and H.26x [2] are well developed and widely deployed. These standards are developed mainly for applications such as DVDs where the compressed video is played over many times by the consumer. Since compression only needs to be performed once while decompression (playback) is performed many times, it is desirable that the decoding/decompression process can be done as simply and quickly as possible. Therefore, essentially all current video compression schemes, such as the various MPEG standards as well as H.264 [1, 2] involve a complex encoder and a simple decoder. The exploitation of spatial and temporal redundancies for data compression at the encoder causes the encoding process to be typically 5 to 10 times more complex computationally than the decoder [3]. In order that video encoding can be performed in real time at frame rates of 30 frames per second or more, the encoding process has to be performed by specially designed hardware, thus increasing the cost of cameras.

In the past ten years, we have seen substantial research and development of large sensor networks where a large number of sensors are deployed. For some applications such as video surveillance and sports broadcasting, these sensors are in fact video cameras. For such systems, there is a need to re-evaluate conventional strategies for video coding. If the encoders are made simpler, then the cost of a system involving tens or hundreds of cameras can be substantially reduced in comparison with deploying current camera systems. Typically, data from these cameras can be sent to a single decoder and aggregated. Since some of the scenes captured may be correlated, computational gain can potentially be achieved by decoding these scenes together rather than separately. . Decoding can be simple reconstruction of the video frames or it can be combined with detection algorithms specific to the application at hand. Thus there are benefits in combing reduced complexity cameras with flexible decoding processes to deliver modern applications which are not anticipated when the various video coding standards are developed.

Recently, a new theory called Compressed Sensing (CS) [4, 5, 6] has been developed which provides us with a completely new approach to data acquisition. In essence, CS tells us that for signals which possess some "sparsity" properties, the sampling rate required to reconstruct these signals with good fidelity can be much lower than the lower bound specified by Shannon's sampling theorem. Since video signals contain substantial amounts of redundancy, they are sparse signals and CS can potentially be applied. The simplicity of the encoding process is traded off by a more complex, iterative decoding process. The reconstruction process of CS is usually formulated as an optimization problem which potentially allows one to tailor the objective function and constraints to the specific application. Even though practical cameras that make use of CS are still in their very early days, the concept can be applied to video coding. A lower sampling rate implies less energy required for data processing, leading to lower power requirements for the camera. Furthermore, the complexity of the encoder can be further simplified by making use of distributed source coding [21, 22]. The distributed approach provides ways to encode video frames without exploiting any redundancy or correlation between video frames captured by the camera. The combined use of CS and distributed source coding can therefore serve as the basis for the development of camera systems where the encoder is less complex than the decoder.

We shall first provide a brief introduction to Compressed Sensing in the next Section. This is followed by a review of current research in video coding using CS.

2. Compressed sensing

Shannon's uniform sampling theorem [7, 8] provides a lower bound on the rate by which an analog signal needs to be sampled in order that the sampled signal fully represents the original. If a signal $f(t)$ contains no frequencies higher than ω_{max} radians per second, then it can be completely determined by samples that are spaced $T = 2\pi/\omega_{max}$ seconds apart. $f(x)$ can be reconstructed perfectly using the these samples $f(nT)$ by

$$f(t) = \sum_{\{k \in z\}} f(kT) sinc\ (t/T - k) \tag{1.1}$$

The uniform samples $f(nT)$ of $f(t)$ may be interpreted as coefficients of basis functions obtained by shifting and scaling of the sinc function. For high bandwidth signals such as video, the amount of data generated based on a sampling rate of at least twice the bandwidth is very high. Fortunately, most of the raw data can be thrown away with almost no perceptual loss. This is the result of lossy compression techniques based on orthogonal transforms. In image and video compression, the discrete cosine transform (DCT) and wavelet transform have been found to be most useful. The standard procedure goes as follows. The orthogonal transform is applied to the raw image data, giving a set of transform coefficients. Those coefficients that have values smaller than a certain threshold are discarded. Only the remaining significant coefficients, typically only a small subset of the original, are encoded, reducing the amount of data that represents the image. This means that if there is a way to acquire only the significant transform coefficients directly by sampling, then the sampling rate can be much lower than that required by Shannon's theorem.

Emmanuel Candes, together with Justin Romberg and Terry Tao, came up with a theory of Compressed Sensing (CS) [9] that can be applied to signals, such as audio, image and video that are *sparse* in some domain. This theory provides a way, at least theoretically, to acquire signals at a rate potentially much lower than the Nyquist rate given by Shannon's sampling theorem. CS has already inspired more than a thousand papers from 2006 to 2010 [9].

2.1 Key Elements of compressed sensing

Compressed Sensing [4-6, 10] is applicable to signals that are sparse in some domain. Sparsity is a general concept and it expresses the idea that the information rate or the signal significant content may be much smaller than what is suggested by its bandwidth. Most natural signals are redundant and therefore compressible in some suitable domain. We shall first define the two principles, sparsity and incoherence, on which the theory of CS depends.

2.1.1 Sparsity

Sparsity is important in Compressed Sensing as it determines how efficient one can acquire signals non-adaptively. The most common definition of sparsity used in compressed sensing is as follows. Let $f \in R^n$ be a vector which represents a signal which can be expanded in an orthonormal basis $\psi = [\psi_1 \psi_2 \cdots \psi_n]$ as

$$f(t) = \sum_{i-1}^{n} x_i \psi_i \tag{1.2}$$

Here, the coefficients $x_i = \langle f, \psi_i \rangle$. In matrix form, (1.2) becomes

$$\boldsymbol{f} = \boldsymbol{\Psi x} \tag{1.3}$$

When all but a few of the coefficients x_i are zero, we say that f is sparse in a strict sense. If S denotes the number of non-zero coefficients with $S \ll n$, then f is said to be S-sparse. In practice, most compressible signals have only a few significant coefficients while the rest have relatively small magnitudes. If we set these small coefficients to zero in the way that it is done in lossy compression, then we have a sparse signal.

2.1.2 Incoherence

We start by considering two different orthonormal bases, Φ and Ψ, of R^n. The coherence between these two bases is defined in [10] by

$$\mu(\Phi, \Psi) = \sqrt{n} \cdot \max_{1 \le k,j \le n} |\langle \phi_k, \psi_k \rangle| \tag{1.4}$$

which gives us the largest correlation between any two elements of the two bases. It can be shown that

$$\mu(\Phi, \Psi) \in [1, \sqrt{n}] \tag{1.5}$$

Sparsity and incoherence together quantify the compressibility of a signal. A signal is more compressible if it has higher sparsity in some representation domain Ψ that is less coherent to the sensing (or sampling) domain Φ. Interestingly, random matrices are largely incoherent with any fixed basis [18].

2.1.3 Random sampling

Let X be a discrete time random process and let $\boldsymbol{x} = \{x[1], \ldots x[N]\}$ be a vector of N real-valued samples of X. If the representation of x in a transform domain Ψ given by s, then

$$\boldsymbol{x} = \boldsymbol{\Psi s} = \sum_{i-1}^{N} s_i \psi_i \tag{1.6}$$

Here $\boldsymbol{\Psi} = [\psi_1, \psi_2 \ldots \psi_N]$ is the transform basis matrix and $\boldsymbol{s} = [s_1 \ldots s_N]$ is the vector of weighted coefficients where $s_i =< x, \psi_i >$.

Consider a general linear measurement process that computes $M < N$ inner products of $y_i = \langle x, \phi_j \rangle$ between $\boldsymbol{x}$ and a collection of vectors $\{\phi_j\}_1^M$. Let $\boldsymbol{\Phi}$ denote the $M \times N$ matrix with the measurement vectors ϕ_j as rows. Then $\boldsymbol{y}$ is given by

$$\boldsymbol{y} = \boldsymbol{\Phi x} = \boldsymbol{\Phi \Psi x} = \boldsymbol{\Theta s} \tag{1.7}$$

where $\boldsymbol{\Theta} = \boldsymbol{\Phi\Psi}$. If $\boldsymbol{\Phi}$ is fixed, then the measurements are not adaptive or depend on the structure of the signal $\boldsymbol{x}$ [6]. The minimum number of measurements needed to reconstruct the original signal depends on the matrices $\boldsymbol{\Phi}$ and $\boldsymbol{\Psi}$.

Theorem 1 [11]. Let $f \in R^N$ has a discrete coefficient sequence $\boldsymbol{x}$ in the basis $\boldsymbol{\Psi}$. Let $\boldsymbol{x}$ be S-sparse. Select M measurements in the domain $\boldsymbol{\Phi}$ uniformly at random. Then if

$$M \geq C \cdot \mu^2(\Phi, \Psi) \cdot S \log N \tag{1.8}$$

for some positive constant C, then with high probability, x can be reconstructed using the following convex optimization program:

$$\min_{\tilde{x}} \|\tilde{x}\|_{l1} \; subject\ to\ y_k = \langle \phi_k, \Psi\tilde{x} \rangle, \forall\, k \in J \tag{1.9}$$

where J denotes the index set of the M randomly chosen measurements.

This is an important result and provides the requirement for successful reconstruction. It has the following three implications [10]:

i. The role of the coherence in above equation is transparent – the smaller the coherence between the sensing and basis matrices, the fewer the number of measurements needed.
ii. It provides support that there will be no information loss by measuring any set of m coefficients, which may be far less than the original signal size.
iii. The signal f can be exactly recovered without assuming any knowledge about the non-zero coordinates of x or their amplitudes.

2.1.4 CS Reconstruction

The reconstruction problem in CS involves taking the M measurements $\boldsymbol{y}$ to reconstruct the length-N signal x that is K-sparse, given the random measurement matrix $\boldsymbol{\Phi}$ and the basis matrix $\boldsymbol{\Psi}$. Since $M < N$, this is an ill-conditioned problem. The classical approach to solving ill-conditioned problems of this kind is to minimize the l_2 norm. The general problem is given by

$$\hat{s} = \arg\min \|s'\|_2 \ such\ that\ \mathbf{\Theta}s' = \mathbf{y} \quad (1.10)$$

However, it has been proven that this l_2 minimization will never return a K-sparse solution. Instead, it can only produce a non-sparse solution [6]. The reason is that the l_2 norm measures the energy of the signal and signal sparsity properties could not be incorporated in this measure.

The l_0 norm counts the number of non-zero entries and therefore allows us to specify the sparsity requirement. The optimization problem using this norm can be stated as

$$\hat{s} = \arg\min\|s'\|_0 \ such\ that\ \mathbf{\Theta}s' = \mathbf{y} \quad (1.11)$$

There is a high probability of obtaining a solution using only $M = K + 1$ i.i.d Gaussian measurements [10]. However, the solution produced is numerically unstable [6]. It turns out that optimization based on the l_1 norm is able to exactly recover K sparse signals with high probability using only $M \geq cK \log N/K$ i.i.d Gaussian measurements [4, 5]. The convex optimization problem is given by

$$\hat{s} = \arg\min\|s'\|_1 \ such\ that\ \Theta s' = y \quad (1.12)$$

Which can be reduced to a linear program. Algorithms based on Basis Pursuit [12] can be used to solve this problem with a computational complexity of $O(N^3)$ [4].

3. Compressed Video Sensing (CVS)

Research into the use of CS in video applications has only started very recently. We shall now briefly review what has been reported in the open literature.

The first use of CS in video processing is proposed in [13]. Their approach is based on the single pixel camera [14]. The camera architecture employs a digital micro mirror array to perform optical calculations of linear projections of an image onto pseudo-random binary patterns. It directly acquires random projections. They have assumed that the image changes slowly enough across a sequence of snapshots which constitutes one frame. They acquired the video sequence using a total of M measurements, which are either 2D or 3D random measurements. For 2D frame-by-frame reconstruction, 2D wavelets are used as the sparsity-inducing basis. For 3D joint reconstruction, 3D wavelets are used. The Matching Pursuit reconstruction algorithm [15] is used for reconstruction.

Another implementation of CS video coding is proposed in [16]. In this implementation, each video frame classified as a reference or non-reference frame. A reference frame (or key frame) is sampled in the conventional manner while non-reference frames are sampled by CS techniques. The sampled reference frame is divided into B non-overlapping blocks each of size $n \times n = N$ pixels whereby discrete cosine transform (DCT) is applied. A compressed sensing test is applied to the DCT coefficients of each block to identify the sparse blocks in the non-reference frame. This test basically involves comparing the number of significant DCT coefficients against a threshold T. If the number of significant coefficients is small, then the block concerned is a candidate for CS to be applied. The sparse blocks are compressively sampled using an i.i.d. Gaussian measurement matrix and an inverse DCT sensing matrix. The remaining blocks are sampled in the traditional way. A block diagram of the encoder is shown in Figure 1.

Signal recovery is performed by the OMP algorithm [17]. In reconstructing compressively sampled blocks, all sampled coefficients with an absolute value less than some constant C are set to zero. Theoretically, if there are $N - K$ non significant DCT coefficients, then at least $M = K + 1$ samples are needed for signal reconstruction [10]. Therefore the threshold is set to $T < N - K$. The choice of values for M, T, and C depends on the video sequence and the size of the blocks. They have proved experimentally that up to 50% of savings in video acquisition is possible with good reconstruction quality.

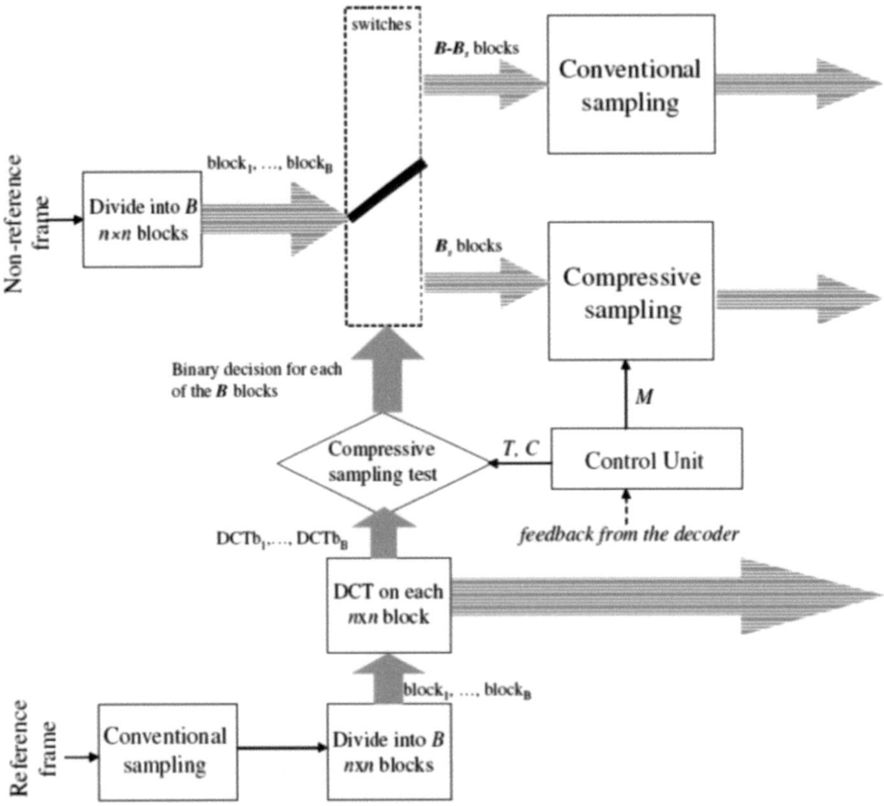

Fig. 1. System Block Diagram of Video Coding Scheme Proposed in [16]

Another technique which uses motion compensation and estimation at the decoder is presented in [18]. At the encoder, only random CS measurements were taken independently from each frame with no additional compression. A multi-scale framework has been proposed for reconstruction which iterates between motion estimation and sparsity-based reconstruction of the frames. It is built around the LIMAT method for standard video compression [19].

LIMAT [19] uses a second generation wavelets to build a fully invertible transform. To incorporate temporal redundancy, LIMAT adaptively apply motion-compensated lifting steps. Let k-th frame of the n frame video sequence is given by x_k , where $k \in \{1,2, ...\}$. The lifting transform partitions the video into even frames $\{x_{2k}\}$ and odd frames $\{x_{2k+1}\}$ and attempts to predict the odd frames from the even ones using a forward motion compensation operator. Suppose $\{x_{2k}\}$ and $\{x_{2k+1}\}$ differ by a 3-pixel shift that is captured precisely by a motion vector v_f, then it is given by $\{x_{2k+1}\} = F(x_{2k}, v_f)$ exactly.

The proposed algorithm in [18] uses block matching (BM) to estimate motion between a pair of frames. Their BM algorithm divides the reference frame into non-overlapping blocks. For each block in the reference frame the most similar block of equal size in the destination frame is found and the relative location is stored as a motion vector. This approach overcomes previous approaches such as [13] where the reconstruction of a frame depends only on the individual frame's sparsity without taking into account any temporal motion. It is also better than using inter-frame difference [20] which is insufficient for removing temporal redundancies.

3.2 Distributed Compressed Video Sensing (DCVS)

Another video coding approach that makes use of CS is based on the distributed source coding theory of Slepian and Wolf [21], and Wyner and Ziv [22]. Source statistics, partially or totally, is only exploited at the decoder, not at the encoder as it is done conventionally. Two or more statistically dependent source data are encoded by independent encoders. Each encoder sends a separate bit-stream to a common decoder which decodes all incoming bit streams jointly, exploiting statistical dependencies between them.

In [23], a framework called Distributed Compressed Video Sensing (DISCOS) is introduced. Video frames are divided into key frames and non-key frames at the encoder. A video sequence consists of several GOPs (group of pictures) where a GOP consists of a key frame followed by some non-key frames. Key frames are coded using conventional MPEG intra-coding. Every frame is both block-wise and frame-wise compressively sampled using structurally random matrices [25]. In this way, more efficient frame based measurements are supplemented by block measurement to take advantage of temporal block motion.

At the decoder, key frames are decoded using a conventional MPEG decoder. For the decoding of non-key frames, the block-based measurements of a CS frame along with the two neighboring key frames are used for generating sparsity-constraint block prediction. The temporal correlation between frames is efficiently exploited through the inter-frame sparsity model, which assumes that a block can be sparsely represented by a linear combination of few temporal neighboring blocks. This prediction scheme is more powerful than conventional block-matching as it enables a block to be adaptively predicted from an optimal number of neighboring blocks, given its compressed measurements. The block-based prediction frame is then used as the side information (SI) to recover the input frame from its measurements. The measurement vector of the prediction frame is subtracted from that of the input frame to form a new measurement vector of the prediction error, which is sparse if the prediction is sufficiently accurate. Thus, the prediction error can be faithfully recovered. The reconstructed frame is then simply the sum of the prediction error and the prediction frame.

Another DCVS scheme is proposed in [24]. The main difference from [23] is that both key and non-key frames are compressively sampled and no conventional MPEG/H.26x codec is required. However, key frames have a higher measurement rate than non-key frames.

The measurement matrix Φ is the scrambled block Hadamard ensemble (SBHE) matrix [28]. SBHE is essentially a partial block Hadamard transform, followed by a random permutation of its columns. It provides near optimal performance, fast computation, and memory efficiency. It outperforms several existing measurement matrices including the Gaussian i.i.d matrix and the binary sparse matrix [28]. The sparsifying matrix used is derived from the discrete wavelet transform (DWT) basis.

At the decoder, the key frames are reconstructed using the standard Gradient Projection for Sparse Reconstruction (GPSR) algorithm. For the non-key frames, in order to compensate for lower measurement rates, side information is first generated to aid in the reconstruction. Side information can be generated from motion-compensated interpolation from neighboring key frames. In order to incorporate side information, GPSR is modified with a special initialization procedure and stopping criteria are incorporated (see Figure 3). The convergence speed of the modified GPSR has been shown to be faster and the reconstructed video quality is better than using original GPSR, two-step iterative shrinkage/thresholding (TwIST) [29], and orthogonal matching pursuit (OMP) [30].

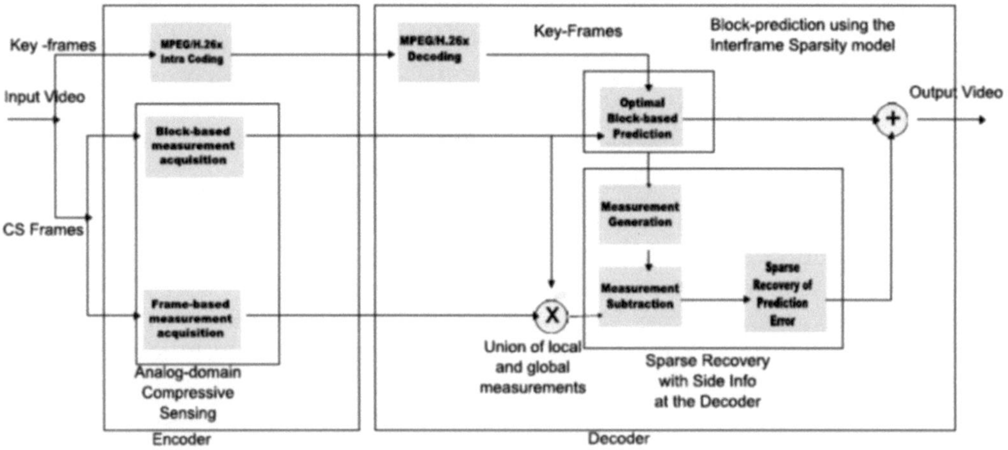

Fig. 2. Architecture of DISCOS [23]

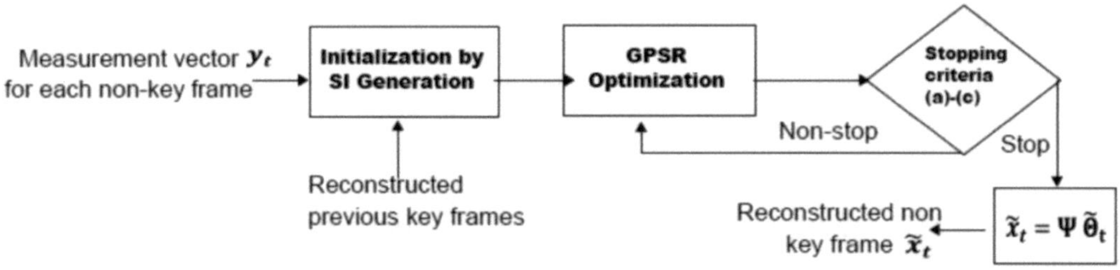

Fig. 3. Distributed CS Decoder [24]

3.3 Dictionary based compressed video sensing

In dictionary based techniques, a dictionary (basis) is created at the decoder from neighbouring frames for successful reconstruction of CS frames.

A dictionary based distributed approach to CVS is reported in [32]. Video frames are divided into key frames and non-key frames. Key frames are encoded and decoded using conventional MPEG/H.264 techniques. Non-key frames are divided into non-overlapping blocks of n pixels. Each block is then compressively sampled and quantized. At the decoder, key frames are MPEG/H.264 decoded while the non-key frames are dequantized and recovered using a CS reconstruction algorithm with the aid of a dictionary. The dictionary is constructed from the decoded key frame. The architecture of this system is shown in Figure 4.

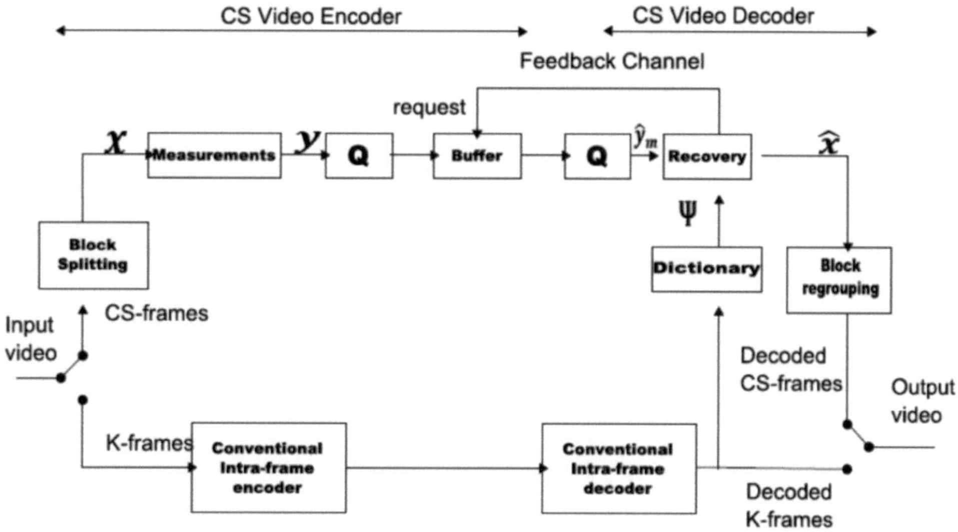

Fig. 4. A Dictionary-based CVS System [32]

Two different coding modes are defined. The first one is called the SKIP mode. This mode is used when a block in a current non-key frame does not change much from the co-located decoded key frame. Such a block is skipped for decoding. This is achieved by increasing the complexity at the encoder since the encoder has to estimate the mean squared error (MSE) between decoded key frame block and current CS frame block. If the MSE is smaller than some threshold, the same decoded block is simply copied to current frame and hence the decoding complexity is very minimal. The other coding mode is called the SINGLE mode. CS measurements for a block are compared with the CS measurements in a dictionary using the MSE criterion. If it is below some pre-determined threshold, then the block is marked as a decoded block. Dictionary is created from a set of spatially neighboring blocks of previous decoded neighboring key frames. A feedback channel is used to communicate with the encoder that this block has been decoded and no more measurements are required. For blocks that are not encoded by either SKIP or SINGLE mode, normal CS reconstruction is performed.

Another dictionary based approach is presented in [33]. The authors proposed the idea of using an adaptive dictionary. The dictionary is learned from a set of blocks globally extracted from the previous reconstructed neighboring frames together with the side information generated from them is used as the basis of each block in a frame. In their encoder, frame are divided as Key-frames and CS frames. For Key-frames, frame based CS measurements are taken and for CS frames, block based CS measurements are taken. At the decoder, the reconstruction of a frame or a block can be formulated as an l_1-minimization problem. It is solved by using the sparse reconstruction by separable approximation (SpaRSA) algorithm [34]. Block diagram of this system is shown in Figure 5.

Adjacent frames in the same scene of a video are similar, therefore a frame can be predicted by its side information which can be generated from the interpolation of its neighboring reconstructed frames. at decoder in [33], for a CS frame x_t , its side information I_t can be generated from the motion-compensated interpolation (MCI) of its previous x_{t-1} and next reconstructed key frames x_{t+1}, respectively. To learn the dictionary from x_{t-j} , I_t and x_{t+j} , Q training patches were extracted. For each block in the three frames, 9 training patches

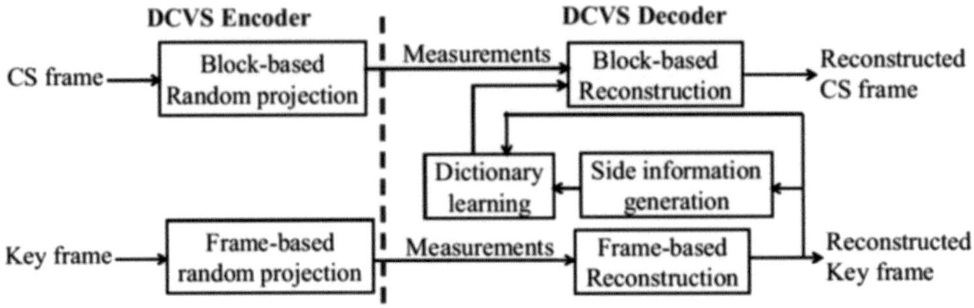

Fig. 5. Distributed Compressed Video Sensing with Dictionary Learning

including the nearest 8 blocks overlapping this block and this block itself are extracted. After that, the K-SVD algorithm [35] is applied to Q training patches to learn the dictionary $D_t \in R^{N_b \times P}$, $N_b \leq P$. D_t is an overcomplete dictionary containing P atoms. By using the learned dictionary D_t, each block b_{ti} in x_t can be sparsely represented as a sparse coefficient vector $\alpha_{ti} \in R^{P \times 1}$. This learned dictionary provides sparser representation for the frame than using the fixed basis dictionary. Same authors have extended their work in [36] for dynamic measurement rate allocation by incorporating feedback channel in their dictionary based distributed video codec.

4. Summary

CS is a new field and its application to video systems is even more recent. There are many avenues for further research and thorough quantitative analyses are still lacking. Key encoding strategies adopted so far includes:

- Applying CS measurements to all frames (both key frames and non-key frames) as suggested by [24].
- Applying conventional coding schemes (MPEG/H.264) to key frames and acquire local block-based and global frame-based CS measurements for non-key frames as suggested in [23, 32].
- Split frames into non-overlapping blocks of equal size. Reference frames are sampled fully. After sampling, a compressive sampling test is carried out to identify which blocks are sparse [16].

Similarly, key decoding strategies includes:

- Reconstructing the key frames by applying CS recovery algorithms such as GPSR and reconstruct the non-key frames by incorporating side information generated by recovered key frames [24].
- Decoding key frames using conventional image or video decompression algorithms and perform sparse recovery with decoder side information for prediction error reconstruction. Add reconstructed prediction error to the block-based prediction frame for final frame reconstruction [23].
- Using a dictionary for decoding [32] where a dictionary is used for comparison and prediction of non-key frames. Similarly, a dictionary can be learned from neighboring frames for reconstruction of non-key frames [33].

These observations suggest that there are many different approaches to encode videos using CS. In order to achieve a simple encoder design, conventional MPEG type of encoding process should not be adopted. Otherwise, there is no point in using CS as an extra overhead. We believe that the distributed approach in which each key-frame and non-key-frame is encoded by CS is able to utilise CS more effectively. While spatial domain compression is performed by CS, temporal domain compression is not exploited fully since there is no motion compensation and estimation performed. Therefore, a simple but effective inter-frame compression will need to be devised. In the distributed approach, this is equivalent to generating effective side information for the non-key frames.

5. References

[1] P. Symes, *Digital Video Compression*. McGraw-Hill, 2004.

[2] ITU, "Advanced video coding for generic audiovisual services," *ITU-T Recommendations for H.264*, 2005.

[3] T.Wiegand, G. Sullivan, G. Bjontegaard, and A. Luthra, "Overview of the H.264/AVC video coding standard," *IEEE Transactions on Circuits and Systems for Video Technology*, vol. 13, no. 7, pp. 560–576, Jul. 2003.

[4] D. Donoho, "Compressed sensing," *IEEE Transactions on Information Theory*, vol. 52, no. 4, pp. 1289–1306, Apr. 2006.

[5] E. Candes, J. Romberg, and T. Tao, "Robust uncertainty principles: Exact signal reconstruction from highly incomplete frequency information," *IEEE Transactions on Information Theory*, vol. 52, no. 2, pp. 489–509, Feb. 2006.

[6] R. Baraniuk, "Compressive sensing [lecture notes]," *IEEE Signal Processing Magazine*, vol. 24, no. 4, pp. 118–121, Jul. 2007.

[7] C. Shannon, "Communication in the presence of noise," *Proceedings of IRE*, vol. 37, pp. 10–21, Jan. 1949.

[8] — —, "Classic paper: Communication in the presence of noise," *Proceedings of the IEEE*, vol. 86, no. 2, pp. 447–457, Feb. 1998.

[9] J. Ellenberg, "Fill in the blanks: Using math to turn lo-res datasets into hi-res samples," *Wired Magazine*, vol. 18, no. 3, Mar. 2010.

[10] E. Candes and M. Wakin, "An introduction to compressive sampling," *IEEE Signal Processing Magazine*, pp. 21–30, Mar 2008.

[11] E. Candes and J. Romberg, "Sparsity and incoherence in compressive sampling," *Inverse Problems*, vol. 23, no. 3, pp. 969–985, 2007.

[12] S. Chen and D. Donoho, "Basis pursuit," in *Proceedings of IEEE Asilomar Conference on Signals, Systems and Computers*, vol. 1, Nov. 1994, pp. 41–44.

[13] M. B. Wakin, J. N. Laska, M. F. Duarte, D. Baron, S. Sarvotham, D. Takhar, K. F. Kelly, and R. G. Baraniuk, "Compressive imaging for video representation and coding," in *Proceedings of Picture Coding Symposium*, Beijing, China, 24-26 April 2006.

[14] D. Takhar, J. N. Laska, M. B. Wakin, M. F. Duarte, D. Baron, S. Sarvotham, K. F. Kelly, and R. G. Baraniuk, "A new camera architecture based on optical domain compression," in *Proceedings of SPIE Symposium on Electronic Imaging: Computational Imaging*, vol. 6065, 2006.

[15] S. Mallat and Z. Zhang, "Matching pursuit with time-frequency dictionaries," *IEEE Transactions on Signal Processing*, vol. 41, no. 2, pp. 3397–3415, Dec. 1993.

[16] V. Stankovic, L. Stankovic, and S. Chencg, "Compressive video sampling," in *Proceedings of 16th European Signal Processing Conference*, Lausanne, Switzerland, Aug. 2008.

[17] J. Tropp and A. Gilbert, "Signal recovery from partial information via orthogonal matching pursuit," *IEEE Transactions on Information Theory*, vol. 53, no. 12, pp. 4655–4666, Dec. 2007.

[18] J.Y.Park and M. B. Wakin, "A Multiscale Framework for Compressive Sensing of Video," Picture Coding Symposium Chicago, Illinois, 2009.
[19] A. Secker and D. Taubman, "Lifting-based invertible motion adaptive transform (LIMAT) framework for highly scalable video compression," *Image Processing, IEEE Transactions on,* vol. 12, pp. 1530-1542, 2003.
[20] R. Marcia and R. Willett, "Compressive Coded Aperture Video Reconstruction," in *16th European Signal Processing Conference, EUSIPCO-2008* Lausanne, Switzerland, 2008.
[21] J. Slepian and J. Wolf, "Noiseless coding of correlated information sources," *IEEE Transactions on Information Theory,* vol. 19, no. 4, pp. 471–480, Jul. 1973.
[22] A. Wyner, "Recent results in the Shannon theory," *IEEE Transactions on Information Theory,* vol. 20, no. 1, pp. 2–10, Jan. 1974.
[23] T. T. Do, C. Yi, D. T. Nguyen, N. Nguyen, G. Lu, and T. D. Tran, "Distributed Compressed Video Sensing," in *Information Sciences and Systems, 2009. CISS 2009. 43rd Annual Conference on,* 2009, pp. 1-2.
[24] K. Li-Wei and L. Chun-Shien, "Distributed compressive video sensing," in *Acoustics, Speech and Signal Processing, 2009. ICASSP 2009. IEEE International Conference on,* 2009, pp. 1169-1172.
[25] T.T.Do, L.Gan, and T.D.Tran, "Fast and efficient compressive sampling using structural Random Matrices," *To be submitted to IEEE Trans. of Information Theory, 2008,* 2008.
[26] T. T. Do, L. Gan, N. Nguyen, and T. D. Tran, "Sparsity adaptive matching pursuit algorithm for practical compressed sensing," in *Aslimore Conference on Signals, Systems and Computers* Pacific Grove, California, 2008.
[27] M. A. T. Figueiredo, R. D. Nowak, and S. J. Wright, "Gradient Projection for Sparse Reconstruction: Application to Compressed Sensing and Other Inverse Problems," *Selected Topics in Signal Processing, IEEE Journal of,* vol. 1, pp. 586-597, 2007.
[28] L. Gan, T.T.Do, and T.D.Tran, "Fast compressive imaging using scrambled hadamard block ensemble," in *16th Eurpoian Signal Processing Conference,* Lausanne, Switzerland, 2008.
[29] J. M. Bioucas-Dias and M. A. T. Figueiredo, "A New TwIST: Two-Step Iterative Shrinkage/Thresholding Algorithms for Image Restoration," *Image Processing, IEEE Transactions on,* vol. 16, pp. 2992-3004, 2007.
[30] T. Blumensath and M. E. Davies, "Gradient Pursuits," *Signal Processing, IEEE Transactions on,* vol. 56, pp. 2370-2382, 2008.
[31] K. Simonyan and S. Grishin, "AviSynth MSU frame rate conversion filter." http://www. compression.ru/video/frame_rate_conversion/index_en_msu.html.
[32] J. Prades-Nebot, M. Yi, and T. Huang, "Distributed video coding using compressive sampling," in *Proceedings of Picture Coding Symposium,* Chicago, IL, USA, 6-8 May 2009.
[33] Hung-Wei Chen, K. Li-Wei and L. Chun-Shien, "Dictionary Leraning-Based Distributed Compressive Video Sensing," in 28th Picture Coding Symposium. PCS 2010. *Dec 8-10, 2010* , pp. 210-213.
[34] S. J. Wright, R. D. Nowak, and M. A. T. Figueiredo, "Sparse reconstruction by separable approximation," *IEEE Trans. on Signal Processing,* vol. 57, no. 7, pp. 2479-2493, July 2009.
[35] M. Aharon, M. Elad, and A. M. Bruckstein, "The K-SVD: an algorithm for designing of overcomplete dictionaries for sparse representation," *IEEE Trans. on Signal Processing,* vol. 54, no. 11, pp. 4311-4322, Nov. 2006.
[36] Hung-Wei Chen, Li-Wei Kang, and Chun-Shien Lu, "Dynamic Measurement Rate Allocation for Distributed Compressive Video Sensing," *Proc. IEEE/SPIE Visual Communications and Image Processing (VCIP): special session on Random Projection and Compressive Sensing,* July 2010

2

Mobile Video Communications Based on Fast DVC to H.264 Transcoding

Alberto Corrales Garcia[1], Gerardo Fernandez Escribano[1],
Jose Luis Martinez[2] and Francisco Jose Quiles[1]
[1]*Instituto de Investigación en Informática de Albacete,*
University of Castilla-La Mancha Albacete,
[2]*Architecture and Technology of Computing Systems Group,*
Complutense University, Madrid,
Spain

1. Introduction

Nowadays, mobile devices demand multimedia services such as video communications due to the advances in mobile communications systems (such us 4G) and the integration of video cameras into mobile devices. However, these devices have some limitations of computing power, resources and complexity constraints for performing complex algorithms. For this reason, in order to establish a video communications between mobile devices, it is necessary to use low complex encoding techniques. In traditional video codecs (such as H.264/AVC (ISO/IEC, 2003)) these low complexity requirements have not been met because H.264/AVC is more complex at the encoder side. Then, mobile video communications based on H.264/AVC low complexity imply a penalty in terms of Rate - Distortion (RD). However, Distributed Video Coding (DVC) (Girod et al., 2005), and particularly Wyner-Ziv (WZ) video coding (Aaron et al., 2002), provides a novel video paradigm where the complexity of the encoder is reduced by shifting the complexity of the encoder to the decoder (Brites et al., 2008). Taking into account the benefits of both paradigms, recently WZ to H.26X transcoders have been proposed in the multimedia community to support mobile-to-mobile video communications. The transcoding framework provides a scheme where transmitter and receiver execute lower complexity algorithms and the majority of the computation is moved to the network where the transcoder is allocated. This complexity is thus assumed by a transcoder, which has more resources and no battery limitations. Nevertheless, for real time communications it is necessary to perform this conversion from WZ to H.264/AVC with a short delay, and then the transcoding process must be executed as efficiently as possible.

At this point, this work presents a WZ to H.264/AVC transcoding framework to support mobile-to-mobile video communications. In order to provide a faster transcoding process both paradigms involve in the transcoder (WZ decoding and H.264/AVC encoding) are accelerated. On the one hand, nowadays parallel programming is becoming more important to solve high complexity computation tasks and, as a consequence, the computing market is full of multicore systems, an approach is proposed to execute WZ decoding in a parallel way. On the other hand, at the same time WZ is decoding, some information could be gathered are sent to the H.264/AVC encoder in order to reduce the encoding algorithm complexity. In this work, the search area of the Motion Estimation (ME) process is reduced by means of Motion Vectors (MVs) calculated in the WZ decoding algorithm. In this way, the complexity of the two most complex tasks of this framework (WZ decoding and H.264/AVC encoding) are largely reduced making the transcoding process more efficient.

2. Background

2.1 Wyner-Ziv video coding

The first practical Wyner-Ziv framework was proposed by Stanford in (Aaron et al., 2002), and this work was widely referenced and improved in later proposals. As a result, in (Artigas et al., 2007) an architecture called DISCOVER was proposed which outperforms the previous Stanford one. This architecture provided a reference for the research community and finally it was later improved upon with the VISNET-II architecture (Ascenso et al., 2010), which is depicted in Figure 1. In this architecture, the encoder splits the sequence into two kinds of frames: Key Frames (K) and Wyner-Ziv Frames (WZ) in module (1). K frames are encoded by an H.264/AVC encoder in (2). On the other hand, WZ frames are sent to the WZ encoder, where the information is firstly quantized (3a), and BitPlanes (BPs) are extracted in (3b); in (3c) each BP is independently channel encoded and several parity bits, which are stored in a buffer (3d), are calculated. On the decoder side, initially K frames are decoded by an H.264/AVC decoder (4). From these frames, Side Information (SI) is calculated in (5), which represents an estimation for each non-present original WZ frame. For this estimation, the Correlation Noise Model (CNM) module (6) generates a Laplacian distribution, which models the residual between SI and the original frame. Afterwards, SI and CNM are sent to the turbo decoder, which corrects differences of SI and the original frame by means of iterative decoding (requesting several parity bits from the encoder through the feedback channel). Finally, decoding bitplanes are reconstructed in module (7c).

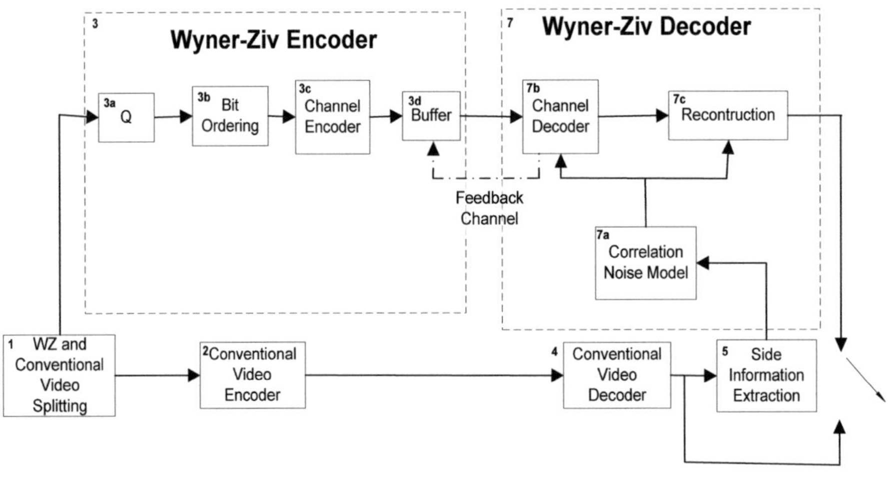

Fig. 1. Block diagram of the reference WZ architecture [Ascenso et al. 2010].

2.2 H.264/AVC

H.264/AVC or MPEG-4 part 10 Advanced Video Coding (AVC) is a compression video standard developed by the ITU-T Video Coding Experts Group (ITU-T VCEG) together with the ISO/IEC Moving Picture Experts Group (MPEG). In fact, both standards are technically identical (ISO/IEC, 2003).

The main purpose of H.264/AVC is to offer a good quality standard able to considerably reduce the output bit rate of the encoded sequences, compared with previous standards, while exhibiting a substantially increasing definition of quality and image. H.264/AVC promises a significant advance compared with the commercial standards currently most in use (MPEG-2 and MPEG-4). For this reason H.264/AVC contains a large amount of compression techniques and innovations compared to previous standards; it allows more compressed video sequences to be obtained and provides greater flexibility for implementing the encoder. Figure 2 shows the block diagram of the H.264/AVC encoder.

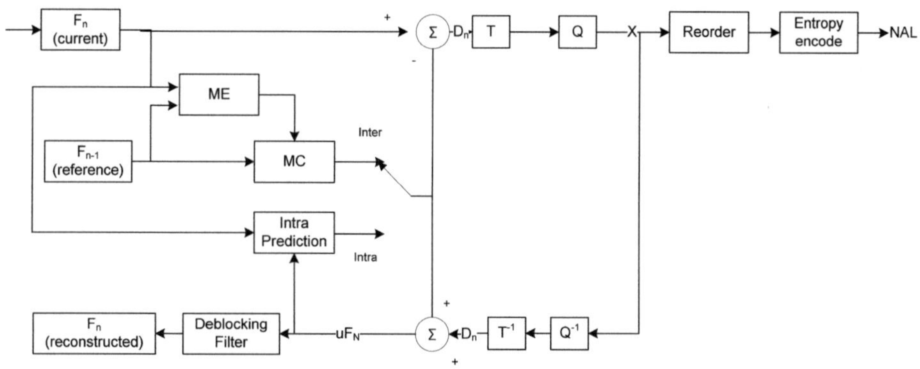

Fig. 2. H.264/AVC encoder diagram

The ME is the most time-consuming task in the H.264/AVC encoder. It is a process which removes the temporal redundancy between images, comparing the current one with previous or later images in terms of time (reference images), looking for a pattern that indicates how the movement is produced inside the sequence.

To improve the encoding efficiency, H.264/AVC allows the use of partitions resulting from dividing the MB in different ways. Greater flexibility for the ME and Motion Compensated (MC) processes and greater motion vector precision give greater reliability to the H.264/AVC encoding process. The ME process is thus carried out many times per each partition and sub-partition. This feature is known as variable block size for the ME.

3. Related work

3.1 Parallel Wyner-Ziv

The DVC framework is based on displacing the complexity from encoders to decoders. However, reducing the complexity of decoders as much as possible is desirable. In traditional feedback-based WZ architectures (Aaron et al., 2002), the rate control is performed at the decoder and is controlled by means of the feedback channel; this is the main reason for the decoder complexity, as once a parity chunk arrives at the decoder, the turbo decoding algorithm (one of the most computationally-demanding tasks (Brites et al., 2008) is called. Taking this fact into account, there are several approaches which try to reduce the complexity of the decoder, which usually induces a rate distortion penalty. However, due to technological advances, new parallel hardware is beginning to be introduced into practical video coding solutions. These new features of computers offer a new challenge to the research community with regards to integrating their algorithms into a parallel framework; this opens a new door in multimedia research. It is true that, with regards to traditional standards, several approaches have been proposed since multicores appeared on the market, but this chapter focuses on parallel computing applied to the WZ framework.

Having said this, in 2010 several different parallel solutions for WZ were proposed. In particular, in (Oh et al., 2010) Oh et al. proposed a WZ parallel execution carried out by Graphic Processing Units (GPUs). In this proposal, the authors focus on designing a parallel distribution for a Slepian-Wolf decoder based on rate Adaptative Low Density Check Code (LDPC) with Accumulator (LDPCA). LDPC codes are composed of many bit-nodes which do not have many dependencies between each node, so they propose a parallel execution in three kernels (steps): i) kernels for check node calculations, ii) kernels for bit node calculations, and iii) kernels for termination condition calculations. In a GPU they achieve a decoding 4~5 times faster for QCIF and 15~20 for CIF. On the other hand, in (Momcilovic et al., 2010) Momcilovic et al. proposed a WZ LDPC parallel decoding based on multicore processors. In this work, the authors parallelize several LDPC approaches. On a Quad-Core machine, they achieve a speedup of about 3.5. Both approaches propose low-level parallelism for a particular LDPC/LDPCA implementation.

This chapter presents a WZ to H.264/AVC transcoder which includes a higher-level parallel WZ video decoding algorithm implemented on a multicore system. The reference WZ decoding algorithm is adapted to a multicore architecture, which divides each frame into several slices and distributes the work among available cores. In addition, the proposed algorithm is scalable because it does not depend on the hardware architecture, the number of cores or even on the implementation of the internal Wyner-Ziv decoder. Therefore, the time reduction can be increased simply by increasing the number of cores, as technology advances. Furthermore, the proposed method can also be applied to WZ architectures with or without a feedback channel (Sheng et al., 2010).

3.2 WZ to H.26x transcoding

Nowadays, mobile-to-mobile video communications are getting more and more common. Transcoding from a low cost encoder format to a low cost decoder provides a practical solution for these types of communications. Although H.264/AVC has been included in multiple transcoding architectures from other coding formats (such as MPEG-2 to H.264/AVC (Fernandez-Escribano et al., 2007, 2008) or even homogeneous H.264/AVC (De Cock et al., 2010), proposals in WZ to H.26x to support mobile communications are rather recent and there are only a few approaches so far.

In 2008, the first WZ transcoder architecture was introduced by Peixoto et al. in (Peixoto et al., 2010). In this work, they presented a WZ to H.263 transcoder for mobile video communications. However, H.263 offers lower performance than other codecs based on H.264/AVC and they did not exploit the correlation between the WZ MVs and the traditional ME successfully and only used them to determine the starting centre of the ME process.

In our previous work, we proposed the first transcoding architecture from WZ to H.264/AVC (Martínez et al., 2009). This work introduced an improvement to accelerate the H.264/AVC ME stage using the Motion Vectors (MV) gathered in the WZ decoding stage. Nevertheless, this transcoder is not flexible since it only applies the ME improvement for transcoding from WZ frames to P frames. In addition, it only allows transcoding from WZ GOPs of length 2 to IPIP H.264/AVC GOP patterns, so it does not use practical patterns due to the high bit rate generated neither flexible. Furthermore, this work used a less realistic WZ implementation. For this reason, the approach presented in this chapter improves this part by introducing a better and more realistic WZ implementation based on the VISNET-II codec (Ascenso et al., 2010), which implements lossy key frame coding, on-line correlation noisy modeling and uses a more realistic procedure call at the decoder for the stopping criterion.

4. Transcoding for mobile to mobile communications

4.1 Introduction

The main task of a transcoder is to convert a source coding format into another one. In the case of mobile video communications, the transcoding process should be done as fast as possible. In addition, a flexible transcoder should take into account the conversion between the input and the output patterns. In order to provide a flexible and fast transcoding architecture, it is proposed the architecture displayed in Figure 3.

This architecture is composed of a Wyner-Ziv decoder and a H.264/AVC encoder with several modifications or extra modules. In particular, the WZ decoder is redesigned to parallelize the decoding process and the black modules in Figure 3 have been included or modified to obtain a faster H.264/AVC encoding. Details will be given in the following subsections.

4.2 Parallelization of WZ decoding

WZ video coding accumulates the majority of the complexity on the decoder side. If you study each module inside the decoder scheme (Figure 1), you discover that most of this complexity is concentrated in the Channel Decoder module (Brites et al., 2008). This module receives successive chunks of parity bits. Then, the quantized symbol stream associated to each bitplane is obtained in an iterative process, which is based on the residual statistics calculated by the CNM. This procedure stops when a condition based on probabilities is satisfied. Obviously, the complexity of the decoder increases when more bitplanes (in the pixel domain) or coefficient bands (for the transform domain) are decoded. At this point, as a first stage on the transcoding process, it is proposed a WZ decoding architecture which distributes decoding complexity across several processing units. The proposed architecture is shown in Figure 3. The approach is a flexible and scalable architecture which distributes the parallel decoding between two parallelism levels: GOPs and frames. First, the input bitstream composed of K frames is stored in a K-frame buffer. Then, at the first parallelism level, the WZ frames inside two K frames delimit a GOP structure, and therefore each GOP decoding procedure is carried out independently by a different core. Additionally, for each WZ frame inside a GOP, an SI is calculated and then split into several parts. Then each portion of the frame is assigned to any core which executes the iterative turbo decoding procedure in order to decode the corresponding part of the WZ reconstructed frame. Therefore, each spatial division of the frame is decoded in an independent way by using the feedback channel to request parity bits from the encoder. When each part of a given frame is decoded, these parts are joined in spatial order and the frame is reconstructed. Finally, a sequence joiner receives each decoded frame and key frames in order to reorganize the sequence in its temporal order.

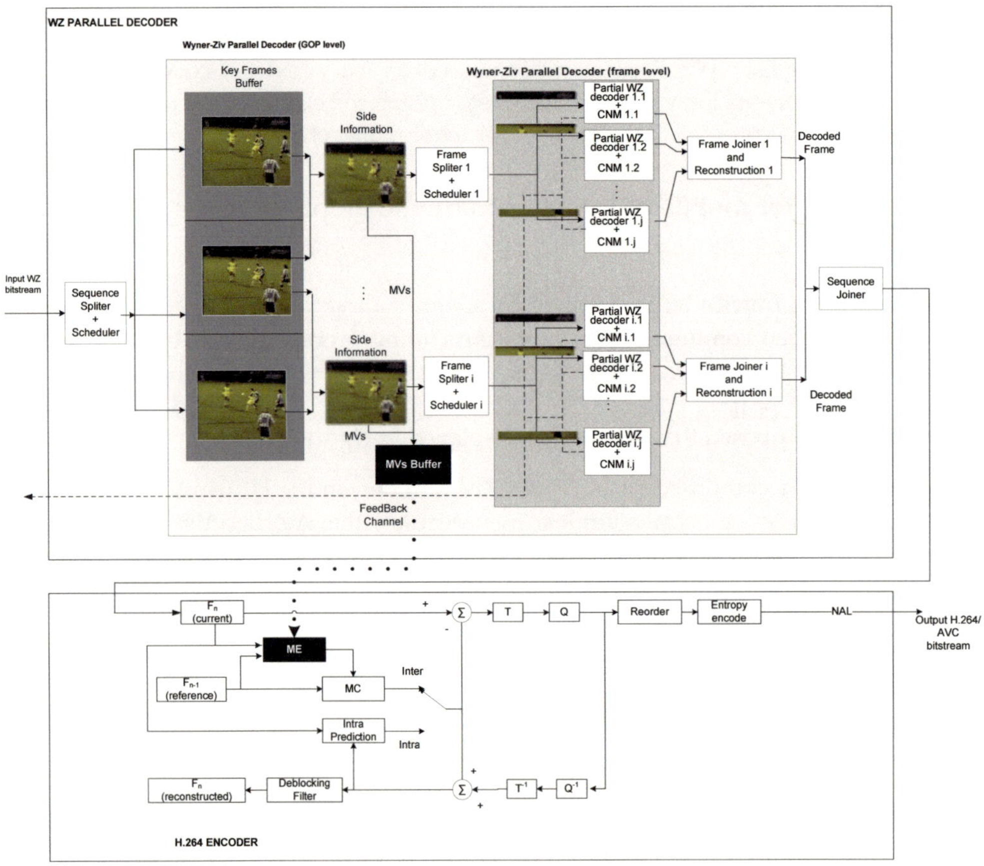

Fig. 3. Proposed WZ-to-H.264/AVC transcoding achitecture

Concerning the scheduler, a dynamic scheduler is implemented. That means that whenever a core is free and there is no pending task, it is assigned to the idle core. The number of tasks is always equal to, or bigger than, the number of cores. So that means there are always tasks in the scheduler queue until the end of the decoding stage is reached. However, partial decoding for each frame requires a synchronization barrier. To illustrate this, Figure 4 shows the decoding time line for a sequence composed of 5 GOPs (with length = 2) on a multicore with four cores. As can be seen, decoder initialization takes some time at the beginning of the decoder process. After that, each core receives a task (defined by a thread) from the scheduler. When a thread finishes the decoding of a part of a frame, it can continue decoding other parts of the same frame. In the case of there being no more parts of this frame for decoding, this core has to wait until the rest of parts of the same frame are decoded. This is a consequence of the synchronization barrier implicit for each frame to be reconstructed. In Figure 4, when a thread is waiting it is labeled as being in an idle state. In addition, while the sequence decoding process is finishing, there are not enough tasks for available cores, so several cores change their status to idle until the decoding process finishes. Nevertheless, real sequences are composed of many GOPs and decoder initialization and ending times are quite shorter than the whole decoding time.

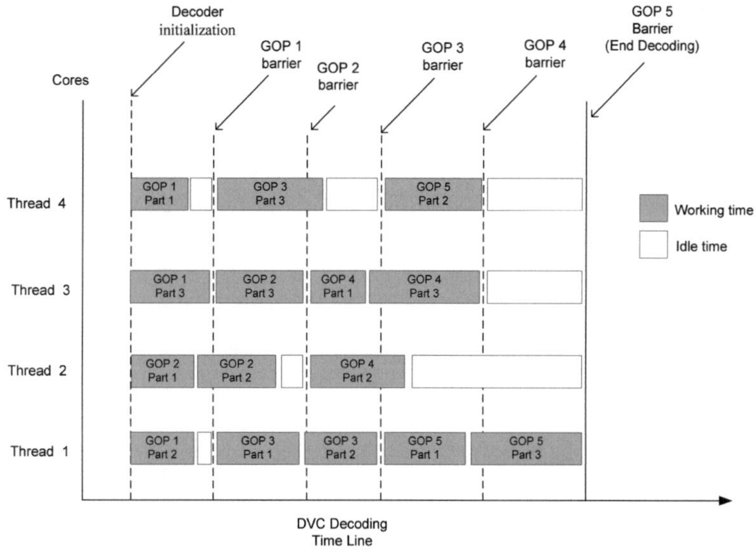

Fig. 4. Timeline for the proposed parallel WZ decoding with a sequence with 5 GOPs (GOP length = 2) and 4 cores.

The size of the K-frame buffer S is defined by Equation 1, where i is the number of GOPs which can be executed in parallel. For example, in the execution in Figure 4, a 4-core processor can execute two GOPs at the same time, so three stored K frames are providing enough tasks for four cores. In addition, it is not necessary to fill the buffer fully and it could be filled progressively during the decoding process. For different GOP lengths, the buffer size would be the same, since every WZ GOP length only needs two K frames to start the first WZ decoding frame.

$$S = i + 1 \tag{1}$$

Finally, considering that the parity bits could be requested to the encoder without following a sequential order, it calculates the Parity Position (PP) which determinates the parity bit position to start to send. PP is calculated by Equation 2, where I is the Intra period, P is the position of the current GOP, Q is the quantification parameter, and W is the width of the image and H the height.

$$PP = (I - 1) * P * Q * \left(\left(\frac{W * H * 2}{8} \right) + 1 \right) \tag{2}$$

4.3 H.264/AVC transcoding approach

In order to provide fast and flexible transcoding at the H.264/AVC encoder side, we have to study two issues: firstly, how MVs generated during the SI process could help to reduce the time used in ME; secondly, taking into account that DVC and H.264/AVC can build different GOPs, how to map MVs between different GOP combinations in order to provide flexibility.

4.3.1 Reducing motion estimation complexity

Within the WZ decoding process, an important task is the SI generation stage, which is the first step in the process for generating the WZ frames from K frames. VISNET-II performs Motion Compensated Temporal Interpolation (MCTI) to estimate the SI. The first step of this method is shown in Figure 5, which consists in matching each forward frame MB with a backward frame MB inside the search area. The process checks all the possibilities inside the search area and chooses the MV that generates the lowest residual. The middle of this MV represents the displacement for the MB interpolated (more details about the SI generation process in (Ascenso et al., 2005)).

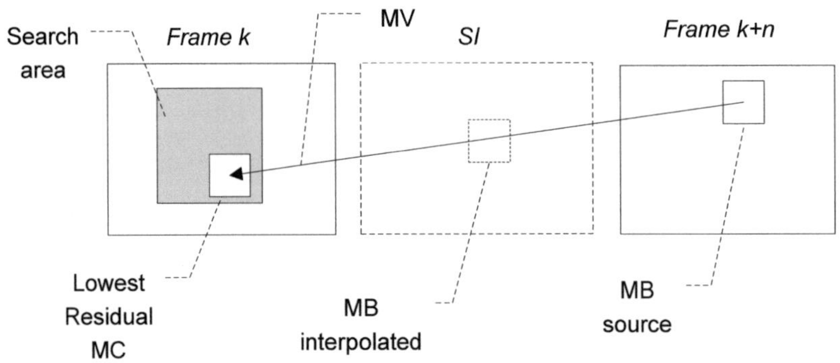

Fig. 5. First step of SI generation process.

Obviously, MVs generated in the WZ decoding stage contain approximated information about the quantity of movement of the frame. Following this idea, the present approach proposes to reuse the MVs to accelerate the H.264/AVC encoding stage by reducing the search area of the ME stage. Moreover, the present reduction is adjusted for every input DVC GOP to every H.264/AVC GOP in an efficient and dynamic way. As is shown in Figure 6, the search area for each MB is defined by a circumference with a radius dependent on the incoming SI MV (*Rmv*). This search area can oscillate between a minimum (defined by *Rmin*) and a maximum (limited by the H.264 search area). In particular, the length will vary depending on the type of frame and the length of the reference frame, as will be explained in section 4.2.2. Furthermore, a minimum area is considered since MVs are calculated from 16x16 MBs in the SI process, and H.264/AVC can even work with smaller partitions than 16x16. Besides, SI is an approximation of the frame, so some changes could occur when the fame is completely reconstructed. For these reasons, this minimum was set at 4 pixels.

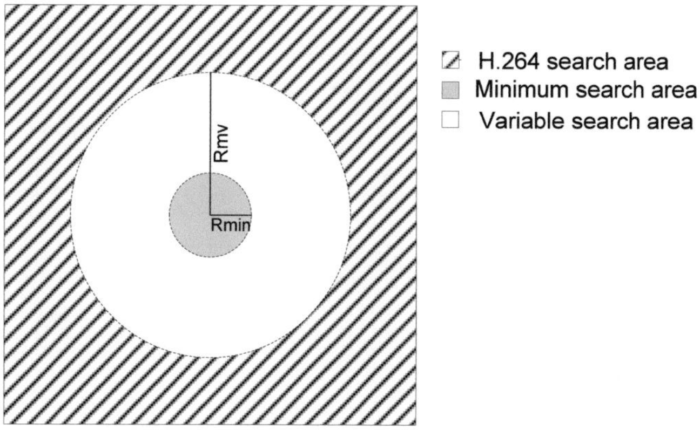

Fig. 6. Search area reduction for H.264 encoding stage.

4.3.2 Mapping GOPs from DVC to H.264

One desired feature of every transcoder is flexibility. To achieve it, an important process is to perform a with care known as GOP mapping. On the second part of the transcoder, it is proposed a DVC to H.264/AVC conversion which allows every mapping combination by performing this task using techniques to improve the time spending by the transcoding process. To extract MVs, first the distance used to calculate the SI is considered. For example, Figure 7 shows the transcoding process for a DVC GOP of length 4 to a H.264/AVC pattern IPPP (baseline profile). In step 1, DVC starts to decode the frame labeled as WZ_2 and the MVs generated in its SI generation are discarded because they are not closely correlated with the proper movement (low accuracy). When the WZ_2 frame is reconstructed (through the entire WZ decoding algorithm, WZ'_2) in step 2, the WZ decoding algorithm starts to decode frames WZ_1 and WZ_3 by using the reconstructed frame WZ'_2. At this point, the MVs $V_{0\text{-}2}$ and $V_{2\text{-}4}$ generated in this second iteration of the DVC decoding algorithm are stored. These MVs will be used to reduce the H.264/AVC ME process. Notice that in the case of higher GOP sizes the procedure is the same. In other words, MVs are stored and reused when the distance between SI and the two reference frames is 1. Finally, $V_{0\text{-}2}$ and $V_{2\text{-}4}$ are divided into two halves because P frames have the reference frame with distance one and MVs were calculated for a distance of two during the SI process.

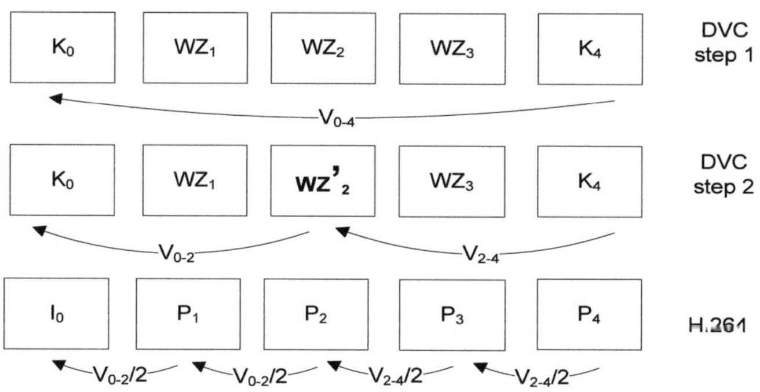

Fig. 7. Mapping from DVC GOP of length 4 to H.264 GOP IPPP.

For more complex patterns, which include mixed P and B frames (main profile), this method can be extended in a similar way with some changes. Figure 8 shows the transcoding from a DVC GOP of length 4 to a H.264 pattern IBBP. MVs are also stored by always following the same procedure. However, in this case the way to apply them in H.264/AVC changes.

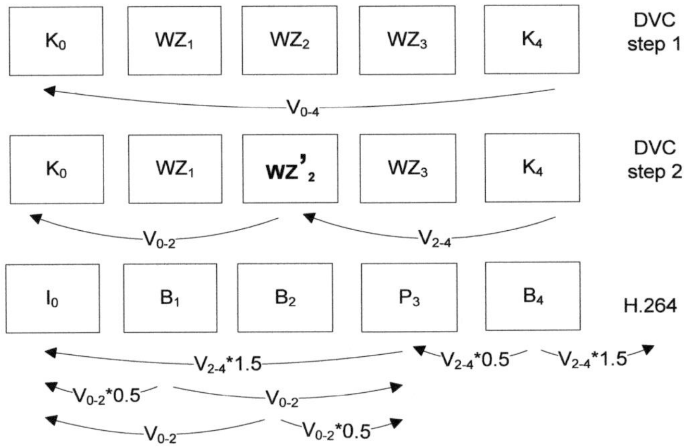

Fig. 8. Mapping from DVC GOP of length 4 to H.264 GOP IBBP.

For P frames, MVs are multiplied by a factor of 1.5 because MVs were calculated for a distance of 2 and P frames have their references with a distance of 3. For B frames, it depends on the position that they are allocated and it changes for backward and forward searches.

As can be observed, this procedure can be applied to both K and WZ frames. Therefore, following this method the proposed transcoder can be used for transcoding from every DVC GOP to every H.264/AVC GOP.

5. Experimental results

The proposed transcoder has been evaluated by using four representative QCIF sequences with different motion levels were considered. These sequences were coded at 15 fps and 30 fps using 150 frames and 300 respectively. In the DVC to H.264/AVC transcoder applied, the DVC stage was generated by the VISNET II codec using PD with BP = 3 as quantification in a trade-off between RD performance and complexity constraints but with whatever BP could be used. In addition, sequences were encoded in DVC with GOPs of length 2, 4 and 8 to evaluate different patterns. The parallel decoder was implemented by using an Intel C++ compiler (version 11.1) which combines a high-performance compiler as well as Intel Performance Libraries to provide support for creating multi-threaded applications. In addition, it provides support for OpenMP 3.0 (OpenMP, 2011). In order to test the performance of parallel decoding, it was executed over an Intel i7-940 multicore processor (Intel, 2011), although the proposal is not dependent on particular hardware. For the experiments, the parallel decoding was split into 9 parts where each core has thus a ninth part of the frame. This value is a good selection for QCIF frames (176x144), 16x16 macroblocks (this is the size of the block in the SI generation and thus a QCIF frame has 99 16x16 blocks) and 4 processors (4 cores, 8 simultaneous processes with hyper-threading).

During the decoding process, the MVs generated by the SI generation stage were sent to the H.264/AVC encoder; hence it does not involve any increase in complexity. In the second stage, the transcoder performs a mapping from every DVC GOP to every H.264/AVC GOP using QP = 28, 32, 36 and 40. In our experiments we have chosen different H.264/AVC patterns in order to analyze the behavior for the baseline profile (IPPP GOP) and the main profile (IBBP pattern). These patterns were transcoded by the reference and the proposed transcoder. The H.264/AVC reference software used in the simulations was theJM reference software (version 17.1). As mentioned in the introduction, the framework described is focused on communications between mobile devices; therefore, a low complexity configuration must be employed. For this reason, we have used the default configuration for the H.264/AVC main and baseline profile, only turning off the RD Optimization. The reference transcoder is composed of the whole DVC decoder followed by the whole H.264/AVC encoder. In order to analyze the performance of the proposed transcoder in detail we have taken into account the two halves and global results are also presented.

Furthermore, the performance of the proposed DVC parallel decoding is shown in Tables 1 (for 15 and 30fps sequences). PSNR and bitrate (BR) display the quality and bitrate measured by the reference WZ decoding. To calculate the PSNR difference, the PSNR of each sequence was estimated before transcoding starts and after transcoding finishes. Then the PSNR of the proposed transcoding was subtracted from the reference one for each H.264/AVC RD point, as defined by Equation 3. However, Table 1 do not include results for ΔPSNR because the quality obtained by DVC parallel decoding is the same as the reference decoding, it iterates until a given threshold is reached (Brites et al., 2008).

$$\Delta PSNR(db) = PSNR_{reference} - PSNR_{porposed} \tag{3}$$

Equation 4 was applied in order to calculate the Bitrate increment (ΔBR) between reference and proposed DVC decoders as a percentage. Then a positive increment means a higher bitrate is generated by the proposed transcoder. As the results of Table 1 show, when DVC decodes smaller and less complex parts, sometimes the turbo decoder (as part of the DVC decoder) converges faster with less iterations and it implies less parity bits requested and thus a bitrate reduction. However, generally speaking the turbo codec yields a better performance for longer inputs. For this reason, the bitrate is not always positive or negative. Comparing different GOP lengths, in short GOPs most of the bitrate is generated by the K frames. When the GOP length increases, the number of K frames is reduced and then WZ frames contribute to reducing the global bitrate in low motion sequences (like Hall) or increasing it in high motion sequences (Foreman or Soccer). Generally, decoding smaller pieces of frame (in parallel) works better for high motion sequences, where the bitrate is similar or even lower in some cases.

$$\Delta BR(\%) = 100 * \frac{(BR_{porposed} - BR_{reference})}{BR_{reference}} \tag{4}$$

Concerning the time reduction (TR), it was estimated as a percentage by using Equation 5. In this case, negative time reduction means decoding time saved by the proposed DVC decoding. As is shown in Table 1, DVC decoding time is reduced by up to 70% on average. TR is similar for different GOP lengths, but it works better for more complex sequences.

$$TR(\%) = 100 * \frac{(Time_{porposed} - Time_{reference})}{Time_{reference}} \quad (5)$$

		15 fps sequences				30 fps sequences			
		Reference DVC decoder		Proposed DVC parallel decoder		Reference DVC decoder		Proposed DVC parallel decoder	
Sequence	GOP	PSNR (dB)	BR (kbps)	ΔBR (%)	TR (%)	PSNR (dB)	BR (kbps)	ΔBR (%)	TR (%)
Foreman	2	30.25	295.58	0.66	-75.99	32.41	504.93	-2.37	-74.29
	4	29.73	450.59	-0.05	-70.88	31.95	648.69	-1.91	-74.7
	8	28.96	571.31	-1.04	-76.98	30.87	804.73	-0.88	-73.23
Hall	2	32.81	222.24	-2.52	-75.14	36.4	439.74	1.33	-70.89
	4	33.1	224.09	7.99	-70.47	36.34	412.8	1.27	-70.83
	8	33.06	224.13	9.05	-69.34	36.03	384.31	6.49	-68.96
Coast Guard	2	30.14	289.84	1.11	-72.8	33.84	592.64	4.69	-71.88
	4	30.13	371.62	1.38	-74.46	33.32	608.2	5.88	-72.51
	8	29.65	437.85	1.91	-74.73	32.24	661.11	4.72	-70.92
Soccer	2	29.56	377.15	-2.67	-74.17	30.52	532.94	1.2	-74.86
	4	29.05	593.66	-2.82	-75.81	30.21	855.23	-0.58	-75.41
	8	28.34	735.48	-3.2	-73.94	29.53	1069.21	-1.19	-74.65
mean				0.82	-73.73			1.55	-72.76

Table 1. Performance of the proposed DVC parallel decoder for 15 and 30 fps sequences (first stage of the proposed transcoder).

Results for the second stage of the transcoder are shown in Tables 2 and 3. In this case, both H.264/AVC encoders (reference and proposed) start from the same DVC output sequence (as DVC parallel decoding obtains the same quality as the reference DVC decoding), which is quantified with four QP values. For these four QP values, ΔPSNR and ΔBRare calculated as specified in Bjøntegaard and Sullivan's common test rule (Sullivan et al., 2001). TR is given by Equation 5. In Table 2, DVC decoded sequences are mapped to an IPPP pattern. In this case RD loss is negligible and TR is around 40%. For 30 fps sequences, the accuracy of the proposed method works better and RD loss is even lower. In addition, Figure 9 displays each plot for each of the four 4 QP values simulated. As can be observed, all RD points are much closer. For the IBBP pattern (Table 3), the conclusions are similar. Comparing both patterns, the IBBP pattern generates a slightly higher RD loss, but H.264/AVC encoding is performed faster (up to 48%). This is because B frames have two reference frames, but dynamic ME search area reduction is carried out in both of them. Figure 10 displays plots for each of the four QP points when an IBBP pattern is performed. As can be observed, the RD drop penalty is negligible.

IPPP H.264 pattern							
		15fps			30fps		
Sequence	GOP	$\Delta PSNR$(db)	ΔBR(%)	TR (%)	$\Delta PSNR$(db)	ΔBR(%)	TR (%)
Foreman	2	-0.02	0.57	-41.57	-0.01	0.31	-42.54
	4	-0.03	0.86	-44.62	0.00	0.18	-41.81
	8	-0.04	1.11	-45.85	-0.01	0.36	-43.71
Hall	2	-0.01	0.41	-30.04	0.00	0.05	-30.50
	4	0.00	0.12	-30.77	0.00	0.06	-29.28
	8	0.00	0.17	-27.21	0.00	0.01	-27.81
Coast Guard	2	-0.01	0.27	-47.46	-0.01	0.19	-46.39
	4	-0.01	0.33	-46.15	0.00	0.08	-45.59
	8	-0.01	0.20	-47.61	0.00	0.09	-45.23
Soccer	2	-0.01	0.19	-38.85	-0.01	0.15	-37.86
	4	-0.04	1.18	-43.35	-0.03	0.84	-40.61
	8	-0.05	1.63	-44.98	-0.03	0.90	-42.35
mean		-0.02	0.59	-40.70	-0.01	0.27	-39.47

Table 2. Performance of the proposed transcoder mapping method for IPPP H.264 pattern with 15fps and 30fps sequences.

IBBP H.264 pattern							
		15fps			30fps		
Sequence	GOP	$\Delta PSNR$(db)	ΔBR(%)	TR (%)	$\Delta PSNR$(db)	ΔBR(%)	TR (%)
Foreman	2	-0.06	1.51	-48.86	-0.08	2.31	-48.17
	4	-0.08	2.00	-51.11	-0.07	2.18	-49.56
	8	-0.07	2.18	-52.19	0.00	0.00	-37.71
Hall	2	-0.01	0.21	-39.06	-0.01	0.24	-37.31
	4	-0.01	0.55	-37.11	-0.01	0.13	-35.74
	8	-0.01	0.48	-36.15	0.00	0.01	-52.41
Coast Guard	2	-0.04	1.13	-49.44	-0.01	0.26	-51.14
	4	-0.04	1.24	-49.90	-0.01	0.37	-50.62
	8	-0.05	1.40	-51.07	-0.05	1.59	-45.19
Soccer	2	-0.02	0.43	-42.93	-0.08	2.63	-46.90
	4	-0.05	1.54	-46.03	-0.08	2.57	-48.52
	8	-0.08	2.52	-48.71	-0.04	1.21	-45.93
mean		-0.04	1.27	-46.05	-0.08	2.31	-48.17

Table 3. Performance of the proposed transcoder mapping method for IBBP H.264 pattern with 15fps and 30fps sequences.

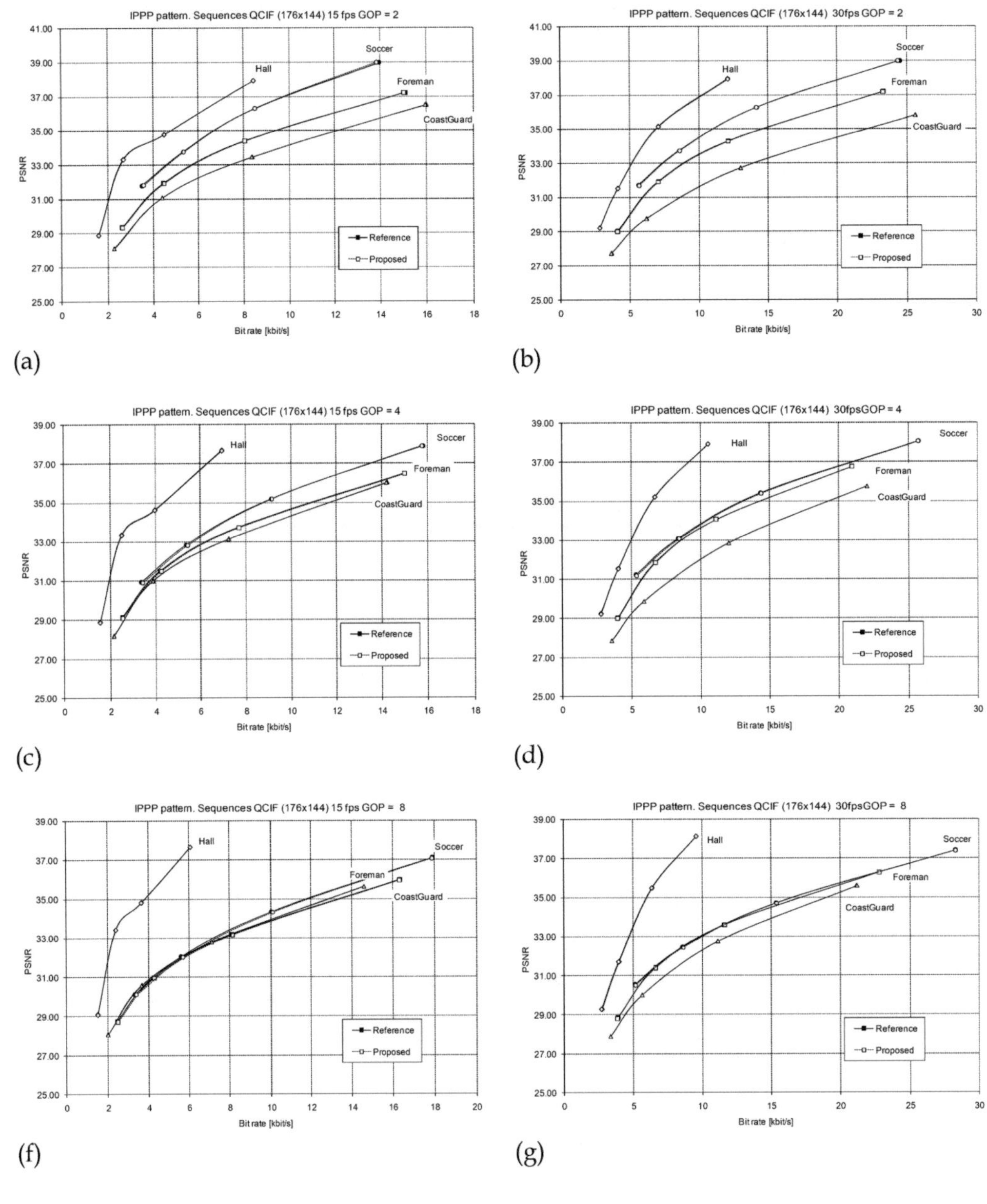

Fig. 9. PSNR/bitrate results transcoding to H.264 IPPP GOP from DVC GOP = 2, 4, and 8 in sequences with 15 and 30 fps. Reference symbols: ■Foreman ♦Hall ▲CoastGuard ●Soccer

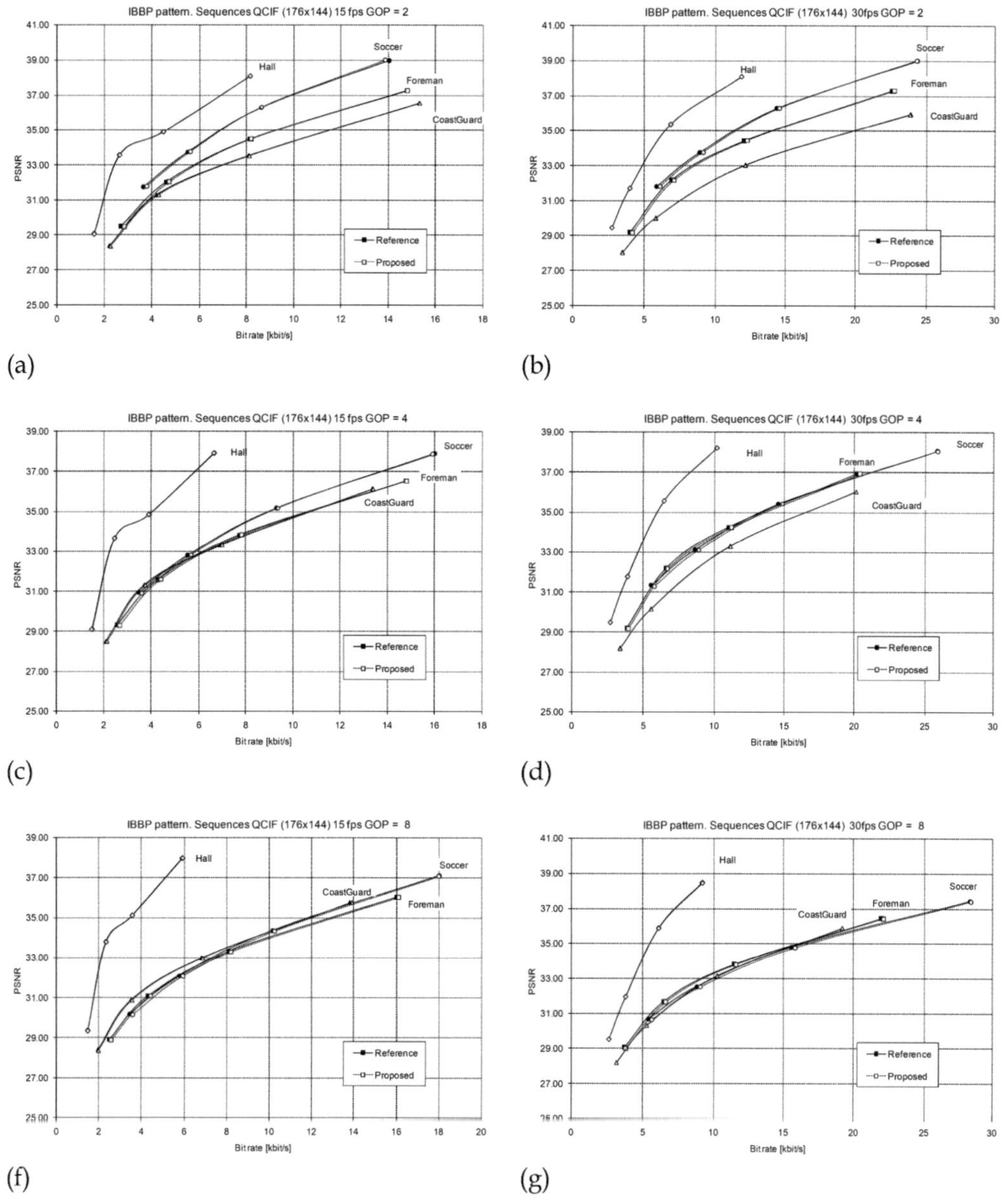

Fig. 10. PSNR/bitrate results transcoding to H.264 IBBP GOP from DVC GOP = 2, 4, and 8 in sequences with 15 and 30 fps. Reference symbols: ■Foreman ♦Hall ▲CoastGuard ●Soccer

15 fps for IPPP H.264 pattern				
Sequence	GOP	$\Delta\overline{PSNR}$ (dB)	$\Delta\overline{BR}$ (%)	$\overline{TR}$ (%)
Foreman	2	-0.02	0.64	-75.50
	4	-0.02	-0.05	-70.66
	8	-0.01	-1.02	-76.78
Hall	2	0	-2.47	-74.48
	4	0	7.86	-70.01
	8	0	8.91	-68.92
Coast Guard	2	0	1.07	-72.41
	4	0	1.35	-74.18
	8	0	1.88	-74.52
Soccer	2	-0.03	-2.62	-73.82
	4	-0.03	-2.78	-75.61
	8	-0.03	-3.15	-73.79
mean		-0.01	0.80	-73.39

Table 4. Performance of the proposed transcoder for 15fps sequences and IPPP pattern.

30 fps for IPPP H.264 pattern				
Sequence	GOP	$\Delta\overline{PSNR}$ (dB)	$\Delta\overline{BR}$ (%)	$\overline{TR}$ (%)
Foreman	2	-0.01	-2.32	-73.72
	4	0	-1.88	-74.34
	8	0	-0.87	-72.99
Hall	2	0	1.31	-70.03
	4	0	1.25	-70.24
	8	0	6.40	-68.48
Coast Guard	2	0	4.59	-71.31
	4	-0.01	5.78	-72.15
	8	-0.01	4.65	-70.65
Soccer	2	-0.02	1.16	-74.39
	4	-0.02	-0.57	-75.15
	8	-0.02	-1.17	-74.45
mean		-0.01	1.53	-72.33

Table 5. Performance of the proposed transcoder for 30fps sequences and IPPP pattern.

15 fps for IBBP H.264 pattern				
Sequence	GOP	$\Delta\overline{PSNR}$ (dB)	$\Delta\overline{BR}$ (%)	$\overline{TR}$ (%)
Foreman	2	-0.03	0.67	-75.12
	4	-0.03	-0.03	-70.51
	8	-0.03	-1.01	-76.63
Hall	2	0	-2.47	-73.99
	4	0	7.86	-69.66
	8	0	8.92	-68.63
Coast Guard	2	-0.01	1.10	-72.00
	4	-0.01	1.37	-73.92
	8	-0.02	1.89	-74.31
Soccer	2	-0.04	-2.61	-73.45
	4	-0.04	-2.77	-75.39
	8	-0.03	-3.15	-73.64
mean		-0.02	0.81	-73.10

Table 6. Performance of the proposed transcoder for 15fps sequences and IBBP pattern.

30 fps for IBBP H.264 pattern				
Sequence	GOP	$\Delta\overline{PSNR}$ (dB)	$\Delta\overline{BR}$ (%)	$\overline{TR}$ (%)
Foreman	2	-0.04	-2.28	-73.25
	4	-0.03	-1.86	-74.06
	8	-0.02	-0.85	-72.80
Hall	2	0	1.31	-69.40
	4	0	1.25	-69.82
	8	0	6.40	-68.13
Coast Guard	2	0	4.60	-70.94
	4	-0.01	5.78	-71.88
	8	0	4.66	-70.46
Soccer	2	-0.04	1.20	-74.01
	4	-0.05	-0.55	-74.92
	8	-0.04	-1.16	-74.29
mean		-0.02	1.54	-72.00

Table 7. Performance of the proposed transcoder for 30fps sequences and IBBP pattern.

Finally, to analyze the global transcoding improvement, Tables 4, 5, 6 and 7 summarize global transcoding performance. In this case, Bjøntegaard and Sullivan´s common test rule (Sullivan et al., 2001) was not used because it is a recommendation only for H.264/AVC. Then, to estimate the PSNR obtained by the transcoder, the original sequences were compared with the output sequences after transcoding. For each four QP points, the PSNR measured is displayed as an average ($\Delta\overline{PSNR}$)). To estimate the BR generated by the reference and the proposed transcoder, the BR generated by both stages (DVC decoding and H.264/AVC encoding) was added. Then equation (1) was applied and it was averaged for each four H.264/AVC QPs ($\Delta\overline{BR}$). As the DVC decoding contributes with most of the bitrate, results are very similar to those in Tables 1. In order to evaluate the TR, total transcoding time was measured for the reference and proposed transcoder. Then Equation 5 was applied and a mean was calculated for each of the four H.264/AVC QPs ($\overline{TR}$). As DVC decoding takes up most of the transcoding time, improvements in this stage have a bigger influence on the overall transcoding time, and so the TR obtained is similar to that in Table 1, reducing the complexity of the transcoding process by up to 73% (on average).

6. Conclusions

In this chapter it is analyzed the transcoding framework for video communications between mobile devices. In addition, it is proposed a WZ to H.264/AVC transcoder designed to support mobile-to-mobile video communications. Since the transcoder device accumulates the highest complexity from both video coders, reducing the time spent in this process is an important goal. With this aim, in this chapter two approaches are proposed to speed-up WZ decoding and H.264/AVC encoding. The first stage is improved by using parallelization techniques as long as the second stage is accelerated by reusing information generated during the first stage. As a result, with both approaches a time reduction of up to 73% is achieved for the complete transcoding process with negligible RD losses. In addition, the presented transcoder performs a mapping for different GOP patterns and lengths between the two paradigms by using an adaptive algorithm, which takes into account the MVs gathered in the side information generation process.

7. Acknowledgements

This work was supported by the Spanish MICINN, Consolider Programme and Plan E funds, as well as European Commission FEDER funds, under Grants CSD2006-00046 and TIN2009-14475-C04-03. It was also supported by JCCM funds under grant PEII09-0037-2328 and PII2I09-0045-9916, and the University of Castilla-La Mancha under Project AT20101802. The work presented was performed by using the VISNET2-WZ-IST software developed in the framework of the VISNET II project.

8. References

Aaron, A., Rui, Z. & Girod, B. (2002). Wyner-Ziv coding of motion video. In: Asilomar Conference on Signals, Systems and Computers, pp. 240-244.

Artigas, X., Ascenso, J., Dalai, M., Klomp, S., Kubasov, D. & Ouaret, M. (2007). The DISCOVER codec: architecture, techniques and evaluation. In: Picture Coding Symposium (PCS), pp. 1-4. Citeseer.

Ascenso, J., Brites, C. & Pereira, F. (2005). Improving frame interpolation with spatial motion smoothing for pixel domain distributed video coding. 5th EURASIP Conference on Speech and Image Processing, Multimedia Communications and Services, Smolenice, Slovak Republic.

Ascenso, J., Brites, C., Dufaux, F., Fernando, A., Ebrahimi, T., Pereira, F. & Tubaro, S. (2010). The VISNET II DVC Codec: Architecture, Tools and Performance. In: European Signal Processing Conference (EUSIPCO).

Brites, C., Ascenso, J., Quintas Pedro, J. & Pereira, F. (2008). Evaluating a feedback channel based transform domain Wyner-Ziv video codec. Signal Processing: Image Communication 23, 269-297.

De Cock, J., Notebaert, S., Vermeirsch, K., Lambert, P. & Van de Walle, R. (2010). Dyadic spatial resolution reduction transcoding for H.264/AVC - Multimedia Systems, 16(2): 139-149.

Fernández-Escribano, G., Kalva, H., Cuenca, P. & Orozco-Barbosa L. (2007). A first approach to speeding-up the inter mode selection in MPEG-2/H.264 transcoders using machine learning. Multimedia Tools Appl. 35(2): 225-240.

Fernández-Escribano, G., Cuenca, P., Orozco-Barbosa, L., Garrido del Solo, A. J. & Kalva, H. (2008). Simple intra prediction algorithms for heterogeneous MPEG-2/H.264 video transcoders. Multimedia Tools Appl. 38(1): 1-25.

Girod, B., Aaron, A.M., Rane, S. & Rebollo-Monedero, D. (2005) Distributed Video Coding. Proceedings of the IEEE 93, 71-83.

Intel Processor Core family. (2011). URL: http://www.intel.com/.

ISO/IEC International Standard 14496-10 (2003). Information Technology - Coding of Audio - Visual Objects - Part 10: Advanced Video Coding.

Martínez, J. L., Kalva, H., Fernández-Escribano, G., Fernando, W.A.C. & Cuenca, P. (2009). Wyner-Ziv to H.264 video transcoder, 16th IEEE International Conference on Image Processing (ICIP), Cairo, Egypt. pp. 2941-2944.

Momcilovic, S., Wang, Y., Rane, S. & Vetro, A. (2010). Toward Realtime Side Information Decoding on Multi-core Processors, IEEE International Workshop on Multimedia Signal Processing (MMSP), Saint-Malo, France.

Oh, R., Park, J. & Jeon, B. (2010). Fast implementation of Wyner-Ziv Video codec using GPGPU, IEEE International Symposium on Broadband Multimedia Systems and Broadcasting (BMSB), Shangai, China.

OpenMP. (2011) The OpenMP API specification for parallel programming. URL: http://openmp.org

Peixoto E., Queiroz R. L. & Mukherjee, D. (2010). A Wyner-Ziv Video Transcoder, Circuits and Systems for Video Technology, IEEE Transactions on , vol.20, no.2, pp.189-200.

Sheng, T., Zhu, X., Hua, G., Guo, H., Zhou, J. & Chen, C. (2010). Feedback-free rate-allocation scheme for transform domain Wyner-Ziv video coding - Multimedia Systems, 16(2): 127-137.

Sullivan G. & Bjøntegaard G. (2001). Recommended Simulation Common Conditions for H.26L Coding Efficiency Experiments on Low-Resolution Progressive-Scan Source Material. ITU-T VCEG, Doc. VCEG-N81.

3

Quantifying Interpretability Loss due to Image Compression

John M. Irvine[1] and Steven A. Israel[2]
[1]*Draper Laboratory, Cambridge, MA,*
[2]*Scientist,*
USA

1. Introduction

Video imagery provides a rich source of information for a range of applications including military missions, security, and law enforcement. Because video imagery captures events over time, it can be used to monitor or detect activities through observation by a user or through automated processing. Inherent in these applications is the assumption that the image quality of the video data will be sufficient to perform the required tasks. However, the large volume of data produced by video sensors often requires data reduction through video compression, frame rate decimation, or cropping the field-of-view as methods for reducing data storage and transmission requirements. This paper presents methods for analyzing and quantifying the information loss arising from various video compression techniques. The paper examines three specific issues:

- **Measurement of image quality**: Building on methods employed for still imagery, we present a method for measuring video quality with respect to performance of relevant analysis tasks. We present the findings from a series of perception experiments and user studies which form the basis for a quantitative measure of video quality.
- **User-based assessments of quality loss**: The design, analysis, and findings from a user-based assessment of image compression are presented. The study considers several compression methods and compression rates for both inter- and intra-frame compression.
- **Objective measures of image compression**: The final topic is a study of video compression using objective image metrics. The findings of this analysis are compared to the user evaluation to characterize the relationship between the two and indicate a method for performing future studies using the objective measures of video quality.

1.1 Information content and analysis

Video data provides the capability to analyze temporal events which enables far deeper analysis than is possible with still imagery. At the primitive level, analysis of still imagery depends on the static detection, recognition, and characterization of objects, such as people or vehicles. By adding the temporal dimension, video data reveals information about the movement of objects, including changes in pose and position and changes in the spatial configuration of objects. This additional information can support the recognition of basic activities, associations among objects, and analysis of complex behavior (Fig. 1).

Fig. 1 is a hierarchy for target recognition information complexity. Each box's color indicates the ability of the developer community to assess the performance and provide confidence measures. The first two boxes on the left exploit information in the sensor phenomenology domain. The right two boxes exploit extracted features derived from the sensor data.

To illustrate the concept, consider a security application with a surveillance camera overlooking a bank parking lot. If the bank is robbed, a camera that collects still images might acquire an image depicting the robbers exiting the building and show several cars in the parking lot. The perpetrators have been detected but additional information is limited. A video camera might collect a clip showing these people entering a specific vehicle for their getaway. Now both the perpetrators and the vehicle have been identified because the activity (a getaway) was observed. If the same vehicle is detecting on other security cameras throughout the city, analysis of multiple videos could reveal the pattern of movement and suggest the location for the robbers' base of operations. In this way, an association is formed between the event and specific locations, namely the bank and the robbers' hideout. If the same perpetrators were observed over several bank robberies, one could discern their pattern of behavior, i.e. their *modus operandi*. This information could enable law enforcement to anticipate future events and respond appropriately (Gualdi *et al.* 2008; Porter *et al.* 2010).

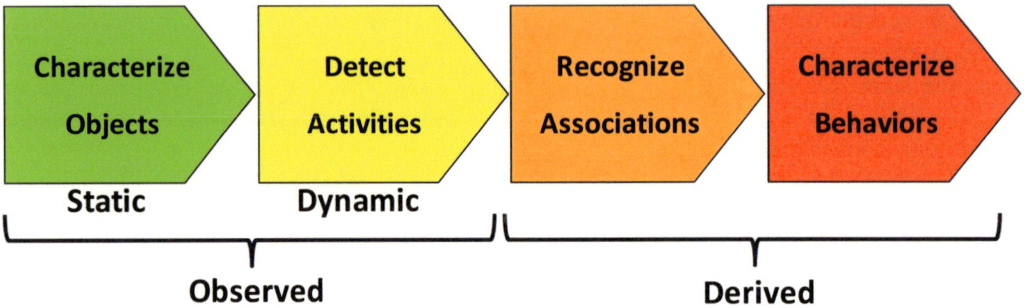

Fig. 1. Image Exploitation and Analysis

1.2 Image interpretability

A fundamental premise of the preceding example is that the imagery, whether a still image or a video clip, is of sufficient quality that the appropriate analysis can be performed (Le Meur *et al.* 2010; Seshadrinathan *et al.* 2010; Xia *et al.* 2010). Military applications have led to the development of a set of standards for assessing and quantifying this aspect of the imagery. The National Imagery Interpretability Rating Scale (NIIRS) is a quantification of image interpretability that has been widely applied for intelligence, surveillance, and reconnaissance (ISR) missions (Irvine 2003; Leachtenauer 1996; Maver *et al.* 1995). Each NIIRS level indicates the types of exploitation tasks an image can support based on the expert judgments of experienced analysts. Development of a NIIRS for a specific imaging modality rests on a perception-based approach. Additional research has verified the relationship between NIIRS and performance of target detection tasks (Baily 1972; Driggers *et al.* 1997; Driggers *et al.* 1998; Lubin 1995). Accurate methods for predicting NIIRS from the sensor parameters and image acquisition conditions have been developed empirically and substantially increase the utility of NIIRS (Leachtenauer *et al.* 1997; Leachtenauer and Driggers 2001).

The NIIRS provides a common framework for discussing the interpretability, or information potential, of imagery. NIIRS serves as a standardized indicator of image interpretability within the community. An image quality equation (IQE) offers a method for predicting the NIIRS of an image based on sensor characteristics and the image acquisition conditions (Leachtenauer *et al.* 1997; Leachtenauer and Driggers 2001). Together, the NIIRS and IQE are useful for:

- Communicating the relative usefulness of the imagery,
- Documenting requirements for imagery,
- Managing the tasking and collection of imagery,
- Assisting in the design and assessment of future imaging systems, and
- Measuring the performance of sensor systems and imagery exploitation devices.

The foundation for the NIIRS is that trained analysts have consistent and repeatable perceptions about the interpretability of imagery. If more challenging tasks can be performed with a given image, then the image is deemed to be of higher interpretability. A set of standard image exploitation tasks or "criteria" defines the levels of the scale. To illustrate, consider Fig. 2. Several standard NIIRS tasks for visible imagery appear at the right. Note that the tasks for levels 5, 6, and 7 can be performed, but the level 8 task cannot. The grill detailing and/or license plate on the sedan are not evident. Thus, an analyst would assign a NIIRS level 7 to this image.

Rating level 5:

Detect open bay doors of vehicle storage buildings

Rating Level 6:

Identify automobiles as sedans or station wagons.

Rating level 7:

Detect individual steps on stairway.

Rating Level 8:

Identify grill detailing and/or the license plate on a passenger/truck type vehicle

Fig. 2. Illustration of NIIRS for a still image

Recent studies have extended the NIIRS concept to motion imagery (video). In exploring avenues for the development of a NIIRS-like metric for motion imagery, a clearer understanding of the factors that affect the perceived quality of motion imagery was needed (Irvine *et al.* 2006a; Young *et al.* 2010b). Several studies explored specific aspects of this problem, including target motion, camera motion, and frame rate, and the nature of the analysis tasks (Hands 2004; Huynh-Thu *et al.* 2011; Moorthy *et al.* 2010). Factors affecting perceived interpretability of motion imagery include the ground sample distance (GSD) of the imagery, motion of the targets, motion of the camera, frame rate (temporal resolution), viewing geometry, and scene complexity. These factors have been explored and characterized in a series of evaluations with experienced imagery analysts:

- Spatial resolution: Evaluations shows that for motion imagery the interpretability of an video clip exhibits a linear relationship with the natural log of the ground sample distance (GSD), at least for clips where the GSD is fairly constant over the clip (Cermak *et al.* 2011; Irvine *et al.* 2004; Irvine *et al.* 2005; Irvine *et al.* 2007b) .
- Motion and Complexity: User perception evaluations assessed the effects of target motion, camera motion, and scene complexity on perceived image quality (Irvine *et al.* 2006b). The evaluations indicated that target motion has a significant positive effect on perceived image quality, whereas camera motion has a barely discernable effect.
- Frame Rate: These evaluations assessed object detection and identification and other image exploitation tasks as a function of frame rate and contrast (Fenimore *et al.* 2006). The study demonstrated that an analyst's ability to detect and recognize objects of interest degrades at frame rates below 15 frames per second. Furthermore, the effect of reduced frame rate is more pronounced with low contrast targets.
- Task Performance: The evaluations assessed the ability of imagery analysts to perform various image exploitation tasks with motion imagery. The tasks included detection and recognition of objects, as might be done with still imagery and the detection and recognition of activities, which relies on the dynamic nature of motion imagery (Irvine *et al.* 2006b; Irvine *et al.* 2007c). Analysts exhibited good consistency in the performance of these tasks. In addition, dynamic exploitation tasks that require detection and recognition of activities are sensitive to the frame rate of the video clip.

Building on these perceptions studies, a new Video NIIRS was developed (Petitti *et al.* 2009; Young *et al.* 2009). The work presented in this paper quantifies video interpretability using a 100-point scale described in Section 3 (Irvine *et al.* 2007a; Irvine *et al.* 2007b; Irvine *et al.* 2007c). The scale development methodologies imply that each scale is a linear transform of the other, although this relationship has not been validated (Irvine *et al.* 2006a; Irvine *et al.* 2006b). Other methods for measuring video image quality frequently focus on objective functions of the imagery data, rather than perception of the potential utility of the imagery to support specific types of analysis (Watson *et al.* 2001; Watson and Kreslake 2001; Winkler 2001; Winkler *et al.* 2001).

2. Image compression

A recent study of compression for motion imagery focused on objective performance of target detection and target tracking tasks to quantify the information loss due to compression (Gibson *et al.* 2006). Gibson *et al.* (2006) leverage recent work aimed at quantification of the interpretability of motion imagery (Irvine *et al.* 2007b). Using techniques developed in these earlier studies, this paper presents a user evaluation of the interpretability of motion imagery compressed under three methods and various bitrates. The interpretability of the native, uncompressed imagery establishes the reference for comparison (He and Xiong 2006; Hewage *et al.* 2009; Yang *et al.* 2010; Yasakethu *et al.* 2009).

2.1 Data compression

The dataset for the study consisted of the original (uncompressed) motion imagery clips and clips compressed by three compression methods at various compression rates (Abomhara *et al.* 2010). The three compression methods were:

- Motion JPEG 2000 – intraframe only
- MPEG-2 – intraframe and interframe
- H.264 – intraframe and interframe

All three were exercised in intraframe mode. Each of the parent clips was compressed to three megabits per second, representing a modest level of compression. In addition, each parent clip was severely compressed to examine the limits of the codecs. Actual bitrates for these severe cases depend on the individual clip and codec. The choice of compression methods and levels supports two goals: comparison across codecs and comparisons of the same compression method at varying bitrates. Table 1 shows the combinations represented in the study. We recorded the actual bit rate for each product and use this as a covariate in the analysis.

The study used the Kakadu implementation of JPEG2000, the Vanguard Software Solutions, Inc. implementation of H.264, and the Adobe Premiere's MPEG-2 codec. In each case, the 300 key frame interval was used for interframe compression unless otherwise noted. Intraframe encoding is comparable to interframe encoding with 1 key frame interval.

The study used progressive scan motion imagery in a 848 x 480 pixel raster at 30 frames per second (f/s). Since most of the desirable source material was available to us in 720 P HD video, a conversion process was employed to generate the lower resolution/lower frame rate imagery. We evaluated the conversion process to assure the goals of the study could be met. The video clips were converted using Adobe Premiere tools.

Bitrate	**Uncompressed**	**H.264 (VSS)**		**JPEG 2000 (KDU)**	**MPEG 2 (Premiere)**	
		Inter-frame	**Intra-frame**	**Intra-frame**	**Inter-frame**	**Intra-frame**
Native	X					
3 MB/sec		X	X	X	X	X
Severe		X		X	X	

Note: the severe bitrate represents the limit of the specific codec on a given clip.

Table 1. Codecs and Compression Rates

2.2 Experimental design

The study consists of two parts. Both parts used the set of compression products described above. The first part was an evaluation in which trained imagery analysts viewed the compressed products and the original parent clip to assess the effects of compression on interpretability. The second part of the study implemented a set of computational image metrics and examined their behavior with respect to bitrate and codec. The typical duration of each clip is 10 seconds. Ten video clips were used for this study.

3. User-based evaluation of compression

To quantify image interpretability, subjective rating scale was developed by Irvine *et al.* (2007c), based on consistent ratings by trained imagery analysts. The scale assigns the values 0 to a video clip of no utility and 100 to clips that could support any of the analysis tasks under consideration (Fig. 3). Three additional clips identified in this study formed markers to evenly divide the subjective interpretability space. Thus, reference clips were available at subjective rating levels of 0, 25, 50, 75, and 100.

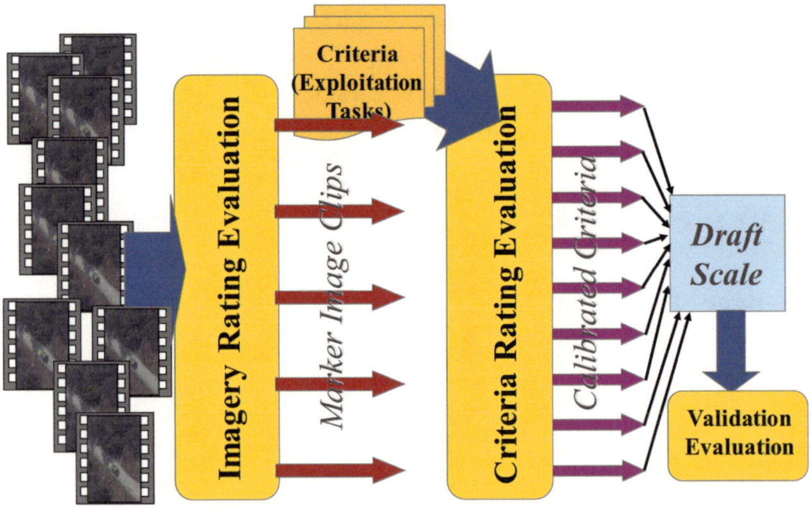

Fig. 3. NIIRS Development Functional Decomposition

A set of specific image exploitation tasks were reviewed by imagery analysts and rated relative to these marker video clips. In this way, these analysis tasks were calibrated to the subjective rating scale. A subset of these "calibrated" analysis tasks were used to evaluate the compressed video products (Table 2). Note that some of these tasks do not require analysis of temporal activity and could be performed with still imagery. We label these as "static" tasks. A second set of tasks are "dynamic" because they require direct observation or inference about movements of objects.

Image analysts rated their confidence in performing each image exploitation task with respect to each compression product, including the original (uncompressed) clip. We calculated an overall interpretability rating from each analyst for each clip.

3.1 Approach

For each parent clip, three criteria (image exploitation tasks) were assigned. The considerations for selecting the criteria were:

- The criteria should "bound" the interpretability of the parent clip, i.e. at least one of the three should be difficult to do and one should be easy
- The criteria (or at least some of the criteria) should reference objects and activity that are comparable to the content of the clip
- The criteria should have exhibited low rater variance in the previous evaluations

Static Criteria	Detect large buildings (e.g. hospitals, factories)
	Identify individual rail cars (e.g. gondola, flat, box) and locomotives by type (e.g. steam, diesel)
	Identify vehicles by general class (civilian, military tracked, artillery, construction)
	Detect presence of freight in open-bed trucks
	Detect gatherings of 5 or more people
Dynamic Criteria	Determine motion and direction of large vehicles (e.g. trains, barges, 18-wheelers)
	Track a civilian-size moving vehicle (e.g., car, truck, SUV)
	Distinguish between an orderly assembly and a panicked crowd
	Distinguish among a person walking, a person running, and a person riding a small vehicle (bicycle, moped, or motorcycle)
	Determine whether a person is getting into or out of a vehicle

Table 2. Video Analysis Tasks

3.2 Analysis and findings

The data analysis progresses through several stages: verification and quality control, exploratory analysis to uncover interesting relationships, and statistical modeling to validate findings and formally test hypotheses of interest. The initial analysis examined the data for anomalies or outliers. None were found in this case.

Next, we calculated an overall interpretability rating from each analyst for each clip. The method for calculating these ratings was as follows: Each of the three criteria used to rate each clip was calibrated (on a 0-100 scale) in terms of interpretability, where this calibration was derived from an earlier evaluation (Irvine *et al.* 2007c). Multiplying the interpretability level by the IA's confidence rating produces a score for each criterion. The final interpretability score (Equation 1) was the maximum of the three scores for a given clip.

$$\text{Interpretability Score}(j, k) = \max \{C_{i,j,k}\, I_{i,k} : i=1,2,3\} / 100 \qquad (1)$$

Where $C_{i,j,k}$ is the confidence rating by the jth IA on the kth clip for the ith criterion and $I_{i,k}$ is the calibrated interpretability level for that criterion. All subsequent analysis presented below is based on this final interpretability score. The remaining analysis is divided into two sections: interframe compression and intraframe compression. Ultimately, we compared the analyst derived utility measures, as a NIIRS surrogate, to the automated computational values.

All three codecs yielded products for the evaluation. However, MPEG-2 would not support extreme compression rates. Bitrate was the dominant factor, but pronounced differences among the codecs emerged too (Fig. 6 and Fig. 7). At modest compression rates, MPEG-2 exhibited a substantial loss in interpretability compared to either H.264 or JPEG-2000. Only JPEG-2000 supported more extreme intraframe compression. A computational model was developed to characterize the significance among codec, scene, and bitrate's effect on data quality. There were systematic differences across the clips, as expected, but the effects of the codecs and bitrates were consistent. When modeled as a covariate, the effects of bitrate dominate. The effect due to codec is modest, but still significant. As expected, there is a significant main effect due to scene, but no scene-by-codec interaction.

3.3 Interframe compression

Analysis of the interframe ratings shows a loss in image interpretability for both MPEG-2 and H.264 as a function of bitrate (Fig. 4). The initial compression from the native rate to 3 MB per second corresponds to a modest loss in interpretability. This finding is consistent with previous work. At extreme compression levels (below 1 MB per second), the interpretability loss is substantial. H.264 generally supported more extreme compression levels, but the interpretability degrades accordingly. Although the exact compression level

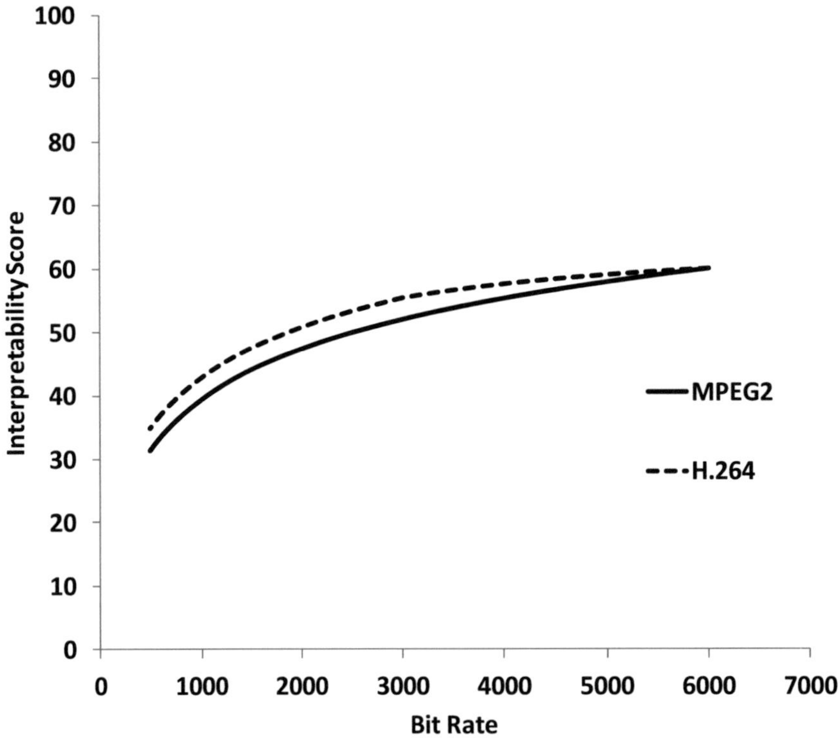

Fig. 4. Summary Comparison Across Codec and Bitrate

varies by clip, the pattern is clear for all clips. Statistical analysis shows that bitrate, modeled as a covariate, is the primary factor affecting interpretability. For interframe compression, the differences between H.264 and MPEG-2 are small but statistically significant (Table 3). The pattern holds across all scenes, as indicated by the lack of a codec-by-scene interaction effect.

Source	Deg. Of Freedom	F-statistic	Significance <0.025
Intercept	1	6.2	0.0033
BitRate	1	59.7	0.00003
Codec	2	5.7	0.015
Scene	4	15.4	0.00028
Codec * Scene	8	0.5	0.82

Table 3. Analysis of Covariance for Interframe Comparisons

3.4 Intraframe compression

In the case of intraframe compression, all three codecs yielded products for the evaluation, although MPEG-2 would not support extreme compression rates. The findings in this case are slightly different than interframe compression. Bitrate remained the dominant factor, but more pronounced differences among the codecs emerged (Figure 4). At modest compression rates, MPEG-2 exhibited a substantially loss in interpretability compared to either H.264

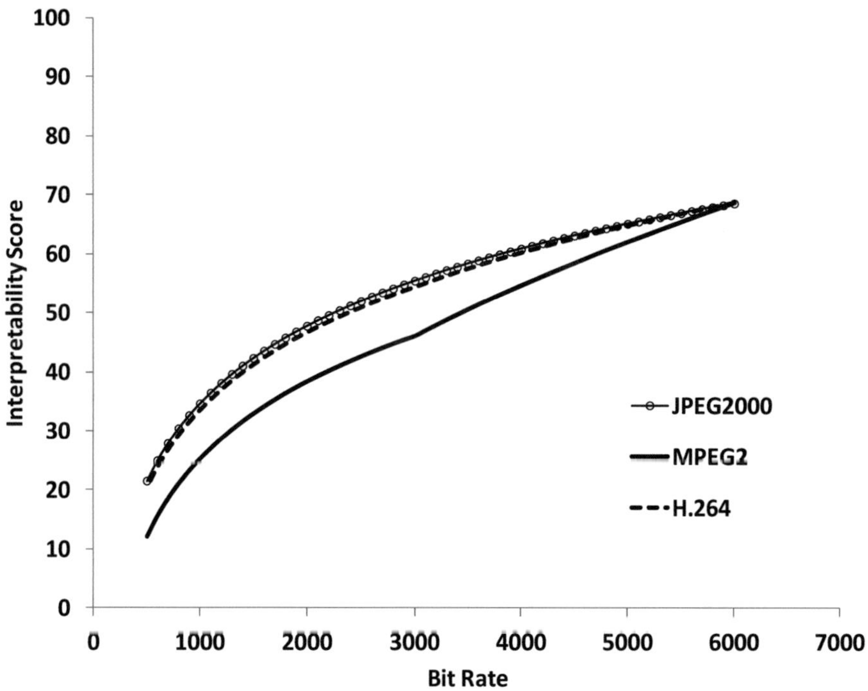

Fig. 5. Summary Comparison Across Codec and Bitrate

or JPEG-2000. Only JPEG-2000 supported more extreme intraframe compression and highly compressed renditions were produced from all of the parent clips. As with the interframe comparisons, there were systematic differences across the clips, as expected, but the effects of the codecs and bitrates were consistent. The analysis of covariance confirms these statistical effects (Table 4). When modeled as a covariate, effects of bitrate dominate. The effect due to codec is modest, but still significant. As expected, there is a significant main effect due to scene, but no scene-by-codec interaction.

Source	Deg. of Freedom	F-statistic	Significance < 0.025
Intercept	1	0.9	0.0038
BitRate	1	24.4	0.0078
Codec	3	5.6	0.001
Scene	4	26.2	0.00001
Codec * Scene	12	0.5	0.84

Table 4. Analysis of Variance for Interframe Comparisons

4. Computational measures and performance assessment

In the previous section, analyst assessments of image quality were characterized. This section identifies computational attributes for image quality that can be extracted from video clips. Performance measures will evaluate the computational image quality metrics and provide an understanding of how well they compare to codec, bitrate, and scene parameters.

4.1 Computational image metrics

We reviewed a variety of image metrics to quantify image quality (Bhat *et al.* 2010; Chikkerur *et al.* 2011; Culibrk *et al.* 2011; Huang 2011; Sohn *et al.* 2010). Based on a review of the literature and assessment of the properties of these metrics, we selected four measures for this study: two edge-based metrics, structural similarity image metric (SSIM), and SNR. SSIM and edge metrics are performed at each pixel location. The resultant can be viewed as an image (Fig. 6). SNR metrics deal with overall information content and cannot be visualized as an image. These metrics were computed for the original (uncompressed) clips and for all of the compressed products. We will present the computation methods and the results.

The color information was transposed into panchromatic (intensity) using either a HSI transformation or luminance. Intensity was computed using (2):

$$I = \frac{R + G + B}{3} \tag{2}$$

Luminance was computed (3)

$$Y = 0.299R + 0.587G + 0.114B \tag{3}$$

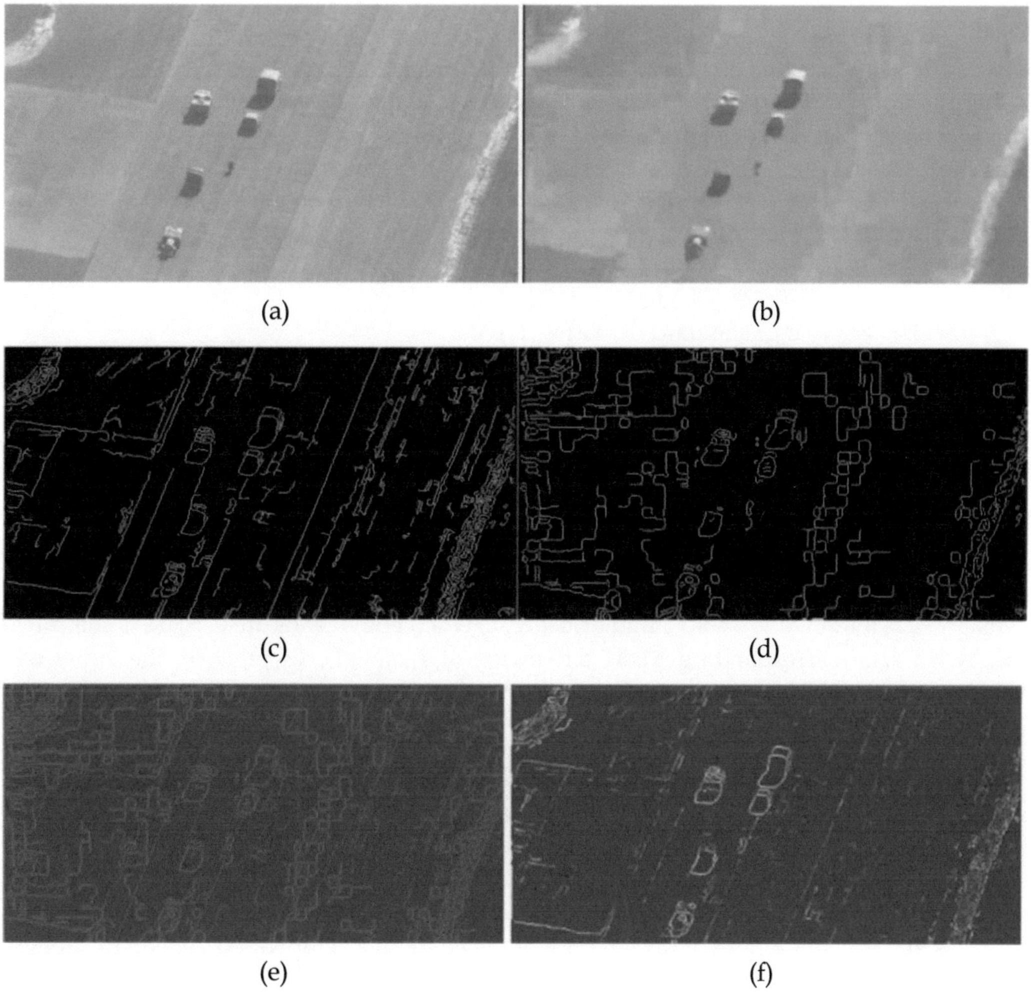

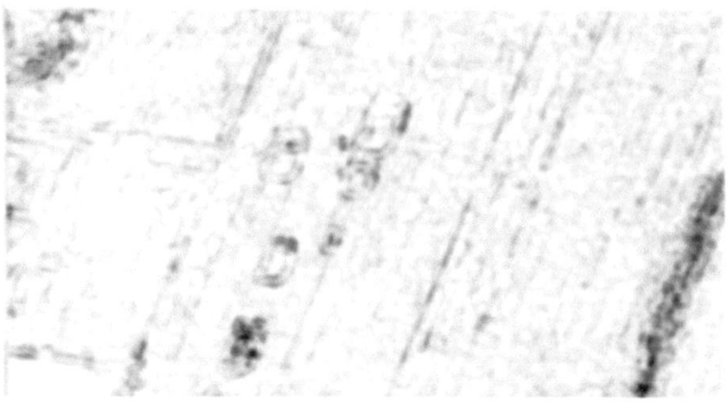

Imagery extracted from the VIVID Public Release Data set provided by Air Force Research Laboratory

(g)

Fig. 6. (a) Original, (b) Compressed version, (c,d) original edge images, (e) edge images displayed together where Red, Blue, Magenta are from the original, the compressed, both edge images respectively (f) edge intensities, and (g) is the SSIM image darker areas represent more noticeable differences.

4.1.1 SSIM

The first metric for image quality is the Structural Similarity Image Metric (Wang *et al.* 2004). SSIM quantifies differences between two images, I_1 and I_2, by taking three variables into consideration, luminance, contrast, and spatial similarity. For grey level images, those variables are measured in the images as the mean, standard deviation, and Pearson's correlation coefficient between the two images respectively. For our application, the RGB data was converted to grey level using the standard Matlab function. Let:

$$\mu = mean(I_1)$$

$$\sigma_1 = \text{standard deviation}(I_1)$$

$$\sigma_{12} = \frac{1}{N-1}\sum_{i.j}(I_1(i,j)-\mu_1)(I_2(i,j)-\mu_2) : \text{covariance}$$

then

$$\text{SSIM}(I_1, I_2) = \frac{2\mu_1\mu_2}{\mu_1^2+\mu_2^2} * \frac{2\sigma_1\sigma_2}{\sigma_1^2+\sigma_2^2} * \frac{\sigma_{12}}{\sigma_1^2\sigma_2^2} \quad (4)$$

Equation 4 is modified to avoid singularities, e.g., when both means are 0. SSIM is computed locally on each corresponding MxM sub-image of I_1 and I_2. In practice, the sub-image window size is 11x11, implemented as a convolution filter. The SSIM value is the average across the entire image.

4.1.2 Edge metrics

Two edge metrics were examined. The first is denoted by CE for Common Edges and the second is denoted SE for strength of edges (O'Brien *et al.* 2007). Heuristically, CE measures the ratio of the number edges in a compressed image to the number of edges in the original; whereas SE measures a ratio of the strength of the edges in a compressed version to strength of the edges in the original.

Given two images I_1 and I_2 CE(I_1, I_2) and SE(I_1, I_2) are computed as follows. From the grey level images, edge images are constructed using the Canny edge operator. The edge images are designated as E_1 and E_2. Assume that the values in E_1 and E_2 are 1 for an edge pixel and 0 otherwise. Let "*" denote the pixel wise product. Let G_1 and G_2 denote the gradient images of I_1 and I_2 respectively. G(m,n) was approximated as the maximum of absolute value of the set {I(m,n) - I(m+t1,n + t2) | -6 < t1 < 6 and -6< t2 < 6}, i.e. the maximum difference between the center value and all values in a 5x5 neighborhood around it. With that notation,

$$CE(I_1, I_2) = \frac{2 * \sum(E_1 * E_2)}{\sum E_1 + \sum E_2} \quad (5)$$

where the sum is taken over all the pixels within a given frame.

$$SE(I_1, I_2) = \frac{\sum(E_2 * G_2)}{\sum E_1 * G_1} \quad (6)$$

where the sum is taken over all the pixels within a given frame.

An additional set of edge operators were also applied. These operators are called edge strength (ES) metrics. Let Y_1 be the luminance component of an original frame from an clip and let Y_2 be the corresponding frame after compression processing, also in luminance. We apply a Sobel filter, S, to both Y_1 and Y_2, where for a grayscale frame F:

$$S(F) = \sqrt{(H * F)^2 + (V * F)^2} \tag{7}$$

The filters H and V used in the Sobel edge detector are:

$$H = \begin{matrix} -1 & 0 & 1 \\ -2 & 0 & 2 \\ -1 & 0 & 1 \end{matrix} \tag{7.1}$$

$$V = H^T \tag{7.2}$$

We define two metrics, one for local loss of edge energy (EL) (thus finding blurred edges from Y_1 in Y_2) and the other for the addition of edge energy (thus finding edges added to Y_2 that are weaker in Y_1). Each metric examines the strongest edges in one image (either Y_1 or Y_2) and compares them to the edges at the corresponding pixels in the other (Y_2 or Y_1).

For the grayscale image F, let I(F,f) be the set of image pixels, p, where F (p) is at least as large as f * max(F). That is:

$$I(F,f) = \{Pixels : F(p) \geq f * \max(F)\} \tag{8}$$

Using the definition of Y(F,f), the two edge metrics are:

$$BlurIndex = \frac{mean(S(Y_2))}{mean(S(Y_1))} \tag{9}$$

where the means are taken over the set $I(S(I_1), 0.99)$

$$AddedEdgeEnergy = \frac{mean(S(Y_1))}{mean(S(Y_2))} \tag{10}$$

where the means are taken over the set $I(S(Y_2), 0.99)$.

4.1.3 SNR

Finally, we examined the peak signal to noise ratio (PSNR). The PSNR is defined for a pair of m×n luminance images, Y_1 and Y_2. Let MSE be defined by,

$$MSE - \frac{1}{mn}\sum_{i=0}^{m-1}\sum_{j=0}^{n-1}\left\|Y_1(i,j)\quad Y_2(i,j)\right\|^2 \tag{11}$$

The PSNR is defined as:

$$PSNR = 10\log_{10}\frac{MAX_I^2}{MSE} = 20\log_{10}\frac{MAX_I}{\sqrt{MSE}} \qquad (12)$$

where MAX_I is maximum pixel value of the image. In our case, MAX_I is taken to be 255.

4.2 Metrics and performance

The image metrics were plotted (Fig. 7). The image metrics are all highly correlated across both bitrate and codec, for both intraframe and interframe compression techniques. For the set of clips with every 300 key frame interval, the correlation was greater than 0.9. In each case, the lower information content is indicated by lower position on the Y axis, quality. The X axis is the target bitrate. Due to the high correlation a single computational metric was chosen for more detailed analysis to quantify the relationship between image quality and bitrate. SSIM was selected because it generates an image to diagnose unexpected values and the computation is based upon perceptual difference of spatial similarity and contrast.

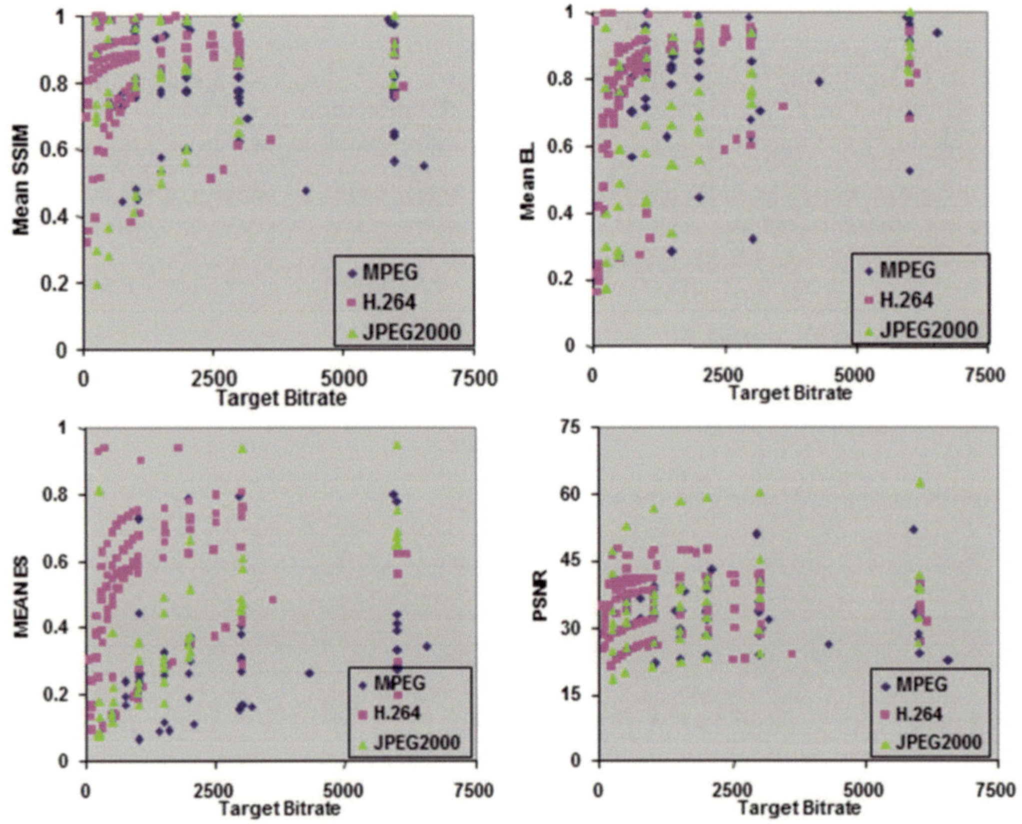

Fig. 7. Target Bitrate (k bps) versus Image Metric: SSIM, EL, ES, and PSNR

Fig. 7 indicates that SSIM, CE, and SE that measures separate image quality based on bitrate. H.264's asymptotic quality improvement observed in the rise in the graph from the initial frames (Fig. 7). This corresponds to exactly where the algorithm is increasing its fidelity of the compressed frames to the original frames. Along this initial portion of the clip the metrics agree with human perception of the image quality increasing.

Fig. 8 plots SSIM versus frame at differeing bitrates for the H.264 codec, which is an interframe codec. The saw-tooth nature of the graph is the result of the group of pictures (GOP) sequence. The peak and trough differences are between bilinear interpolation between key frames (B) and predicted (P) encoded frames.

The observations for the metrics listed above for H.264 were also visually evident in the case of MPEG compression. Close inspection of the clips shows the quality to be lower in the case of MPEG than for H.264. The example in Fig. 9 is taken from a clip that was compressed to 2 Mbits/second using both codecs. While discernable in both the original and the H.264 compressed versions, some of the individuals' heads seem to be nearly totally lost in the MPEG version.

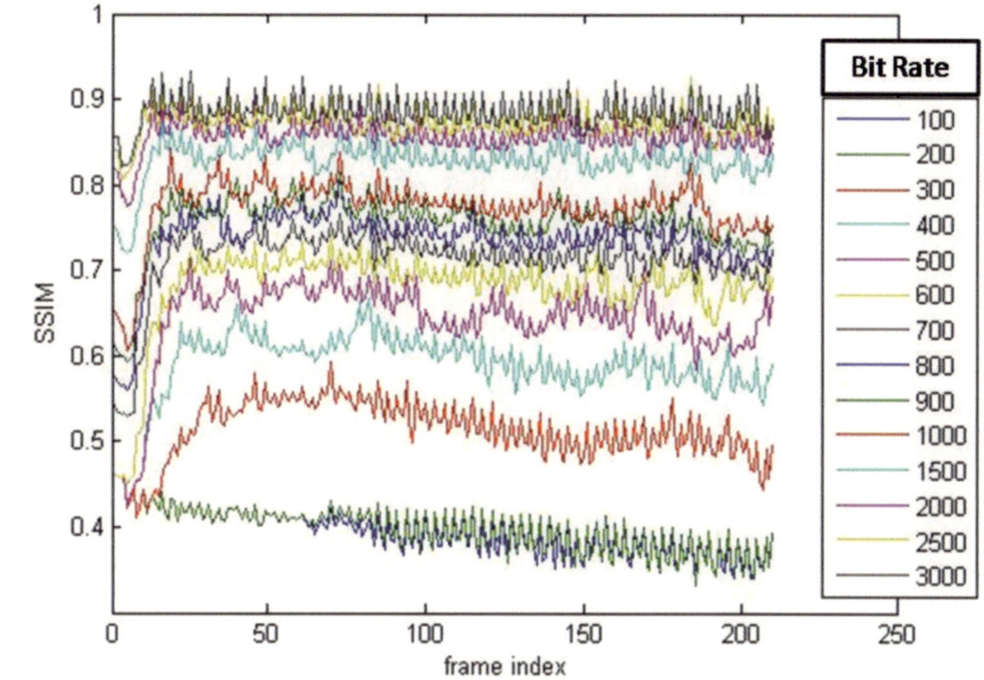

Fig. 8. Plot of the SSIM evaluated on each frame for 11 different bit rates.
Each clip was compressed using H.264 with the key frames 1 every 300 frames.

5. Discussion

These experiments demonstrate the existence of several metrics that are monotonic with bitrate. The metrics showed considerable sensitivity to image quality that matched the authors' observations. Specifically, the MPEG quality was considerably less than H.264 at the same bitrate. The knee of the quality curves exist between 500k and 1000k bps. In addition, the metrics were sensitive to the encoded structure of the individual frames as the saw tooth differences between the B and P frames were readily observable.

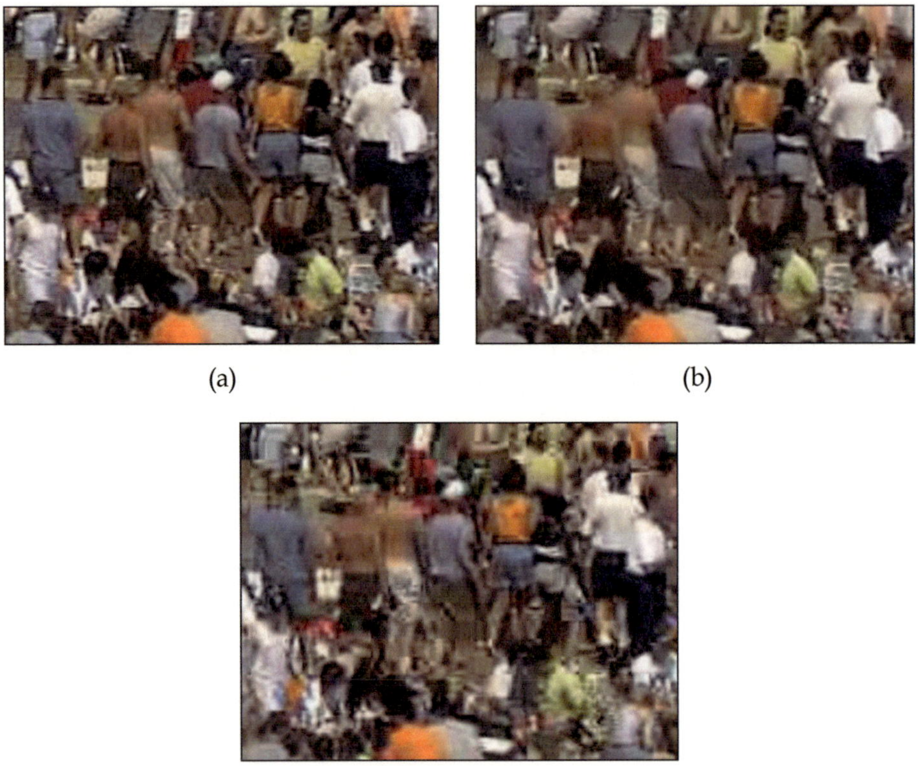

(a) (b)

(c)

Fig. 9. (a) Original frame and compressed using (b) H.264 and (c) MPEG.

A qualitative comparison of the objective metrics to the user assessment of interpretability shows strong consistency. Compression of these video products to bitrates below 1,000k bps yields discernable losses in image interpretability. The objective metrics shows a similar knee in the curve. These data suggest that one could estimate loss in interpretability from compression using the objective metrics and derive a prediction of the loss in Video NIIRS. Development of such a model would require conducting a second user experiment to establish the relationship between the subjective interpretability scale used in this study and the published Video NIIRS. The additional data from such an experiment would also support validation of a model for predicting loss due to compression.

6. Conclusion

The evaluations and analyses presented in this Chapter characterize the loss in perceived interpretability of motion imagery arising from various compression methods and compression rates. The findings build on previous studies (Irvine *et al.* 2007a; O'Brien *et al.* 2007). The findings are consistent with other evaluations of video compression (Gibson *et al.* 2006; Young *et al.* 2010a). Evaluation of image compression for motion imagery illustrates how interpretability-based methods can be applied to the analysis of the image chain. We present both objective image metrics and analysts' assessments of various compressed products. The results show good agreement between the two approaches. Further research is needed to validate a model-based relationship that could predict Video NIIRS loss due to compression using the objective image metrics presented here.

7. References

Abomhara, M., Khalifa, O.O., Zakaria, O., Zaidan, A.A., Zaidan, B.B., and Rame, A. 2010. Video Compression Techniques: An Overview, *Journal of Applied Sciences,* 10(16): 1834-1840.

Baily, H.H. 1972. Target Acquisition Through Visual Recognition: An Early Model, *Target Acquisition Symposium,* Orlando, 14-16 November.

Bhat, A., Richardson, I., and Kannangara, S. 2010. A New Perceptual Quality Metric for Compressed Video Based on Mean Squared Error, *Signal Processing: Image Communication,* 25(7): 588-596.

Cermak, G., Pinson, M., and Wolf, S. 2011. The Relationship Among Video Quality, Screen Resolution, and Bit Rate, *IEEE Transactions on Broadcasting,* 57(2): 258-262.

Chikkerur, S., Sundaram, V., Reisslein, M., and Karam, L.J. 2011. Objective Video Quality Assessment Methods: A Classification, Review, and Performance Comparison, *IEEE Transactions on Broadcasting,* 57(2): 165-182.

Culibrk, D., Mirkovic, M., Zlokolica, V., Pokric, M., Crnojevic, V., and Kukolj, D. 2011. Salient Motion Features for Video Quality Assessment, *IEEE Transactions on Image Processing,* 20(4): 948-958.

Driggers, R.G., Cox, P.G., and Kelley, M. 1997. National Imagery Interpretation Rating System and the Probabilities of Detection, Recognition, and Identification, *Optical Engineering,* 36(7): 1952-1959.

Driggers, R.G., Cox, P.G., Leachtenauer, J., Vollmerhausen, R., and Scribner, D.A. 1998. Targeting and Intelligence Electro-Optical Recognition and Modeling: A Juxtaposition of the Probabilities of Discrimination and the General Image Quality Equation, *Optical Engineering,* 37(3): 789-797.

Fenimore, C., Irvine, J.M., Cannon, D., Roberts, J., Aviles, I., Israel, S.A., Brennan, M., Simon, L., Miller, J., Haverkamp, D., Tighe, P.F., and Gross, M. 2006. Perceptual Study of the Impact of Varying Frame Rate on Motion Imagery Interpretability, *Human Vision and Electronic Imaging XI,* SPIE, San Jose, 16-19 January, 6057: 248-256.

Gibson, L., Irvine, J.M., O'Brien, G., Schroeder, S., Bozell, A., Israel, S.A., and Jaeger, L. 2006. User Evaluation of Differential Compression for Motion Imagery, *Defense and Security Symposium 2006,* SPIE, Orlando, 17-21 April, 6209: paper number 6209-03.

Gualdi, G., Prati, A., and Cucchiara, R. 2008. Video Streaming for Mobile Video Surveillance, *IEEE Transactions on Multimedia,* 10(6): 1142-1154.

Hands, D.S. 2004. A Basic Multimedia Quality Metric, *IEEE Transactions on Multimedia,* 6(6): 806-816

He, Z. and Xiong, H. 2006. Transmission Distortion Analysis for Real-Time Video Encoding and Streaming Over Wireless Networks, *IEEE Transactions on Circuits and Systems for Video Technology,* 16(9): 1051-1062.

Hewage, C.T.E.R., Worrall, S.T., Dogan, S., Villette, S., and Kondoz, A.M. 2009. Quality Evaluation of Color Plus Depth Map-Based Stereoscopic Video, *IEEE Journal of Selected Topics in Signal Processing,* 3(2): 304-318.

Huang, S.C. 2011. An Advanced Motion Detection Algorithm with Video Quality Analysis for Video Surveillance Systems, *IEEE Transactions on Circuits and Systems for Video Technology,* 21(1): 1-14.

Huynh-Thu, Q., Garcia, M.N., Speranza, F., Corriveau, P., and Raake, A. 2011. Study of Rating Scales for Subjective Quality Assessment of High-Definition Video, *IEEE Transactions on Broadcasting,* 57(1): 1-14.

Irvine, J.M. 2003. *National Imagery Interpretability Rating Scale,* 1442-1456. In: Driggers, R.G. *Encyclopedia of Optical Engineering,* Marcel Dekker, Inc., New York.

Irvine, J.M., Fenimore, C., Cannon, D., Roberts, J., Israel, S.A., Simon, L., Watts, C., Miller, J.D., Avilés, A.I., Tighe, P.F., and Behrens, R.J. 2004. Feasibility Study for the Development of a Motion Imagery Quality Metric, *33rd Applied Imagery and Pattern Recognition Workshop: Image and Data Fusion,* IEEE Computer Society, Washington, 13-15 October: 179-183.

Irvine, J.M., Fenimore, C., Cannon, D., Roberts, J., Israel, S.A., Simon, L., Watts, C., Miller, J.D., Avilés, A.I., Tighe, P.F., and Behrens, R.J. 2005. Factors Affecting Development of a Motion Imagery Quality Metric, *Defense & Security Symposium,* SPIE, Orlando, Florida, 29-31 March, 5817: 116-123.

Irvine, J.M., Cannon, D., Miller, J., Bartolucci, J., Gibson, L., Fenimore, C., Roberts, J., Aviles, I., Brennan, M., Bozell, A., Simon, L., and Israel, S.A. 2006a. Methodology Study for Development of a Motion Imagery Quality Metric, *Defense and Security Symposium,* SPIE, Orlando, Florida, 17-21 April.

Irvine, J.M., Fenimore, C., Cannon, D., Haverkamp, D., Roberts, J., Israel, S.A., Simon, L., Miller, J., Avilés, A.I., and Brennan, M. 2006b. Development of a Motion Imagery Quality Metric, *American Society for Photogrammetry and Remote Sensing (ASPRS) Annual Meeting,* ASPRS, Reno, Nevada, 1-5 May.

Irvine, J.M., Avilés, A.I., Cannon, D.M., Fenimore, C., Israel, S.A., O'Brien, G., and Roberts, J. 2007a. Quantifying Interpretability for Motion Imagery: Applications to Image Chain Analysis, *10th International Conference on Information Fusion (Fusion 2007),* IEEE, Quebec, 9-12 July.

Irvine, J.M., O'Brien, G., Israel, S.A., Fenimore, C., Roberts, J., Brennan, M., Bartolucci, J., and Cannon, D.M. 2007b. Perceived interpretability of Motion Imagery: Implications for Scale Development, *SPIE Defense and Security Symposium,* Orlando, 9-13 April.

Irvine, J.M., O'Brien, G., Miller, J., Israel, S.A., Fenimore, C., Roberts, J., Bartolucci, J., and Cannon, D.M. 2007c. User-oriented Evaluation of Compression for Motion Imagery, *SPIE Defense and Security Symposium,* Orlando, 9-13 April.

Le Meur, O., Ninassi, A., Le Callet, P., and Barba, D. 2010. Overt Visual Attention for Free-Viewing and Quality Assessment Tasks: Impact of the Regions of Interest on the Video Quality Metric, *Signal Processing: Image Communications,* 25: 5.

Leachtenauer, J. 1996. National Imagery Interpretability Rating Scale: Overveiw and Product Description, *Annual Meeting,* ASPRS, Baltimore, April.

Leachtenauer, J.C., Malila, W., Irvine, J.M., Colburn, L., and Salvaggio, N. 1997. General Image-Quality Equation: GIQE, *Applied Optics,* 36(32): 8322-8328.

Leachtenauer, J.C. and Driggers, R.G. 2001. *Surveillance and Reconnaissance Imaging Systems: Modeling and Performance,* Artech House, Inc., Boston.

Lubin, J. 1995. *A Visual Discrimination Model for Imaging System Design and Evaluation*. In: Menendez, A.R. and Peli, E. *Vision Models for Target Detection and Recognition*, World Scientific.

Maver, L.A., Erdman, C.D., and Riehl, K. 1995. Image Interpretability Rating Scale, *Digest of Technical Papers: International Symposium Society for Information Display*, Society for Information Display, XXVI: 117-120.

Moorthy, A.K., Seshadrinathan, K., Soundararajan, R., and Bovik, A.C. 2010. Wireless Video Quality Assessment: A Study of Subjective Scores and Objective Algorithms, *IEEE Transactions on Circuits and Systems for Video Technology*, 20(4): 587-599.

O'Brien, G., Israel, S.A., Irvine, J.M., Fenimore, C., Roberts, J., Brennan, M., Cannon, D.M., and Miller, J. 2007. Metrics to Estimate Image Quality in Compressed Video Sequences, *SPIE Defense and Security Symposium*, Orlando, 9-13 April.

Petitti, F., Young, D., Butto, R., Bakir, T., and Brennan, M. 2009. Video-NIIRS RP 0901, *http://www.gwg.nga.mil/misb/rrpubs.html*: 1-13.

Porter, R., Fraser, A.M., and Hush, D. 2010. Wide-Area Motion Imagery: Narrowing the Semantic Gap, *IEEE Signal Processing Magazine*, (September): 56-65.

Seshadrinathan, K., Soundararajan, R., Bovik, A.C., and Cormack, L.K. 2010. Study of Subjective and Objective Quality Assessment of Video, *IEEE Transactions on Image Processing*, 19(6): 1427-1441.

Sohn, H., Yoo, H., De Neve, W., Kim, C.S., and Ro, Y.M. 2010. Full-Reference Video Quality Metric for Fully Scalable and Mobile SVC Content, *IEEE Transactions on Broadcasting*, 56(3): 269-280.

Wang, Z., Bovik, A.C., Sheikh, H.R., and Simoncelli, E.P. 2004. Image Quality Assessment: Form Error Visibility to Structural Similarity, *IEEE Transactions on Image Processing*, 13(4): 600-612.

Watson, A.B., Hu, J., and McGowan III, J.F. 2001. DVQ: A Digital Video Quality Metric Based on Human Vision, *Journal of Electronic Imaging*, 10(1): 20-29.

Watson, A.B. and Kreslake, L. 2001. Measurement of Visual Impairment Scales for Digital Video, *Human Vision, Visual Processing, and Digital Display IX*, SPIE, San Jose, 4299: 11 pages.

Winkler, S. 2001. Visual Fidelity and Perceived Quality: Towards Comprehensive Metrics, *Human Vision and Electronic Imaging*, SPIE, San Jose, California, 21-26 January, 4299: 114-125.

Winkler, S., Sharma, A., and McNally, D. 2001. Perceptual Video Quality and Blockiness Metrics for Multimedia Streaming Applications, *International Symposium on Wireless Personal Multimedia Communications*: 547-552.

Xia, T., Mei, T., Hua, G., Zhang, Y.D., and Hua, X.S. 2010. Visual Quality Assessment for Web Videos, *Journal of Visual Communication and Image Representation*, 21(6): 826-837.

Yang, F., Wan, S., Xie, Q., and Wu, H.R. 2010. No-Reference Quality Assessment for Networked Video via Primary Analysis of Bit Stream, *IEEE Transactions on Circuits and Systems for Video Technology*, 20(11): 1544-1554.

Yasakethu, S.L.P., Fernando, W.A.C., Kamolrat, B., and Kondoz, A.M. 2009. Analyzing Perceptual Attributes of 3D Video, *IEEE Transactions on Consumer Electronics*, 55(2): 864-872.

Young, D., Yen, J., Petitti, F., Bakir, T., Brennan, M., and Butto, R. 2009. Video National Imagery Interpretability Rating Scale Cirterial Survey Results, *Proceedings of the SPIE,* San Diego, 7307.

Young, D., Bakir, T., Butto, R., Duffield, C., and Petitti, F. 2010a. Loss of Interpretability Due to Compression Effects as Measured by the New Video NIIRS, *Proceedings of the SPIE,* 7529.

Young, D., Bakir, T., Butto, R., and Petitti, F. 2010b. Factors Related to Low Slant Angle Affecting Airborne Video Interpretability, *Proceedings of the SPIE,* San Diego, 7668.

Part 2

Motion Estimation

4

H.264 Motion Estimation and Applications

Murali E. Krishnan, E. Gangadharan and Nirmal P. Kumar
Anand Institute of Higher Technology, Anna University, India

1. Introduction

A video signal represented as a sequence of frames of pixels contains vast amount of redundant information that can be eliminated with video compression technology enhancing the total transmission and hence storage becomes more efficient. To facilitate interoperability between compression at the video producing source and decompression at the consumption end, several generations of video coding standards have been defined and adapted by the ITU-G and VCEG etc... Demand for high quality video is growing exponentially and with the advent of the new standards like H.264/AVC it has placed a significant increase in programming and computational power of the processors. In H.264/AVC, the motion estimation part holds the key in capturing the vital motion vectors for the incoming video frames and hence takes very high processing at both encoder and the decoder. This chapter gives an overview of Motion estimation and the various search algorithms and also the scalability of parallelism in their operations to enhance the performance and improve the overall video quality. For low-end applications, software solutions are adequate. For high-end applications, dedicated hardware solutions are needed.

This chapter gives an overview of H.264/AVC video coding in general and its applications in four main sections. Section 1 deals with motion estimation and the types of algorithms one of the key modules of H.264 and the most time-consuming. Section 2 deals with the estimation criterion and their role in determining the complexiety of the estimation algorithms. Section 3 briefly discusses about the scalability of parallelism in H.264 and the final section deals with the applications of H.264 focussing on Aerial video surveillance and its advantages.

1.1 Motion estimation

Motion estimation techniques form the core of H.264/AVC (Iain Richardson, 2010) video compression and video processing applications. It extracts motion information from the video sequence where the motion is typically represented using a motion vector (x, y). The motion vector indicates the displacement of a pixel or a pixel block from the current location due to motion. This information is used in video compression to find best matching block in reference frame to calculate low energy residue to generate temporally interpolated frames. It is also used in applications such motion compensated de-interlacing, video stabilization, motion tracking etc. Varieties of motion estimation techniques are available. There are pel-recursive techniques, which derive motion vector (T.Wiegand et.al, 2003) for each pixel and there is also the phase plane correlation technique, which generates motion vectors via correlation between current frame and reference frame. However, the most popular technique is Block Matching methodology which is the prime topic of discussion here.

1.1.1 Block matching algorithm

Block Matching Algorithm (BMA) (IEG Richardson 2003) is the most popular motion estimation algorithm. BMA calculates motion vector for an entire block of pixels instead of individual pixels. The same motion vector is applicable to all the pixels in the block. This reduces computational requirement and also results in a more accurate motion vector since the objects are typically a cluster of pixels. BMA algorithm is illustrated in figure 1.

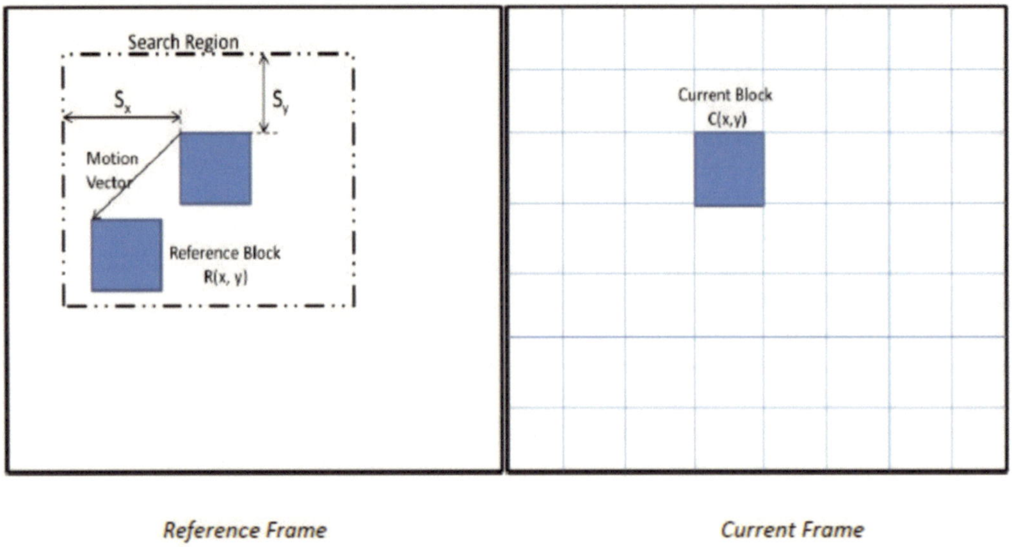

Fig. 1. Block Matching Algorithm

The current frame is divided into pixel blocks and motion estimation is performed independently for each pixel block. Motion estimation is done by identifying a pixel block from the reference frame that best matches the current block, whose motion is being estimated. The reference pixel block is generated by displacement from the current block's location in the reference frame. The displacement is provided by the Motion Vector (MV). MV consists of is a pair (x, y) of horizontal and vertical displacement values. There are various criteria available for calculating block matching.

The reference pixel blocks are generated only from a region known as the search area. Search region defines the boundary for the motion vectors and limits the number of blocks to evaluate. The height and width of the search region is dependent on the motion in video sequence. The available computing power also determines the search range. Bigger search region requires more computation due to increase in number of evaluated candidates. Typically the search region is kept wider (i.e. width is more than height) since many video sequences often exhibit panning motion. The search region can also be changed adaptively depending upon the detected motion. The horizontal and vertical search range, Sx & Sy, define the search area (+/-Sx and +/- Sy) as illustrated in figure 1.

1.1.2 Full search block matching

Full search block matching algorithm (Alois, 2009) evaluates every possible pixel block in the search region. Hence, it can generate the best block matching motion vector. This type of BMA can give least possible residue for video compression. But, the required computations are prohibitively high due to the large amount of candidates to evaluate in a defined search region. The number of candidates to evaluate are ((2*Sx) +1)*((2*Sy) +1) which is predominantly high compared to any of the search algorithms. There are several other fast block-matching algorithms, which reduce the number of evaluated candidates yet try to keep good block matching (Yu-Wen, 2006) accuracy. Note that since these algorithms test only limited candidates, they might result in selecting a candidate corresponding to local minima, unlike full search, which always results in global minima. Some of the algorithms are listed below.

1.1.3 Fast search algorithms

There are many other block matching algorithms (Nuno, 2002) and their variants available, but differs in the manner how they select the candidate for comparison and what is the motion vector resolution. Although, the full search algorithm is the best one in terms of the quality of the predicted image and its resolution of the motion vector it is very computationally intensive. With the realization that motion estimation is the most computationally intensive operation in the coding and transmitting of video streams, people started looking for more efficient algorithms. However, there is a trade-off between the efficiency of the algorithm and the quality of the prediction image. Keeping this trade-off in mind a lot of algorithms have been developed. These algorithms are called Sub-Optimal (Alois, 2009) because although they are computationally more efficient than the Full search, they do not give as good a quality as in the full search.

1.1.4 Three step search

In a three-step search (TSS) algorithm (Alan Bovik, 2009), the first iteration evaluates nine candidates as shown in figure 2. The candidates are centered on the current block's position. The step size for the first iteration is typically set to half the search range. These algorithms operate by calculating the energy measure (e.g. SAD) at a subset of locations within the search window as illustrated (TSS, sometimes described as N-Step Search) in Figure.2. SAD is calculated at position (0, 0) (the centre of the Figure) and at eight locations $\pm 2N-1$ (for a search window of $\pm$ ($2N-1$) samples). The first nine search locations are numbered '1'. The search location that gives the smallest SAE is chosen as the new search centre and a further eight locations are searched, this time at half the previous distance from the search centre (numbered '2' in the figure). Once again, the 'best' location is chosen as the new search origin and the algorithm is repeated until the search distance cannot be subdivided further. This is the last iteration of the three-step search algorithm. The best matching candidate from this iteration is selected as the final candidate. The motion vector corresponding to this candidate is selected for the current block. The number of candidates evaluated during three-step search is very less compared to the full search algorithm. The TSS is considerably simpler than Full Search ($8N + 1$ search compared with ($2N$+1 −1)2 searches for Full Search) but the TSS (and other fast search algorithms) do not usually perform as well as Full Search.

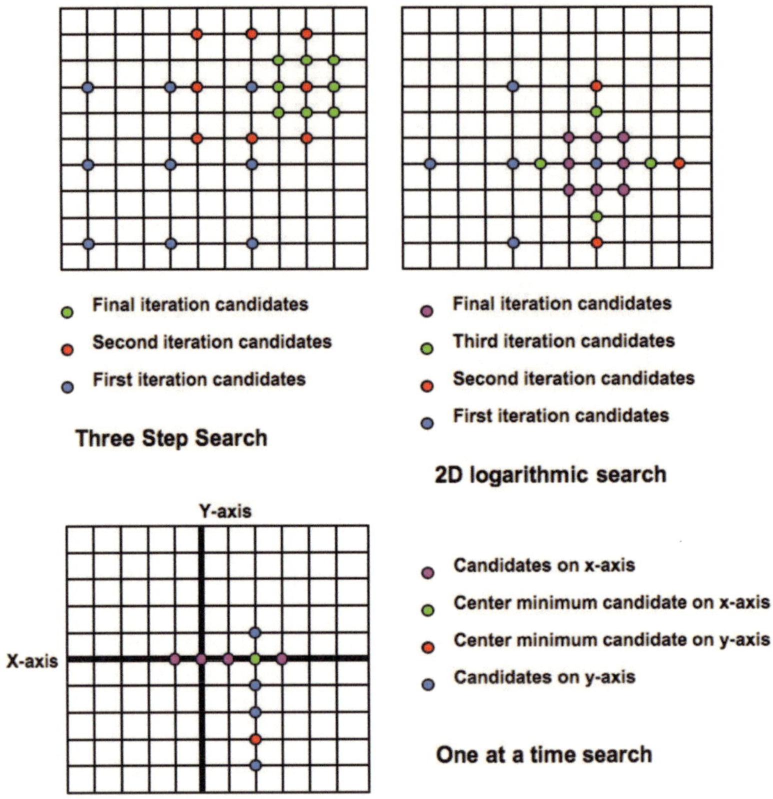

Fig. 2. Fast Search Algorithms

1.1.5 2D logarithmic search

2D Logarithmic (Alois, 2009) search is another algorithm, which tests limited candidates. It is similar to the three-step search. During the first iteration, a total of five candidates are tested. The candidates are centered on the current block location in a diamond shape. The step size for first iteration is set equal to half the search range. For the second iteration, the centre of the diamond is shifted to the best matching candidate. The step size is reduced by half only if the best candidate happens to be the centre of the diamond. If the best candidate is not the diamond centre, same step size is used even for second iteration. In this case, some of the diamond candidates are already evaluated during first iteration. Hence, there is no need for block matching calculation for these candidates during the second iteration. The results from the first iteration can be used for these candidates. The process continues till the step size becomes equal to one pixel. For this iteration all eight surrounding candidates are evaluated. The best matching candidate from this iteration is selected for the current block. The number of evaluated candidate is variable for the 2D logarithmic search. However, the worst case and best case candidates can be calculated.

1.1.6 One at a time search algorithm

The one at a time search algorithm estimates the x-component and the y-component of the motion vector independently. The candidate search is first performed along the x-axis.

During each ite ration, a set of three neighboring candidates along the x-axis are tested in Fig.2. The three-candidate set is shifted towards the best matching candidate, with the best matching candidate forming the centre of the set for the next iteration. The process stops if the best matching candidate happens to be the centre of the candidate set. The location of this candidate on the x-axis is used as the x-component of the motion vector. The search now continues parallel to the y-axis. A procedure similar to x-axis search is followed to estimate y-component of the motion vector. One-step at a time search on average tests less number of candidates. However, the motion vector accuracy is poor.

1.1.7 Sub-pixel motion estimation (Fractional Pel Motion Estimation)

Integer pixel motion estimation (also called as full search method) is carried out in the process of motion estimation that is mainly used to reduce the duplication (redundant data) among adjacent frames. But in practice, the distance of real motion is not always made by multiplier (which is constant) at the sampling interval.The actual motion in the video sequence can be much finer. Hence, the resulting object might not lie on the integer pixel (Iain Richardson, 2010) grid. To get a better match, the motion estimation needs to be performed on a sub-pixel grid. The sub-pixel grid can be either at half pixel resolution or quarter pixel resolution.

Therefore it is advantageous to use the subpixel motion estimation technique to ensure high compression with high PSNR ratio of reconstructed image. The motion vector can be calculated at 1/2, 1/4, 1/8 subpixel (Young et.al 2010) positions. The motion vector is to be calculated at 1/4 pixel gives more detailed information than at 1/2 pixel position. Since, the image has been enlarged, interpolation must be implemented to compensate for the pixel value in case of enlargement.

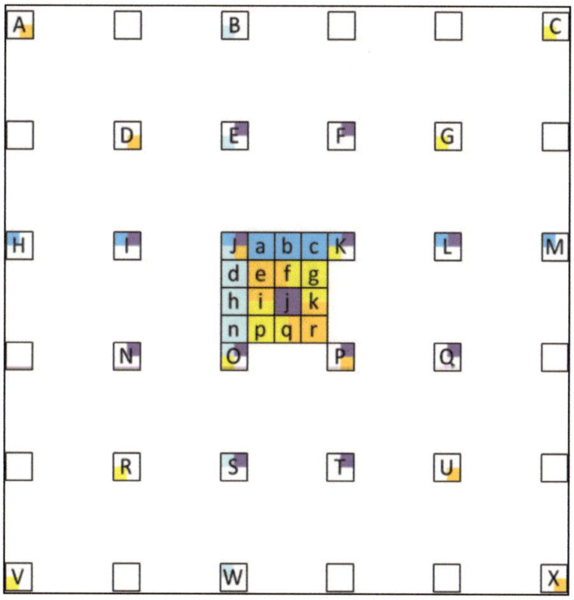

Fig. 3. 6-tap Directional interpolation filter for luma

Figure.3 shows the support pixels for each quarter-pixel position (Young et.al 2010) with different colours. For instance, the blue integer pixels are used to support the interpolation of three horizontal fractional pixels, a, b and c, the light-blue integer pixels for three vertical fractional pixels, d, h and n, the deep-yellow integer pixels for two down-right fractional pixels, e and r, the light-yellow integer pixels for two down-left fractional pixels, g and p, the purple integer pixels for the central fractional pixel j.

For each of the three horizontal fractional (Zhibo et.al.,2007) positions, a, b and c, and the three vertical fractional positions, d, h and n, which are aligned with full pixel positions, a single 6-tap filter is used and their equations are produced . The filter coefficients of DIF are {3, -15, 111, 37, -10, 2}/128 for ¼ position (and mirrored for ¾ position), {3, -17, 78, 78, -17, 3}/128 for ½ position.

$$\begin{aligned} a &= (3H-15I+111J+37K-10L+2M+64)>>7 \\ b &= (3H-17I+78J+78K-17L+3M+64)>>7 \\ c &= (2H-10I+37J+111K-15L+3M+64)>>7 \end{aligned} \qquad (1)$$

$$\begin{aligned} d &= (3B-15E+111J+37O-10S+2W+64)>>7 \\ h &= (3B-17E+78J+78O-17S+3W+64)>>7 \\ n &= (2B-10E+37J+111O-15S+3W+64)>>7 \end{aligned} \qquad (2)$$

For the 4 innermost quarter-pixel positions, e, g, p, and r, the 6-tap filters at +45 degree and -45 degree angles are used respectively.

$$\begin{aligned} e &= (3A-15D+111J+37P-10U+2X+64)>>7 \\ g &= (3C-15G+111K+37O-10R+2V+64)>>7 \\ p &= (2C-10G+37K+111O-15R+3V+64)>>7 \\ r &= (2A-10D+37J+111P-15U+3X+64)>>7 \end{aligned} \qquad (3)$$

For another 4 innermost quarter-pixel positions, f, i, k, and q, a combination of the 6-tap filters at +45 degree and -45 degree angles, which is equivalent to a 12-tap filter, is used.

$$\begin{aligned} f &= (e+g+1)>>1 = ((3A-15D+111J+37P-10U+2X)+(3C-15G+111K+37O-10R+2V)+128)>>8 \\ i &= (e+p+1)>>1 = ((3A-15D+111J+37P-10U+2X)+(2C-10G+37K+111O-15R+3V)+128)>>8 \\ k &= (g+r+1)>>1 = ((3C-15G+111K+37O-10R+2V)+(2A-10D+37J+111P-15U+3X)+128)>>8 \\ q &= (p+r+1)>>1 = ((2C-10G+37K+111O-15R+3V)+(2A-10D+37J+111P-15U+3X)+128)>>8 \end{aligned} \qquad (4)$$

$$j = ((5E+5F) + (5I+22J+22K+5L) + (5N+22O+22P+5Q) + (5S+5T) +64)>>7 \qquad (5)$$

The exception is the central position, j, where a 12-tap non-separable filter is used. The filter coefficients of DIF are {0, 5, 5, 0; 5, 22, 22, 5; 5, 22, 22, 5; 0, 5, 5, 0}/128 for the central position.

1.1.8 Hierarchical block matching

Hierarchical block matching algorithm (Alan Bovik, 2009) is a more sophisticated motion estimation technique which provides consistent motion vectors by successively refining the motion vector at different resolutions. In this, a pyramid fig.4 of reduced resolution video frame is formed from the source video. The original video frame forms the highest resolution image and the other images in the pyramid are formed by down sampling the original image. A simple bi-linear down sampling can be used. This is illustrated in figure 4. The block size of NxN at the highest resolution is reduced to (N/2) x (N/2) in the next resolution level. Similarly, the search range is also reduced. The motion estimation process starts at the lowest resolution. Typically, full search motion estimation is performed for each block at the lowest resolution. Since the block size and the search range are reduced, it does not require large computations. The motion vectors from lowest resolution are scaled and passed on as candidate motion vectors for each block to next level. At the next level, the motion vectors are refined with a smaller search area. A simpler motion estimation algorithm and a small search range is enough at close to highest resolution since the motion vectors are already close to accurate motion vectors.

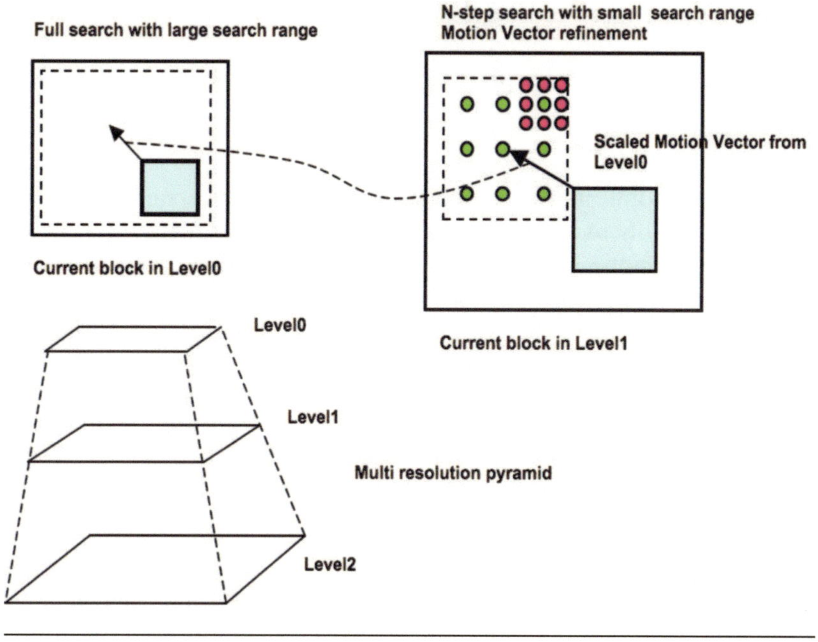

Fig. 4. Hierarchial block matching

1.1.9 Global motion estimation

There is another type of motion estimation technique known as global motion estimation. The motion estimation techniques discussed so far are useful in estimating local motion (i.e. motion of objects within the video frame). However, the video sequence can also contain global motion. For some applications, such as video stabilization, it is more useful to find global motion (Alan Bovik 2009) rather than local motion. In global motion, the same type of motion is applicable to each pixel in the video frame. Some examples of global motion are panning, tilting and zoom in/out. In all these motion, each pixel is moving using the same global motion model. The motion vectors for each pixel or pixel block can be described using following parametric model with four parameters Global motion vector for a pixel or pixel block is given (6) & (7). For pan and tilt global motion, only q0 and q1 are non-zero i.e. constant motion vector for the entire video frame. For pure zoom in/out, only p0 and p1 will be nonzero.

$$G_x = p0 * x + q0 \tag{6}$$

$$G_y = p1 * x + q1 \tag{7}$$

However a combination of all the parameters is usually present. Global motion estimation involves calculation of the four parameters in the model (p0, p1, q0, q1). The parameters can be calculated by treating them as four unknowns. Hence, ideally sample motion vectors at four different locations can be used to calculate the four run known parameters. In practice though, more processing is needed to get good estimate for the parameters. Also, note that still local motion estimation, at least at four locations, is essential to calculate the global motion estimation parameters. However, there are algorithms for global motion estimation, which do not rely on local motion estimation. The above parametric model with four parameters cannot fit rotational global motion. For rotational motion a six-parameter model is needed. However, the same four-parameter model concepts can be extended to the six-parameter model.

1.1.10 True motion estimation

For video compression applications it is enough to get a motion vector corresponding to best match. This in turns results in lower residual energy and better compression. However, for video processing applications, especially for scan rate conversion, true motion estimation is desired. In True Motion estimation, the motion vectors should represent true motion of the objects in the video sequence rather than providing best block match. Hence, it is important to achieve a consistent motion vector field rather that best possible match. True motion estimation can be achieved via both post-processing the motion vectors to get smooth motion vector field as well as building the consistency measures in motion estimation algorithm itself. Three Dimensional Recursive Search (3DRS) in Fig.5 is one such algorithm where the consistency assumption is inbuilt into the motion estimation.

The algorithm works on two important assumptions - objects are larger than block size and objects have inertia. The first assumption suggests that the neighboring block's motion vectors can be used as candidates for the current block. However, for neighboring blocks ahead in raster scan, there is no motion vectors calculated yet. Here, the second assumption is applied and motion vectors from previous frame are for these blocks. 3DRS motion estimator's candidate set consists of only spatial & temporal neighboring motion vectors. This results in a very consistent motion vector field giving true motion. To kick-start the algorithm a random motion vector is also used as a candidate as illustrated in figure 5.

1.2 Distortion metrics role of estimation criteria

The algorithms/techniques discussed above need to be incorporated into an estimation criterion that will subsequently be optimized in order to obtain the prediction error (Young et.al 2009) or the residual energy of the video frames. There is no unique criterion as such for motion estimation because its choice depends on the task/application at hand. For example, in compression an average performance (prediction error) of a motion estimator is important, whereas in motion-compensated interpolation (Philip 2009) the worst case performance (maximum interpolation error) may be of concern. Moreover, the selection of a criterion may be guided by the processor capabilities on which the motion estimation will be implemented. The difficulty in establishing a good criterion is primarily caused by the fact that motion in images is not directly observable and that particular dynamics of intensity in an image sequence may be induced by more than one motion.

Motion estimation therefore aims to find a 'match' to the current block or region that minimizes the energy in the motion compensated residual (the difference between the current block and the reference area). An area in the reference frame centered on the current macro block (Iain Richardson 2010) position (the search area) is searched and the 16 × 16 region within the search area that minimizes a matching criterion is chosen as the 'best match'. The choice of matching criterion is important since block matching might require the distortion measure for 'residual energy' affects computational complexity and the accuracy of the motion estimation process. Therefore, all attempts to establish suitable criteria for motion estimation require further implicit or explicit modeling of the image sequence of the video. If all matching criteria resulted in compressed video of the same quality then, of course, the least complex of these would always be used for block matching.

However matching criteria (IEG Richardson 2003) often differ on the choice of substitute for the target block, with consequent variation in the quality of the coded frame. The MSD, for example, requires many multiplications whereas the MAD primarily uses additions. While multiplication might not have too great an impact on a software (Romuald 2006) coder, a hardware coder using MSE could be significantly more expensive than a hardware implementation of the SAD/MAD function. Equations 8,9,10 describe three energy measures, MSD, MAD and SAD. The motion compensation block size is $N \times N$ samples; Cur $_{i,\ j}$, Ref $_{i,\ j}$ are current and reference area samples respectively.Fig.6 shows the image in macroblock form for the current video frame.(see photo)

Fig. 6. Macroblock view of the Frame

1.2.1 Mean squared difference

$$MSD = \frac{1}{N^2} \sum_{1=0}^{N-1} \sum_{j=0}^{N-1} \left(\mathrm{Cur}_{i,j} - \mathrm{Ref}_{i,j} \right)^2$$

MSD is also called as Mean Square Error (MSE). It is the indication of amount of difference between two macro blocks. Practically, the lower MSD value better is the match.

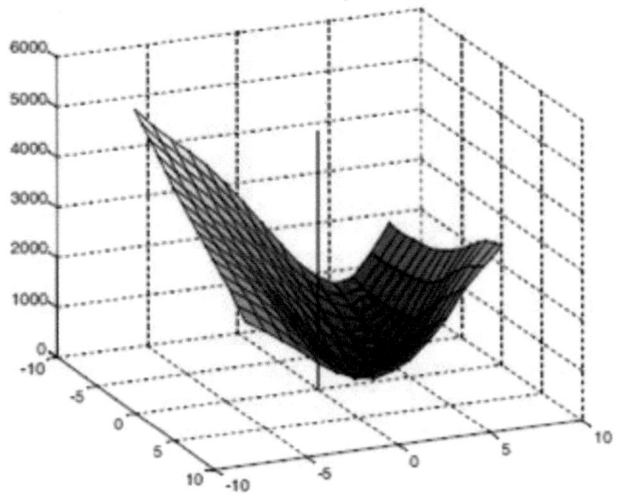

Fig. 7. MSD Map

1.2.2 Mean absolute difference

$$MAD = \frac{1}{N^2} \sum_{1=0}^{N-1} \sum_{j=0}^{N-1} \left| \mathrm{Cur}_{i,j} - \mathrm{Ref}_{i,j} \right|$$

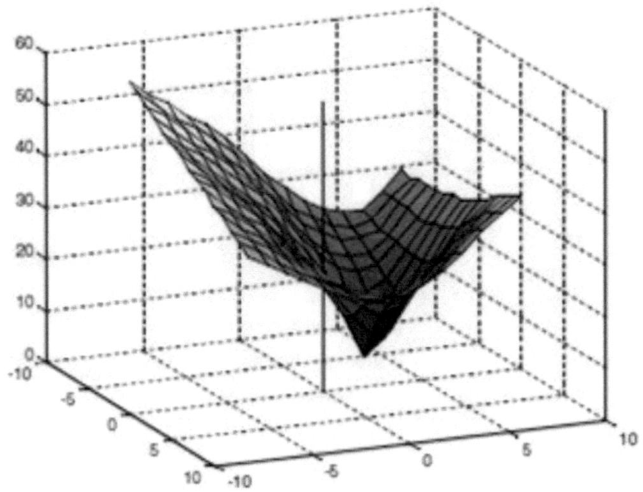

Fig. 8. MAD Map

The lower MAD the better the match and so candidate block with minimum MAD should be chosen. The function is also called as Min Absolute Error (MAE).

1.2.3 Sum of absolute difference

$$SAD = \sum_{1=0}^{N-1} \sum_{j=0}^{N-1} \left| \mathrm{Cur}_{i,j} - \mathrm{Ref}_{i,j} \right|$$

SAD is commonly used as the error estimate to identify the most similar block when trying to obtain the block motion vectoring the process of motion estimation, which requires only easy calculation as in fig.9 without the need for multiplication.

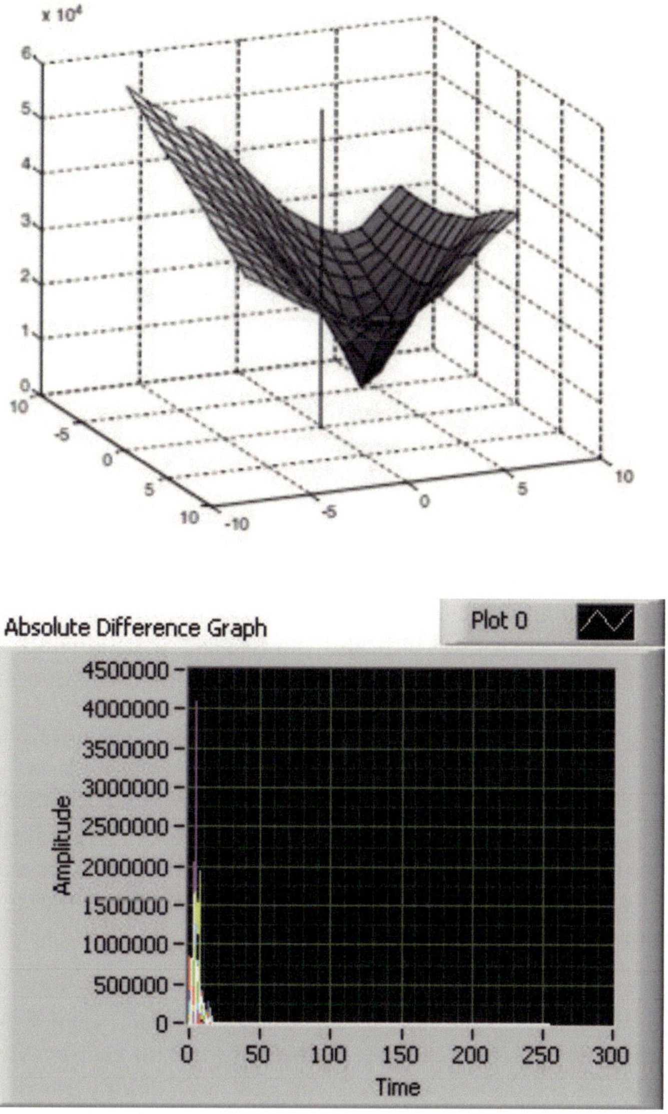

Fig. 9. SAD Map & its PSNR sketch

SAD (Young et.al 2009) is an extremely fast metric due to its simplicity; it is effectively the simplest possible metric that takes into account every pixel in a block. Therefore it is very effective for a wide motion search of many different blocks.

SAD is also easily parallelizable since it analyzes each pixel separately, making it easily implementable with hardware and software coders. Once candidate blocks are found, the final refinement of the motion estimation process is often done with other slower but more accurate metrics like which better take into account human perception. These include the sum of absolute transformed differences (SATD), the sum of squared differences (SSD), and rate-distortion optimization (RDO).

The usual coding techniques applied to moving objects within a video scene lower the compression efficiency as they only consider the pixels at the same position in the video frames. Motion estimation with SAD as the distortion metric used to capture such movements more accurately for better compression efficiency. For example in video surveillance using moving cameras, a popular way to handle translation problems on images, using template matching is to compare the intensities of the pixels, using the SAD measure. The motion estimation on a video sequence using SAD uses the current video frame and a previous frame as the target frame. The two frames are compared pixel by pixel, summing up the absolute values of the differences of each of the two corresponding pixels. The result is a positive number that is used as the score. SAD reacts very sensitively to even minor changes within a scene.

SAD is probably the most widely-used measure of residual energy for reasons of computational simplicity. The H.264 reference model software [5] uses SA (T) D, the sum of absolute differences of the *transformed* residual data, as its prediction energy measure (for both Intra and Inter prediction). Transforming the residual at each search location increases computation but improves the accuracy of the energy measure. A simple multiply-free transform is used and so the extra computational cost is not excessive. The results of the above example in Fig.6 indicate that the best choice of motion vector is (+2, 0). The minimum of the MSE or SAE map indicates the offset that produces a minimal residual energy and this is likely to produce the smallest energy of quantized transform.

1.2.4 Rate distortion optimization

These distortion metrics often play the pivotal role in deciding the quality of the videos viewed when choosing the method of Rate of Distortion Optimization (RDO) (Iain Richardson 2010)which is a technique for choosing the coding mode of a macroblock based on the rate and the distortion cost. Formulating this, we represent bitrate R and distortion cost D combined into a single cost J given by,

$$J = D + \lambda R \tag{11}$$

The bits are mathematically measured by multiplying the bit cost by the Lagrangian λ, a value representing the relationship between bit cost and quality for a particular quality level. The deviation from the source is usually measured in terms of distortion metrics in order to maximize the PSNR video quality metric.

The RDO mode selection algorithm attempts to find a mode that minimizes the joint cost J. The trade-off between Rate and Distortion is controlled by the Lagrange multiplier λ (Alan Bovik 2009). A smaller λ will give more emphasis to minimizing D, allowing a higher rate, whereas a larger λ will tend to minimize R at the expense of a higher distortion. Selecting the best λ for a particular sequence is a highly complex problem. Fortunately, empirical approximations have been developed that provide an effective choice of λ in a practical mode selection scenario.

Good results can be obtained by calculating λ as a function of QP.

$$\lambda = 0.852^{(QP-12)/3} \tag{12}$$

Distortion (D) is calculated as the Sum of Squared Distortion (SSD,

$$D_{SSD} = \sum_{1=0}^{N-1} \sum_{j=0}^{N-1} \left(\text{Cur}_{i,j} - \text{Ref}_{i,j}\right)^2$$

Where i,j are the sample positions in a block, Cur(i,j) are the original sample values and Ref(i,j)

are the decoded sample values at each sample position. Other distortion metrics, such as Sum of Absolute Differences (SAD), Mean of Absolute Difference (MAD) or Mean of Squared errors (MSE) may be used in processes such as selecting the best motion vector for a block [iv]. A different distortion metric typically requires a different λ calculation and indeed will have an impact in the computation process taken as a whole.

A typical mode selection algorithm might proceed as follows:

For every macroblock

- For every available coding mode m
- Code the macroblock using mode m and calculate R, the number of bits required to code the macroblock
- Reconstruct the macroblock and calculate D, the distortion between the original and decoded macroblock
- Calculate the mode cost J_m using (11), with appropriate choice of λ
- Choose the mode that gives the minimum J_m

This is clearly a computationally intensive process, since there is hundreds of possible modes combination and therefore it is necessary to code the macroblock hundreds of times to find the 'best' mode in a rate-distortion sense.

1.2.5 Conclusions and results

Thus a *matching criterion*, or *distortion function*, is used to quantify the similarity between the target block and candidate blocks. If, due to a large search area, many candidate blocks are considered, then the matching criteria will be evaluated many times. Thus the choice of the matching criteria has an impact on the success of the compression. If the matching criterion is slow, for example, then the block matching will be slow. If the matching criterion results in bad matches then the quality of the compression will be adversely affected. Fortunately a number of matching criteria are suitable for use in video compression. Although, the number of matching criteria evaluated by block matching algorithms is largely independent of the sequence coded, the success of the algorithms is heavily dependent on the sequence coded.

1.3 Scalability of parallelism in H.264 video compression

The H.264/AVC standard provides several profiles to define the applied encoding techniques, targeting specific classes of applications. For each profile, several levels are also defined, specifying upper bounds for the bit stream or lower bounds for the decoder capabilities, processing rate, memory size for multipicture buffers, video rate, and motion vector range (Alois 2009) significantly improving the compression performance relative to all existing video coding standards [1]. To achieve the offered encoding performance, this standard incorporates a set of new and powerful techniques: 4×4 integer transform, inter-prediction with variable block-size, quarter-pixel motion estimation (ME), in-loop deblocking filter, improved entropy coding based on Context-Adaptive Variable-Length Coding (CAVLC) or on Content-Adaptive Binary Arithmetic Coding (CABAC), new modes for intra prediction, etc. Moreover, the adoption of bi-predictive frames (B-frames) along with the previous features provides a considerable bit-rate reduction with negligible quality losses.

For instance using Intel VTune software running on a Pentium IV 3 GHz CPU with H.264/AVC SD in main profile encoding solution with Arithmetic, controlling, and data transfer instructions are separated would require about 1,600 billions of operations per second. Table.1 illustrates a typical profile of the H.264/AVC encoder complexity based on the Pentium IV general purpose processor architecture. Notice that motion estimation, macroblock/block processing (including mode decision), and motion compensation modules which take up nearly the entire cycle (78%) of operations and account for higher resource usage.

	Arithmetic		Controlling		Data transfer		
Functions	MIPS	%	MIPS	%	MIPS	Mbytes/s	%
Integer-pel motion estimation	95,491.9	78.31	21,915.1	55.37	116,830.8	365,380.7	77.53
Fractional-pel motion estimation	21,396.6	17.55	14,093.2	35.61	30,084.9	85,045.7	18.04
Fractional-pel interpolation	558.0	0.46	586.6	1.48	729.7	1067.6	0.23
Lagrangian mode decision	674.6	0.55	431.4	1.09	880.7	2642.6	0.56
Intra prediction	538.0	0.44	288.2	0.73	585.8	2141.8	0.45
Variable length coding	35.4	0.03	36.8	0.09	44.2	154.9	0.03
Transform and quantization	3223.9	2.64	2178.6	5.50	4269.0	14,753.4	3.13
Deblocking	29.5	0.02	47.4	0.12	44.2	112.6	0.02
Total	121,948.1	100.00	39,577.3	100.00	153,469.3	471,299.3	100.0

(Baseline profile, 30 CIF frames/s, 5 reference frames, ±16-Pel search range, and QP = 20)

Table 1. Instruction profiling in Baseline Profile H.264

It can be observed that motion estimation, including integer-pel motion estimation, fractional-pel motion estimation, and fractional-pel interpolation in the table, takes up more than 95 percent of the computation in the whole encoder, which is a common characteristic in all video encoders. The total required computing power for a H.264 encoder is more than 300 giga instructions per second (GIPS), which cannot be achieved by existing processors. To account for this problem, several approaches have been adopted, such as the application of new low complexity ME algorithms that have been studied and developed (Yu Wen 2006), dedicated hardware (HW) structures and, more recently, multi-processor solutions.

Nevertheless, the innumerous data dependencies imposed by this video standard frequently inflict a very difficult challenge in order to efficiently take advantage of the several possible parallelization strategies that may be applied. Up recently, most parallelization (Florian et.al 2010) efforts around the H.264 standard have been mainly focused on the decoder implementation [2]. When the most challenging and rewarding goal of parallelizing the encoder is concerned, it has been observed that a significant part of the efforts have been devised in the design of specialized and dedicated systems [7, 6]. Most of these approaches are based on parallel or pipeline topologies, using dedicated HWstructures to implement several parts of the encoder. When only pure software (SW) approaches are considered, fewer parallel solutions have been proposed. Most of them are based on the exploitation of the data independency between Group-of-Pictures (GOPs) of slices. For such a video encoder, it may be probably necessary to use some kind of parallel programming approach to share the encoding application execution time and also to balance the workload among the concurrent processors.

1.3.1 Parallelism in H.264

The primary aim of this section is to provide a deeper understanding of the scalability of parallelism in H.264. Several analyses and parallel optimizations have been presented about H.264/AVC encoders [3, 4, 8]. Due to the encoder's nature, many of these parallelization approaches exploit concurrent execution at: frame-level, slice-level, macroblock-level..The H.264 codec can be parallelized either by task-level and data-level decomposition. In Fig.10 the two approaches are sketched. In task-level decomposition individual tasks of the H.264 Codec are assigned to processors while in data-level decomposition different portions of data are assigned to processors running the same program.

1.3.2 Task-level decomposition

In task-level decomposition the functional partitions of the algorithm are assigned to different processors. As shown in Fig.10 the process of decoding H.264 consists of performing a series of operations on the coded input bitstream. Some of these tasks can be done in parallel. For example, Inverse Quantization (IQ) and the Inverse Transform (IDCT) can be done in parallel with the Motion Compensation (MC) stage. In Fig. 10a the tasks are mapped to a 4-processor system. A control processor is in charge of synchronization and parsing the bitstream. One processor is in charge of Entropy Decoding, IQ and IDCT, another one of the prediction stage (MC or IntraP), and a third one is responsible for the deblocking filter.

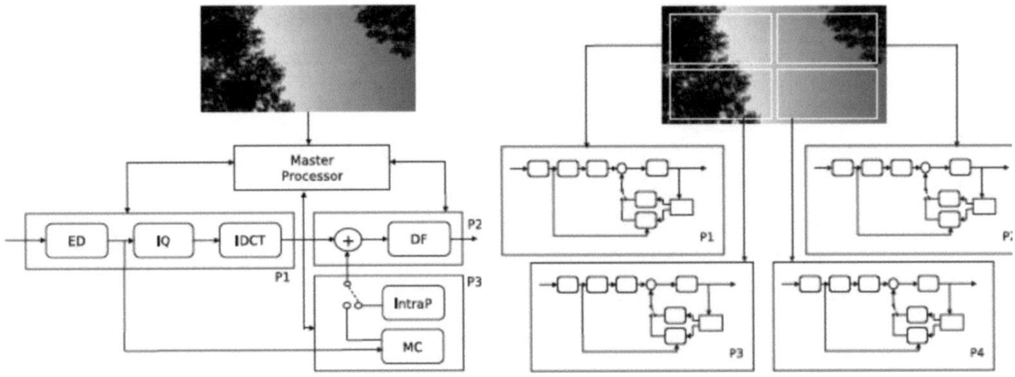

(a) (b)

Fig. 10. H.264 parallelization techniques. **a** Task-level decomposition. **b** Data-level decomposition.

Task-level decomposition requires significant communication between the different tasks in order to move the data from one processing stage to the other, and this may become the bottleneck. This overhead can be reduced using double buffering and blocking to maintain the piece of data that is currently being processed in cache or local memory. Additionally, synchronization is required for activating the different modules at the right time. This should be performed by a control processor and adds significant overhead.

The main drawbacks, however, of task-level decomposition are load balancing and scalability. Balancing the load is difficult because the time to execute each task is not known a priori and depends on the data being processed. In a task-level pipeline the executiontime for each stage is not constant and some stage can block the processing of the others. Scalability is also difficult to achieve. If the application requires higher performance, for example by going from standard to high definition resolution, it is necessary to reimplement the task partitioning which is a complex task and at some point it could not provide the required performance for high throughput demands. Finally from the software optimization perspective the task-level decomposition requires that each task/processor implements a specific software optimization strategy, i.e., the code for each processor is different and requires different optimizations.

1.3.3 Data-level decomposition

In data-level decomposition the work (data) is divided into smaller parts and each assigned to a different processor, as depicted in Fig.10b. Each processor runs the same program but on different (multiple) data elements (SPMD). In H.264 data decomposition can be applied at different levels of the data structure (see Fig.11), which goes down from Group of Pictures (GOP), to frames, slices, MBs, and finally to variable sized pixel blocks. Data-level parallelism can be exploited at each level of the data structure, each one having different constraints and requiring different parallelization methodologies.

1.3.4 GOP-level parallelism

The coarsest grained parallelism is at the GOP level. H.264 can be parallelized at the GOP-level by defining a GOP size of *N* frames and assigning each GOP to a processor. GOP-level

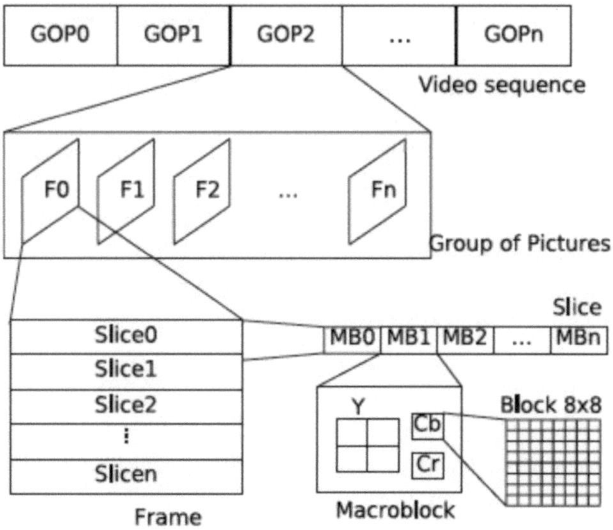

Fig. 11. GOP Structure of H.264 Video

parallelism requires a lot of memory for storing all the frames, and therefore this technique maps well to multicomputers in which each processing node has a lot of computational and memory resources. However, parallelization at the GOP-level results in a very high latency that cannot be tolerated in some applications. This scheme is therefore not well suited for multicore architectures, in which the memory is shared by all the processors, because of cache pollution.

1.3.5 Frame-level parallelism for independent frames

At frame-level in fig.12, the input video stream is divided in GOPs. Since GOPs are usually made independent from each other, it is possible to develop a parallel architecture where a controller is in charge of distributing the GOPs among the available cores.In a sequence of I-B-B-P frames inside a GOP, some frames are used as reference for other frames (like I and P frames) but some frames (the B frames in this case) might not. Thus in this case the B frames can be processed in parallel. To do so, a control/central processor assigns independent frames to different processors.

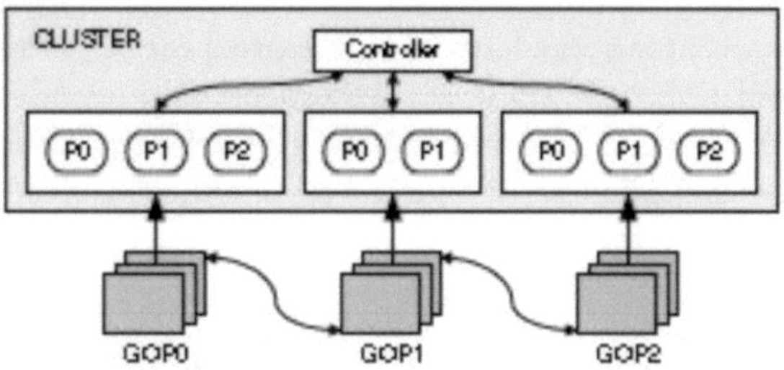

Fig. 12. Frame-level Parallelism

Frame-level parallelism has scalability problems due to the fact that usually there are no more than two or three B frames between P frames. The advantages of this model are clear:

PSNR and bit-rate do not change and it is easy to implement, since GOPs' independency is assured with minimal changes in the code. However, the memory consumption significantly increases, since each encoder must have its own Decoded Picture Buffer (DPB), where all GOP's references are stored. Moreover, real-time encoding is hardly implemented using this approach, making it more suitable for video storage purposes.However, the main disadvantage of frame-level parallelism is that, unlike previous video standards, in H.264 B frames can be used as reference [24]. In such a case, if the decoder wants to exploit frame-level parallelism, the encoder cannot use B frames as reference. This might increase the bitrate, but more importantly, encoding and decoding are usually completely separated and there is no way for a decoder to enforce its preferences to the encoder.

1.3.6 Slice-level parallelism

In slice-level parallelism (Fig. 13), frames are divided in several independent slices, making the processing of macroblocks from different slices completely independent. In the H.264/AVC standard, a maximum of sixteen slices are allowed in each frame. This approach allows exploiting parallelism at a finer granularity, which is suitable, for example, for multicore computers.In H.264 and in most current hybrid video coding standards each picture is partitioned into one or more slices. Slices have been included in order to add robustness to the encoded bitstream in the presence of network transmission errors and losses.

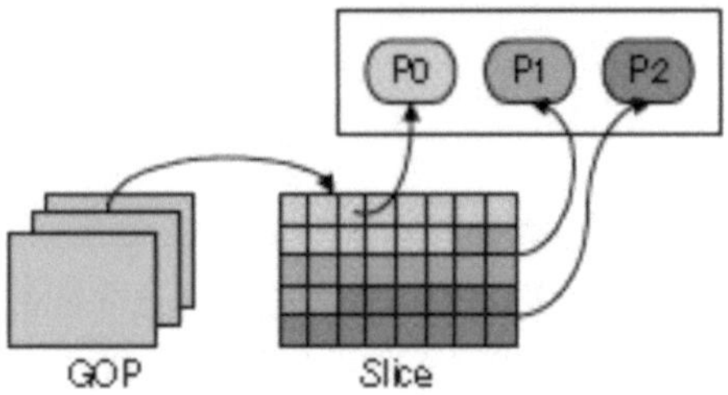

Fig. 13. Slice-level Parallelism

In order to accomplish this, slices in a frame should be completely independent from each other. That means that no content of a slice is used to predict elements of other slices in the same frame, and that the search area of a dependent frame can not cross the slice boundary [10, 16]. Although supports for slices have been designed for error resilience, it can be used for exploiting TLP because slices in a frame can be encoded or decoded in parallel. The main advantage of slices is that they can be processed in parallel without dependency or ordering constraints.This allows exploitation of slice-level parallelism (Rodriguez 2006) without making significant changes to the code.

However, there are some disadvantages associated with exploiting TLP at the slice level. The first one is that the number of slices per frame (sixteen in the H.264 standard) is determined by the encoder. That poses a scalability problem for parallelization at the decoder level. If there is no control of what the encoder does then it is possible to receive sequences with few (or one) slices per frame and in such cases there would be reduced parallelization opportunities. The second disadvantage comes from the fact that in H.264 the encoder can decide that the deblocking filter has to be applied across slice boundaries. This greatly reduces the speedup achieved by slice level parallelism. Another problem is load balancing wherein the slices are created with the same number of MBs, and thus can result in an imbalance at the decoder because some slices are decoded faster than others depending on the content of the slice.

1.3.7 Macroblock level parallelism

There are two ways of exploiting MB-level parallelism: in the spatial domain and/or in the temporal domain. In the spatial domain MB-level parallelism can be exploited if all the intra-frame dependencies are satisfied. In the temporal domainMB-level parallelism can be exploited if, in addition to the intra-dependencies, interframe dependencies are satisfied.

1.3.8 Macroblock-level parallelism in the spatial domain

Usually MBs in a slice are processed in scan order, which means starting from the top left corner of the frame andmoving to the right, row after row. To exploit parallelism between MBs inside a frame it is necessary to take into account the dependencies between them. In H.264, motion vector prediction, intra prediction, and the deblocking filter use data from neighboring MBs defining a structured set of dependencies. These dependencies are shown in Fig. 14.

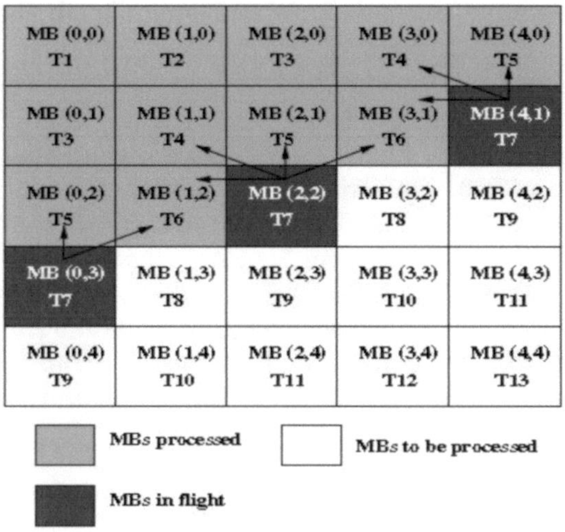

Fig. 14. 2D-Wave approach for exploiting MB parallelism in the spatial domain. The *arrows* indicate dependencies.

MBs can be processed out of scan order provided these dependencies are satisfied. Processing MBs in a diagonal wavefront manner satisfies all the dependencies and at the same time allows to exploit parallelism between MBs. We refer to this parallelization technique as 2D-Wave.

Fig.14 depicts an example for a 5×5 MBs image (80×80 pixels). At time slot T7 three independent MBs can be processed: MB (4,1), MB (2,2) and MB (0,3). The figure also shows the dependencies that need to be satisfied in order to process each of these MBs. The number of independent MBs in each frame depends on the resolution. For a low resolution like QCIF there are only 6 independent MBs during 4 time slots. For High Definition (1920×1080) there are 60 independent MBs during 9 slots of time. Fig. 15 depicts the available MB parallelism over time for a FHD resolution frame, assuming that the time to decode a MB is constant.

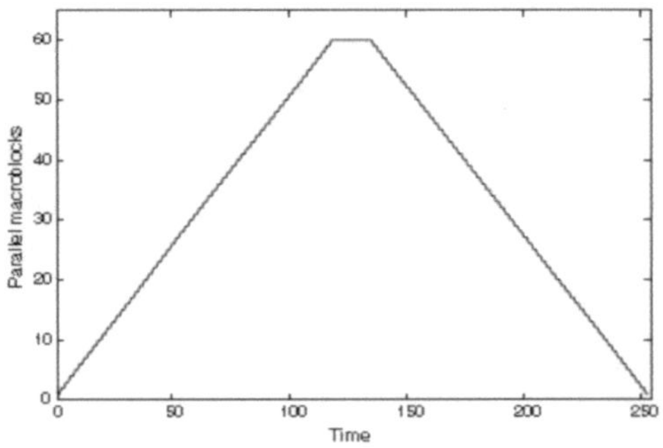

Fig. 15. MB parallelism for a single FHD frame using the 2Dwave approach.

MB-level parallelism in the spatial domain has many advantages over other schemes for parallelization of H.264. First, this scheme can have a good scalability. As shown before the number of independent MBs increases with the resolution of the image. Second, it is possible to achieve a good load balancing if a dynamicscheduling system is used. That is due to the fact that the time to decode a MB is not constant and depends on the data being processed. Load balancing could take place if a dynamic scheduler assigns a MB to a processor once all its dependencies have been satisfied. Additionally, because in MB-level parallelization all the processors/threads run the same program the sameset of software optimizations (for exploiting ILP and SIMD) can be applied to all processing elements. However, this kind ofMB-level parallelism has some disadvantages. The first one is the fluctuating number of independent MBs causing underutilization of cores and decreased total processing rate. The second disadvantage is that entropy decoding cannot be parallelized at the MB level. MBs of the same slice have to be entropy decoded sequentially. If entropy decoding is accelerated with specialized hardware MB level parallelism could still provide benefits.

1.3.9 Macroblock-level parallelism in the temporal domain

In the decoding process the dependency betweenframes is in the MC module only. MC can be regarded as copying an area, called the reference area, from the reference frame, and then to add this predicted area to the residual MB to reconstruct the MB in the current frame. The reference area is pointed to by a Motion Vector (MV). Although the limit to the MV length is defined by the standard as 512 pixels vertical and 2048 pixels horizontal, in practice MVs are within the range of dozens of pixels.

When the reference area has been decoded it can be used by the referencing frame. Thus it is not necessary to wait until a frame is completely decoded before decoding the next frame. The decoding process of the next frame can start after the reference areas of the reference frames are decoded. Figure 16 shows an example of two frames where the second depends on the first. MBs are decoded in scan order and one at a time. The figure shows that MB (2, 0) of frame $i + 1$ depends on MB (2, 1) of frame i which has been decoded. Thus this MB can be decoded even though frame i is not completely decoded.

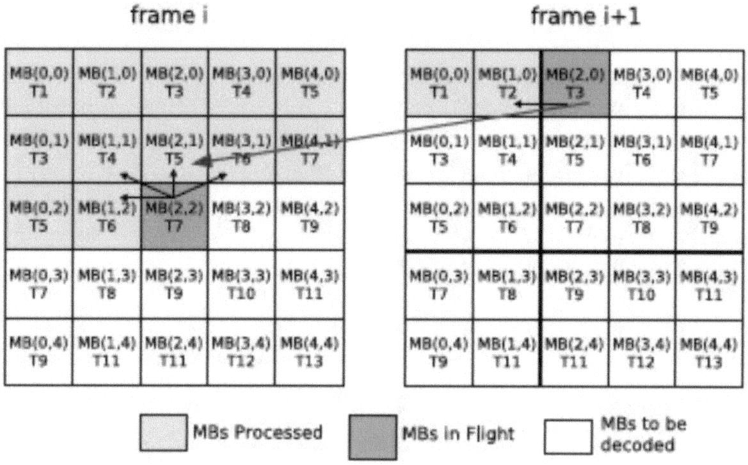

Fig. 16. MB-level parallelism in the temporal domain in H.264.

The main disadvantage of this scheme is the limited scalability. The number of MBs that can be decoded inparallel is inversely proportional to the length of the verticalmotion vector component. Thus for this scheme to be beneficial the encoder should be enforced to heavily restrict themotion search area which in far most cases is not possible. Assuming it would be possible, the minimum search area is around 3 MB rows: 16 pixels for the co-located MB, 3 pixels at the top and at the bottom of the MB for sub-sample interpolations and some pixels for motion vectors (at least 10). As a result the maximum parallelism is 14, 17 and 27MBs for STD, HD and FHD frame resolutions respectively.

The second limitation of this type of MB-level parallelism is poor load-balancing (Lai Ming che 2006) because the decoding time for each frame is different. It can happen that a fast frame is predicted from a slow frame and can not decode faster than the slow frame and remains idle for some time. Finally, this approach works well for the encoder which has the freedom to restrict the range of the motion search area. In the case of the decoder the motion vectors can have large values and the number of frames that can be processed in parallel is reduced.

In summary, parallelizing the entire process of the H.264 encoding particularly motion estimation will definitely end in optimized (Kun et.al 2009) performance provided the hardware/software requirements of the design are required. This will lead to a higher computation throughput achieved at the cost of appreciable load balance among the processor cores.

1.4 Applications

The H.264/AVC (T.Wiegand 2003) standard video format has a very broad application range that covers all forms of digital compressed video from low bit-rate Internet streaming applications to HDTV broadcast and digital cinema applications with nearly lossless coding. With the use of H.264, bit rate savings of 50% or more are reported. H.264 video standard has a broad range of applications like broadcast television, streaming video, video storage and playback, video conferencing, aerial video surveillance, multi-sensor fusion, mobile video, medical imaging, Satellite image processing, video distribution etc..

The H.264/AVC standard was designed to suite a broad range of video application domains. However, each domain is expected to use only a subset of the available options. For this reason profiles and levels were specified to mark conformance points. Encoders and decoders that conform to the same profile are guaranteed to interoperate correctly. Profiles (G.J Sullivan et.al 2004) define sets of coding tools and algorithms that can be used while levels place constraints on the parameters of the bitstream. The standard defines 17 sets of capabilities, which are referred to as *profiles* as seen, targeting specific classes of applications and some of them are listed below in the Table.

	Baseline	Extended	Main	High	High 10	High 4:2:2	High 4:4:4 Predictive
I and P Slices	Yes	Yes	Yes	Yes	Yes	Yes	Yes
B Slices	No	Yes	Yes	Yes	Yes	Yes	Yes
Multiple Reference Frames	Yes	Yes	Yes	Yes	Yes	Yes	Yes
In-Loop Deblocking Filter	Yes	Yes	Yes	Yes	Yes	Yes	Yes
CAVLC Entropy Coding	Yes	Yes	Yes	Yes	Yes	Yes	Yes
CABAC Entropy Coding	No	No	Yes	Yes	Yes	Yes	Yes
Interlaced Coding (PicAFF, MBAFF)	No	Yes	Yes	Yes	Yes	Yes	Yes
8x8 vs. 4x4 Transform Adaptivity	No	No	No	Yes	Yes	Yes	Yes
Quantization Scaling Matrices	No	No	No	Yes	Yes	Yes	Yes
Separate Cb and Cr QP control	No	No	No	Yes	Yes	Yes	Yes
Separate Color Plane Coding	No	No	No	No	No	No	Yes
Predictive Lossless Coding	No	No	No	No	No	No	Yes
	Baseline	Extended	Main	High	High 10	High 4:2:2	High 4:4:4 Predictive

- **Baseline Profile (BP):** The simplest profile mainly used for video conferencing and mobile video.
- **Main Profile (MP):** Intended to be used for consumer broadcast and storage applications, but overtaken by the high profile.
- **Extended Profile (XP):** Intended for streaming video and includes special capabilities to improve robustness.
- **High Profile (HiP)** Intended for high definition broadcast and disc storage, and is used in HD DVD and Blu-ray.

Table 2. H.264 Profiles

Getting the best performance from an H.264/AVC codec generally involves selecting the best coding options or coding mode for each unit of data in the video bitstream. The key considerations in choosing a specific video application (profile/level) depends on the following parameters

- Desired image quality (resolution, frame rate)
- Available bandwidth/storage
- Available processing power
- External factors (camera motion, scene motion,transmission delays)

These variables are vital as they will ultimately impact the performance on which H.264/AVC (profile/level) compression methodology is best for your application. For low lvele applications, the industry uses H.264 Baseline, Constrained Baseline or in some cases, a much lower performance profile with many quality features simply "turned off because they do not have the computer power in the camera (Tiago 2007) to support the higher quality features. Mostly the current profile used in majority is main profile for H.264 encoding, as it provides higher video quality and high performance for the same bandwidth compared to the baseline profile.

Aerial Image Surveillance

Fig. 17. Aerial Video Surveillance

With the development of video coding technologies, digital video surveillance (Nirmal Kumar 2010) has become a very hot application in the recent few years. Specific applications are developed with core functions that extend across civilian and military application areas. Unmanned aerial vehicle (UAV) surveillance and reconnaissance programs increasingly need methods for optimally packaging and distributing information. H.264 supports the collection, formatting, storage and dissemination of "raw" data from real time video capture and image exploitation using embedded technology for surveillance & reconnaissance application, Enhanced fusion vision for situational awareness application, Automatic vision inspection system for quick inspection of components in a manufacturing industry. Also it supports for high-end resolution for remote sensing images and data from satellite.

Airborne surveillance has been widely used in different range of applications in civilian and military applications, such as search and rescue missions, border security, resource exploration, wildfire and oil spill detection, target tracking, surveillance, etc. The unmanned airborne vehicle (UAV) is equipped with special sensors (day / night) to image objects in ground and assigns the actual recognition task (surveillance) to the crew or record image data and analyze them off-line on the ground. Pilot less airborne vehicle with sensor carrying platforms transmit data to a ground control station for analysis and data interpretation.

2. Conclusion

There is likely to be a continued need for better compression efficiency, as video content becomes increasingly ubiquitous and places unprecedented pressure on upcoming new applications in the future. At the same time, the challenge of handling ever more diverse content coded in a wide variety of formats makes reconfigurable coding a potentially useful prospect. To summarize it, we presented an overview of H.264 motion estimation and its types and also the various estimation criterion that decides the complexity of the chosen algorithm. We then probed into the available scalability of parallelism in H.264. Finally we focused on an application which is highly sought in the research environment and its advantages in a more elaborate manner.

3. References

A. Rodr´ıguez, A. Gonz´alez, and M. Malumbres, (2006), Hierarchical parallelization of an H.264/AVC video encoder. *In Int. Conf. on Parallel Computing in Electrical Engineering* (PARLEC), pages 363–368.

Alan Conrad Bovik, (2009). *The Essential Guide to Video processing,* Elsevier, 978-0-12-374456-2, USA.

Alois M.Bock (2009), *"Video Compression Systems from first Principles to Concatenated Codecs"*, The Institution of Engineering and Technology, 978-0-86431-963-6, UK

Florian H. Seitner, Michael Bleyer , Margrit Gelautz · Ralf M. Beuschel, (2010) Evaluation of data-parallel H.264 decoding approaches for strongly resource-restricted architectures, *Springer Science Business Media,* LLC,ISSN 11042-010-0501-7

Gary J. Sullivan, Pankaj Topiwala, and Ajay Luthra, (2004), The H.264/AVC Advanced Video Coding Standard: Overview and Introduction to the Fidelity Range

Extensions, *SPIE Conference on Applications of Digital Image Processing* XXVII, August, 2004.

http://en.wikipedia.org/wiki/H.264

http://en.wikipedia.org/wiki/Video_compression

http://en.www.wikipedia.com

http://www.chiariglione.org

http://www.vodex.com

I.E.G. Richardson, (2003). *H.264 and MPEG-4 Video Compression: Video Coding for Next-generation Multimedia,* John Wiley & Sons, Ltd, 0-470-84837-5, UK

Iain E.Richardson, (2010) .*The H.264 Advanced Video Compression Standard* John Wiley & Sons ltd, 978-0-470-51692-8, UK.

Kue-Hwan Sihn, Hyunki Baik, Jong-Tae Kim, Sehyun Bae, Hyo Jung Song, (2009), Novel Approaches to Parallel H.264 Decoder on Symmetric Multicore Systems, *Proceedings of IEEE.*

Kun Ouyang Qing Ouyang Zhengda Zhou, (2009), Optimization and Implementation of H.264 Encoder on Symmetric Multi- Processor Platform, *Proceedings of IEEE Computer Society, World Congress on Computer Science and Information Engineering.*

Lai Mingche, Dai Kui, Lu Hong-yi, Wang Zhi-ying, 2006, A Novel Data-Parallel Coprocessor for Multimedia Signal Processing",IEEE Computer Society.

Nuno Roma and Leonel Sousa, 2002, Efficient and Configurable Full-Search Block-Matching Processors, *IEEE Transactions on Circuits and Systems for Video Technology,* Vol. 12, No. 12, December 2002.

P.Nirmal Kumar, E.MuraliKrishnan, E.Gangadharan, (2010), Enhanced Performance of H.264 using FPGA Coprocessors in Video Surveillance, *Proceedings of IEEE Computer Society, ICSAP,* India.

Philip P. Dang (2009), Architecture of an application-specific processor for real-time implementation of H.264/AVC sub-pixel interpolation, *Journal of real-time Image Processing,* Vol.4, pp. 43-53

Romuald Mosqueron, Julien Dubois, Marco Mattavelli, and David Mauvilet "Smart Camera Based on Embedded HW/SW Coprocessor", *EURASIP Journal on Embedded Systems,* Hindawi Publishing Corporation, Volume 2008, Article ID 597872, 13 pages,doi:10.1155/2008/597872.

T. Wiegand, G. J. Sullivan, G. Bjontegaard and A. Luthra, (2003), Overview of the H.264 / AVC Video Coding Standard", *IEEE Transactions on Circuit and Systems for Video Technology,* VOL. 13, NO. 7, July 2003.

Tiago Dias ,Nuno Roma , Leonel Sousa, Miguel Ribeiro (2007) Reconfigurable architectures and processors for real-time video motion estimation, *Journal of real-time Image Processing,* Vol.2, pp. 191-205

Youn Long Steve Lin, Chao Yang Kao, Hung-Chih Kuo, Jian-Wen Chen, (2010) "*VLSI Design for Video Coding, H.264/AVC Encoding from Standard Specification to Chip*", Springer, 978-1-4419-0958-9, USA

Yu-Wen Huang, Ching-Yeh Chen, Chen-Han Tsai, Chun-Fu Shen And Liang-Gee Chen, (2006) "Survey on Block Matching Motion Estimation Algorithms and Architectures with New Results, *Journal of VLSI Signal Processing , Springer* Vol.42, pp.297–320, 2006.

Zhibo Chen, Jianfeng Xu, Yun He, Junli Zheng (2006) Fast integer-pel and fractional-pel motion estimation for H.264/AVC, *International Journal of Visual Communication*, Vol.17,pp. 264–29,

5

Global Motion Estimation and Its Applications

Xueming Qian
School of Electronic and Information Engineering, Xi'an Jiaotong University, Xi'an, China

1. Introduction

In this chapter, global motion estimation and its applications are given. Firstly we give the definitions of global motion and global motion estimation. Secondly, the parametric representations of global motion models are provided. Thirdly, global estimation approaches including pixel domain based global motion estimation, hierarchical global motion estimation, partial pixel set based global motion estimation, and compressed domain based global motion estimation are reviewed. Finally, four global motion based applications in video compression, sport video shot classification, video error concealment, and video text occluded region recovery are given.

Motion information is very important for video content analysis. In surveillance video, usually the camera is stationary, and the motions of the video frame are often caused by local motion objects. Thus detecting motions in the video sequences can be utilized in abnormal events detection. In sports video, the heavy motions are also related to highlights. Motion estimation and compensation is the core of video coding. Coding the residual component after motion compensated can save bit-rates significantly. In video sequences, the motion pattern can be classified into two types: local motion and global motion. The global motion is related to camera motion. Integrated with local motion, global motion is widely utilized in video object segmentation, video coding and error concealment. The rest of this chapter is organized as follows: the definition of global motion is given in Section 2. The global motion models are given in Section 3. Global motion estimation approaches are given in Section 4. Four applications based on global motion and local motion (GM/LM) information are introduced in Section 5. The applications are GM/LM based video coding, global view refinement for soccer video, GM/LM based error concealment and GM/LM based text occluded region recovery. And finally conclusions are drawn in Section 6.

2. Definition of global motion

Global motions in a video sequence are caused by camera motion, which can be modeled by parametric transforms [4]. The process of estimating the transform parameters is called global motion estimation.

From the definition, it is clear that global motion is closely related to camera motion. The camera is operated by camera man. Thus the global motion pattern can reveal video shooting style which has some relationship with video contents [18]. The global motion information is especially useful in sport video content analysis [13]-[18].

From the definition, we find that the global motions have certain consistence for the whole frame as shown in Fig.1. The global motion in Fig.1 (a) is a zoom out and that in Fig.1 (b) is a translation respectively. From Fig.1 (a), we find that the motion direction is from outer to inner regions, which means that the coordinates of a current frame t can be generated in the inner regions of the reference frame v ($t > v$). In Fig.l, the motion vectors in the motion field correspond to the global motion vectors at the coordinates.

Global motion vector is the motion vector calculated from the estimated global motion parameters. Global motion vector $(GMVx_t, GMVy_t)$ for the current pixel with its coordinates (x_t, y_t) is determined as

$$\begin{cases} GMVx_t = x'_t - x_t \\ GMVy_t = y'_t - y_t \end{cases} \tag{1}$$

where (x'_t, y'_t) are the warped coordinates in the reference frame by the global motion parameters from the coordinate (x_t, y_t).

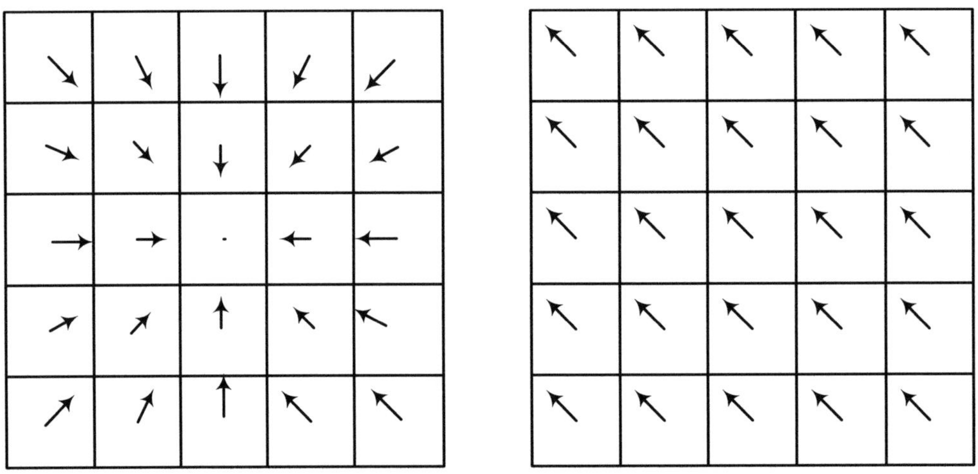

(a)Zoom-out (b) Translation

Fig. 1. Global motion fields. (a) Zoom-out and (b) Translation.

3. Global motion models

Global motion can be represented by global motion models with several parameters. The simplest global motion model is translation with only two parameters. The complex global motion model is quadric model with 12 parameters. Generally, higher order models have more parameters to be estimated, which can represent more complex motions. The lower order models are special cases of the higher ones. The widely used global motion model is perspective model with 8 parameters, which is expressed as follows

$$\begin{cases} x' = \dfrac{m_0 x + m_1 y + m_2}{m_6 x + m_7 y + 1} \\ y' = \dfrac{m_3 x + m_4 y + m_5}{m_6 x + m_7 y + 1} \end{cases} \tag{2}$$

where (x,y) and (x',y') are the coordinates in the current and the reference image respectively, with the set of parameters $\mathbf{m} = [m_0, \cdots, m_7]$ denoting the global motion parameters to be estimated. If m_6=m_7=0, then it is an affine model with 6 parameters. Then Eq.(2) can be simplified as follows

$$\begin{cases} x' = m_0 x + m_1 y + m_2 \\ y' = m_3 x + m_4 y + m_5 \end{cases} \tag{3}$$

When m_0= m_4=1 and ,m_1=m_3=m_6=m_7=0, then the perspective model is actually simplified into a translation model as follows

$$\begin{cases} x' = x + m_2 \\ y' = y + m_5 \end{cases} \tag{4}$$

4. Global Motion Estimation (GME) approaches

Intuitively, global motion estimation can be carried out in pixel domain. In the pixel domain based approaches, all the pixels are involved in the estimation of global motion parameters. There are two shortcomings in pixel domain based approach: 1) it is very computational intensive; 2) it is often sensitive to noises (local object motions).

In order to improve the convergence and speed up the calculation, coarse to fine searching approach is often adopted. Moreover, the subset of pixels having the largest gradient magnitude is adopted to estimate the global motion parameters [6]. Sub-point based global motion estimation approaches are very effective in reducing computational costs. To guarantee the accuracy of global motion estimation, how to determine the optimal sub-sets are the key steps. Except the pixel domain based global motion estimation, compressed domain based global motion estimation approaches are also very popular.

Robust global motion estimation usually carries out by identifying the pixels (blocks or regions) that undergo local motions. Fig.2 shows the global motion and local motions. If the local motion blocks can be determined as outliers, then the global motion performance can be improved significantly.

4.1 Pixel domain based GME

In GME involving two image frames I_k and I_v (with $k<v$), one seeks to minimize the following sum of squared differences between I_v and its predicted image $I_k(x(i, j), y(i, j))$ which is obtained after transforming all the pixels in I_k.

$$E = \sum_i \sum_j e(i,j)^2 \tag{5}$$

where $e(i, j)$ denotes the error of predicting a pixel located at (i, j) of frame Iv, by using a pixel at location $[x(i, j), y(i, j)]$ of previous frame I_k.

$$e(i,j) = I_v(i,j) - I_k(x(i,j), y(i,j)) \tag{6}$$

The transform mapping functions $x(i, j)$ and $y(i, j)$ (with respect to global motion parameters **m**) should be so chosen that E in Eq.(5) is minimized. The well-known Levenberg-Marquard algorithm (LMA) or lest square approach, can be utilized to find the optimal global motion parameters **m** iteratively by minimizing the energy function in Eq.(5) as follows

$$\mathbf{m}^{(n+1)} = \mathbf{m}^{(n)} + \Delta\mathbf{m}^{(n)} \tag{7}$$

where $\mathbf{m}^{(n)}$ and $\Delta\mathbf{m}^{(n)}$ are the global motion parameters and updating vector at iteration n [8].

All the pixels are involved in the global motion parameters optimization in the traditional LMA algorithm [9]. This is very computational intensive. It is impractical for real-time applications. Moreover, the local motions in video frame may also bias the global motion parameters' estimation precision. Thus improvements are carried out by utilizing hierarchical global motion estimation, partial pixel set and compressed domain based approaches.

4.2 Hierarchical global motion estimation

In MPEG-4, GME is performed by a hierarchical approach to reduce computational costs [1]. It is an improvement of pixel domain based approach which consists of following three steps. Firstly, spatial pyramid frames are constructed. Secondly, global motion parameters with the coarsest global motion model are estimated at the top layer of the pyramid images. Then, the estimated global motion parameters at the coarsest level are projected to its next high resolution level to get the refined global motion parameters. Finally, the refined global motion parameters are iteratively updated using a least-square based approach and the process continues until convergence [1]. Fig. 2 shows the illustration of hierarchical global motion estimation approach. The original image and its motion field, the second layer and third layer pyramid images and their motion fields are shown in Fig.2 (a), (b) and (c) respectively. In Fig.2 local motion region (LMR) and global motion region (GMR) of each layer are labeled out respectively.

Global motion parameters at each layer are estimated by minimizing the sum of weighted squared errors over all corresponding pairs of pixels (x_i, y_i) and (x'_i, y'_i) within the current image f and the reference image R as follow.

$$E = \sum_i \sum_j w(i,j) e(i,j)^2 \tag{8}$$

$$E = \sum_i \sum_j w(i,j)[R(x(i,j), y(i,j)) - f(i,j)]^2 \tag{9}$$

where $w(i,j)$ is the corresponding weight of the pixel at coordinate (i,j) with $w(i,j) \in \{0,1\}$. You know, local object motion may create outliers and therefore bias the estimation performance of the global motion parameters. To reduce the influence of such outliers, a robust histogram based technique is adopted to reject the pixel points with large matching errors by setting their weights to be "0".

The hierarchical global motion estimation approach has following advantages: 1) estimating the coarse global motion parameters on the top layer of pyramid is effective for noise filtering; 2) computational cost of coarse global motion estimation is very low at the top layer of pyramid. This is due to the fact that only small resolution images are involved in GME and the global motion model is low order which is easy to get convergence; 3) adaptive model determination with respect to the precisions of global motion parameters, which is also helpful for reducing computational cost. In the enhanced layer, it is only need to updating global motion parameters on the basis of the parameters estimated in its previous layers. The advantages of hierarchical global motion over traditional pixel domain based global motion estimation approach can be shown by the illustrations in Fig.2 respectively.

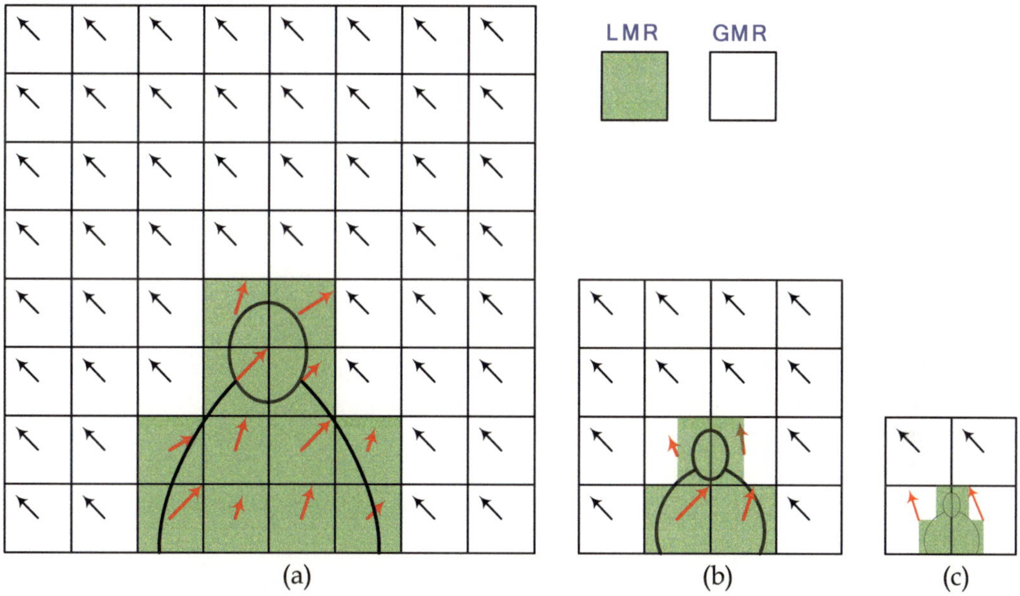

Fig. 2. Illustration of hierarchical global motion estimation approach. (a) Original image and its motion field, (b) and (c) correspond to the second layer and third layer pyramid images and their motion fields.

4.3 Partial pixel points based GME

Just as its name implies, partial pixel points based GME approaches only use sub-set of the whole pixels for estimating global motion parameters. In [6], the subset utilized for GME is selected based on gradient magnitudes information. The top 10% pixels with the largest gradient magnitudes are selected and severed as reliable points for GME. This method divides the whole image into 100 sub-regions and selects the top 10% pixels as feature points which can avoid numerical instability. This subset selection approach reduce the computational cost by reduce the number of pixels at the cost of calculating the gradient image and ranking the gradient of the whole pixels. To further reduce the computational cost, a random subset selection method was proposed in [4] for GME in fast image-based tracking. Pixel selection can also follow certain fixed subsampling pattern. Alzoubi and Pan apply the subsampling method that combines random and fixed subsampling patterns to global motion estimation [9]. The corresponding combined subsampling patterns can provide significantly improved tradeoffs between motion estimation accuracy and complexity than those achievable by using either fixed or random patterns alone. Wang et al., [7] proposed a fast progressive model refinement algorithm to select the appropriate motion model to describe different camera motions. Based on the correlation of motion model and model parameters between neighbor frames, an intermediate-level model prediction method is utilized.

4.4 Compressed domain based GME

In video coding standards, the motion estimation algorithms calculate the motions between successive video frames and predict the current frame from previously transmitted frames using the motion information. Hence, the motion vectors have some relationship with the global motion [10]-[12]. A global motion estimation method is proposed based on randomly selected MV groups from motion vector field with adaptive parametric model determination [5]. A non-iterative GME approach is proposed by Su *et al.* by solving a set of exactly-determined matrix equations corresponding to a set of motion vector groups [4]. Each MV group consists of four MVs selected from the MV field by a fixed spatial pattern. The global motion parameters for each of the MV group are obtained by solving the exactly-determined matrix equation using singular value decomposition (SVD) based pseudo-inverse technique. The final global motion parameters are obtained by a weighted histogram-based method. Moreover, a least-square based GME method by coarsely sampled MVs from the input motion vector field is proposed for compressed video sequences [5]. The global motion parameters are optimized by minimizing the fitting error between the input motion vectors and the wrapped ones from estimated global motion parameters. In order to estimate global motions robustly, motion vectors in local motion region, homogeneous region with zero or near-zero amplitude and regions with larger matching errors are rejected.

The objective function of compressed domain based GME approaches is to minimize the weighted mean matching error (MME) of the input motion vectors and the generated ones by virtue of the estimated global motion parameters, which is expressed as follows

$$MME = \sum_{i=1}^{MVNum} w_i(ex_i^2 + ey_i^2) \Big/ \sum_{i=1}^{MVNum} w_i \tag{10}$$

$$\begin{cases} ex_i = MVx_i - x_i' + x_i \\ ey_i = MVy_i - y_i' + y_i \end{cases} \tag{11}$$

where (MVx_i, MVy_i) denotes the input MV of the i-th macro-block (MB) at the spatial coordinates (x_i, y_i), (ex_i, ey_i) denote the errors vector between the decoded MV and the MV generated by the estimated global motion parameters. And let (x_i', y_i') denote the warped coordinates for (x_i, y_i) with respect to the global motion parameters $\mathbf{m}$. $MVNum$ denotes the number of MVs and $w_i(1 \le i \le MVNum)$ is the weighting factor for the i-th MB, with $w_i \in \{0,1\}$. How to reject the outlier motion vectors is also very important to improve global estimation performances [10]. Intuitively, w_i can be set to be "0" if one of the following three conditions is satisfied: 1) this MB is located in a smooth region (which can be indicated by the standard deviation of the luminance component), 2) the matching error of this MB is large enough (which can be measured by the DC coefficient of the residual component), 3) this MB is intra-coded. Global motion estimation is carried out using the MBs with their weights set to be "1".

5. Applications of global motion estimation

In this Section, four global motion based applications are illustrated. They are 1) the GMC (global motion compensation) and LMC (local motion compensation) based video coding in MPEG-4 advanced simple profile (ASP), 2) GM and LM based mid-level semantic classification for sport video, 3) GM/LM based video error concealment, and 4) GM/LM based text occluded region recovery.

5.1 GMC and LMC based video coding

The aim of this part is to illustrate how video compression performances can be improved by utilizing adaptive GMC/LMC mode determination. GMC/LMC based motion compensation mode selection approach in MPEG-4 is given [1], [2]. Global motion estimation and compensation is used in MPEG-4 advanced simple profiles (ASP) to remove the residual information of global motion. Global motion compensation (GMC) is a new coding technology for video compression in MPEG-4 standard. By extracting camera motion, MPEG-4 coder can remove the global motion redundancy from the video. In MPEG-4 ASP, each macro block (MB) can be selected to be coded use GMC or local motion compensation (LMC) adaptively during mode determination. Intuitively, some types of motion, e.g., panning, zooming or rotation; could be described using one set of motion parameters for the entire VOP (video object plane). For example, each MB could potentially have the exact same MV for the panning. GMC allows the encoder to pass one set of motion parameters in the VOP header to describe the motion of all MBs. Additionally MPEG-4 allows each MB to specify its own MV to be used in place of the global MV.

In MPEG-4 Advanced simple profile, the main target of Global Motion Compensation (GMC) is to encode the global motion in a VOP (video object plane) using a small number of parameters. Each MB can be predicted either from the previous VOP by global motion compensation (GMC) using warping parameters or from the previous VOP by local motion compensation (LMC) using local motion vectors as in the classical scheme. The selection is made based on which predictor leads to the lower prediction error. In this Section we only expressed the GMC/LMC mode selection approach. More detail expression for the INTER4V/INTER/field prediction, GMC/LMC, and INTRA/INTER can be found in the Section 18.8.2 GMC prediction and MB type selection [2]. The pseudo-code of GMC/LMC mode decision in MPEG-4 AS is as follows:

if ($SAD_{GMC} - P < SAD_{LMC}$) then GMC
else LMC

where SAD_{GMC} is defined as the sum of the absolute difference in the luminance block when using GMC prediction, and SAD_{LMC} and P are defined as:
if the previous criterion was INTER4V

$$SAD_{LMC} = SAD_8$$
$$P = N_B * Qp / 16$$

if the previous criterion was INTER

$$SAD_{LMC} = SAD_{16}$$
$$P = N_B * Qp / 64$$

if the previous criterion was INTER and the motion vector was (0,0)

$$SAD_{LMC} = SAD_{16} + (N_B /2 + 1)$$
$$P = NB/2 + 1$$

if the previous criterion was field prediction

$$SAD_{LMC} = SAD_{16*8}$$
$$P = N_B * Qp / 32$$

where SAD_8 (sum of absolute difference for four 8x8 luminance blocks when the INTER4V mode is selected), SAD_{16} (sum of absolute difference for a 16x16 luminance block when the INTER mode is selected) and SAD_{16*8} (sum of absolute difference for two 16x8 interlaced luminance blocks when the field prediction mode is selected) are computed with half pixel motion vectors. N_B indicates the number of pixels inside the VOP. Qp is the quantization parameter.

5.2 Global motion based shot classification for sport video

In [13], Xu et al. classified soccer video shots into the views of global, zoom-in and close-up. From the view sequences, each soccer video clip is classified into either a play or a break. In [14], Duan et al. classified video shots into eight categories by fusing the global motion pattern, color, texture, shape, and shot length information in a supervised learning framework. Ekin and Tekalp utilized shot category and shot duration information to carry out play-break detection according to the dominant related rules and soccer video production knowledge [16]. Similarly, Li et al. classified video shots into event and non-event by identifying the canonical scenes and the camera breaks [15]. Tan et al. also segmented a basketball sequence into wide angle, close-up, fast-break and possible shoot-at-the-basket using motion information [17].

In soccer video, the global views give audiences an overall view of the sport, while the close up and medium views, being complementary to global views, show certain details of the game. Typically the camera men operate cameras, by fast track, or zoom in to provide audiences with clearer views of the games. Based on the view type, camera motion patterns and domain related knowledge, high level semantics can be inferred. The classified shot category information is helpful for highlight events discrimination. In [18], global views of soccer video are further refined into the following three types: stationary, zoom and track in terms of camera motion information using a set of empirical rules with respect to domain and production knowledge. The key-frames of a shot with stationary by means of average motion intensity and average motion intensities of global motion. The local motion information is represented by average motion intensity (AMV) which is expressed as follows

$$AMV = \frac{1}{M}\sum_{j=1}^{M}\sqrt{MVx_j^2 + MVy_j^2} \tag{12}$$

where (MVx_j, MVy_j) is the motion vector (MV) of the block with its coordinates (x_j, y_j) and j is the block index. The average global motion intensity ($AGMV$) is calculated as follows:

$$AGMV = \frac{1}{M}\sum_{j=1}^{M}\sqrt{GMVx_j^2 + GMVy_j^2} \tag{13}$$

where $(GMVx_j, GMVy_j)$ is the global motion vector of the block at (x_j, y_j), M is the total block number. The global motion vector $(GMVx_t, GMVy_t)$ at the coordinates (x_t, y_t) is determined as follows

$$\begin{cases} GMVx_t = x'_t - x_t \\ GMVy_t = y'_t - y_t \end{cases} \tag{14}$$

where (x'_t, y'_t) are the warped coordinates in the reference frame by the global motion parameters from the coordinate (x_t, y_t).

The GM/LM based global view refinement is carried out by the following empirical rules [18]: If the motion energy of a frame satisfies $AMV<0.5$, then it is stationary otherwise non-stationary. The non-stationary shot is further classified into zoom and track. A frame is a zoom-in if $m_0=m_5>1$, a zoom-out if $m_0=m_5<1$, otherwise a track ($m_0=m_5=1$). The track is a slow-track if the average global motion intensity $AGMV$ satisfies $AGMV \le 2$, otherwise a fast-track.

5.3 Global motion and local motion (GM/LM) based application in error concealment

The aim of this sub-chapter is to show how combine global and local motion to improve visual video qualities of corrupted video sequences.

5.3.1 Related work on error concealment (EC)

Temporal recovery (TR) is often utilized to replace the erroneous macro-blocks (EMBs) by their spatially corresponding MBs in the reference frames. TR is efficient for the stationary video sequences. Temporal average (TA) uses the average or medium MV of the correctly received MBs in its neighbors to substitute the losing MVs for the corrupted MBs [19]. Boundary pixels of the top and bottom-, or (and) left and right-adjacent MBs as the references [20], [21]. A recursive block matching (RBM) technique is utilized to recover the error MBs [20]. The correctly received MBs in its neighbors are utilized. Recovery results of the corrupted MBs are improved step by step using the full searching technique within a given searching range. However, this approach is not effective when the reference blocks located in texture-alike or smooth region. There are more than one best matches for the two 8×16 blocks in the smooth regions at reference frames.

A global motion based error concealment method is proposed by Su *et al.*[3,4]. In [3] MVs generated by global motion parameters are utilized to recover the EMBs under the assumption that they are all located in global motion regions. When the EMBs are in LM or GM/LM overlapped regions, usually the MVs generated by global motion parameters are incorrect to recover the lost MVs.

5.3.2 GM/LM based error concealment

Obviously it is more effective to recover MVs of the EMBs in the global motion regions by the global MVs and the EMBs in local motion regions by the local motion compensation. And for the corrupted MBs located in the GM/LM overlapped regions, more accurate boundaries need to be searched using the advanced boundary matching criteria [19]-[21]. We give the detailed steps for the GM/LM based error concealment approach [22]. The detail diagram of the proposed GM/LM based EC method is shown in Fig.3.

GM/LM based EC method consists of the following four steps: 1) Carry out global motion estimation for the corrupted frames using the MVs of the correctly received MBs (CMBs). 2) Classify the CMBs into global motion MBs (GMBs) or local motion MBs (LMBs) types. 3) Determine the type of the erroneous MBs (EMBs) and Step 4. Carry out recovery by using the GM/LM based approach.

Based on the estimated global motion parameters, a CMB is classified into two types: GMB and LMB adaptively with respect to the matching error of the reconstructed MB (from the video streams) and the global motion warped MB. If the matching error is large enough then it is a LMB, otherwise a GMB. Actually this step does not influence the GM/LM based error concealment performances very much [22].

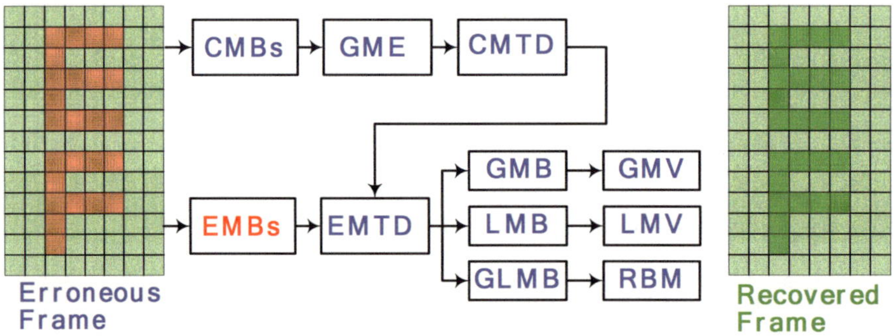

Fig. 3. Diagram of GM/LM based error concealment.

In GM/LM based EC approach, each EMB can be classified into one of the three types: GMB, LMB and GLMB according to the CMBs (including already recovered EMBs) type information in its 8-neighbors as follows:

1. If the CMBs in the neighbors of an EMB are all with the type GMB, then we classify the EMB be a GMB. The corrupted pixels in the EMB are replaced by the warped pixels in their reference frame by utilizing the GMV information.
2. If the CMBs in the neighbors of an EMB are all with the type LMB, then we classify the EMB be a LMB. The corrupted pixels in the EMB can be replaced by the MB in their

reference frame using the average MV of the non-corrupted or recovered MBs in its 8-neighbors. The GMV and LMV based replacement for the EMB are based on the facts that both global motion and local motion have certain consistence.

3. Otherwise the EMB is a GLMB. The EMB may contain both global and local motion regions. Boundaries between background and objects usually exist in the EMB. To determine the accurate boundaries, complicate boundary matching algorithms such as RBM, and AECOD [21] can be adopted. We use RBM method to search the optimal MV to recover the EMB.

5.3.3 Error concealment performance

Objective error concealment performances of the TR, TA, GM, RBM and GM/LM are given. Fig. 4 (a) and (b) show the objective averaged PSNR (peak signal to noise ratio) values of the EC methods applied to each of the P-frame of the testing sequences *flower* and *mobile* under the PER (packet error rates) 15%. From Fig.4, we find that our GM/LM based EC method gives comparatively better recovery results.

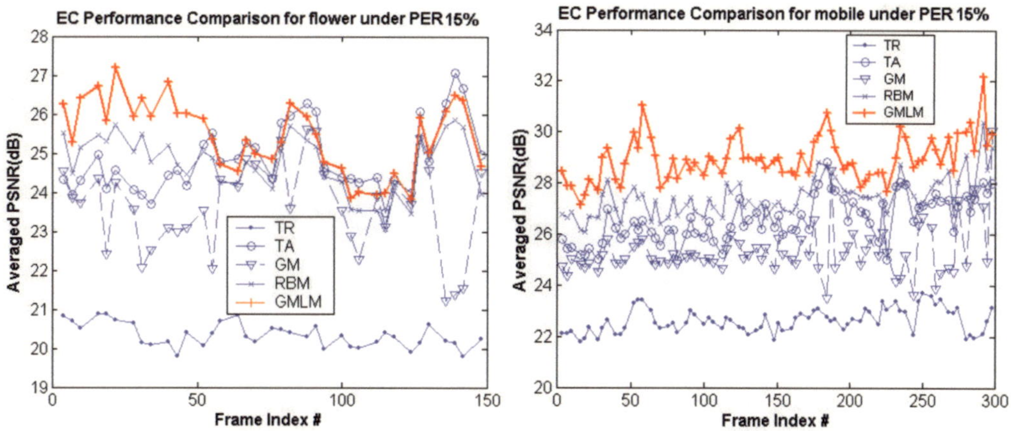

(a) flower (b) mobile

Fig. 4. EC Performances Comparison of the corresponding TR, TA, GM, RBM and GM/LM for the video sequences under PER 15%.

To show the subjective recovery results of the TR, TA, GM, RBM and GM/LM based error concealment approaches, two frames are extracted from the test video sequences with several erroneous slices, as shown in Fig. 5. We find that the recovery results of TR are not so effective. TA is not effective to get accurate motion information for the MBs in heavy motion regions. RBM performs well for the area where non-periodical texture appears. However, it is not so effective in the circumstance that the reference blocks are in smooth and texture similar regions as shown in Fig. 5(b). GM provides better recovery results for the background regions. However, large distortions are produced for recovering the EMBs in local motion regions. Comparatively, better performances are achieved by the proposed GM/LM based EC method.

a) b) c) d) e)

f)

g)

Fig. 5. Subjective error concealment results for #31 of flower and #28 of foreman. (a) non-error frames; (b) corrupted frames; and the corresponding recovery results of (c) TR; (d)TA;(e) GM; (f)RBM and (g) GM/LM respectively.

5.4 GM/LM based text occluded region recovery

The corresponding block diagram of the proposed GM/LM based text occluded region recovery (TORR) approach is shown in Fig.6. It consists of the following steps.

Fig. 6. Block diagram of the GM/LM based text occluded region recovery (TORR). The input video is with text occluded regions and the output video is with text occluded region recovery.

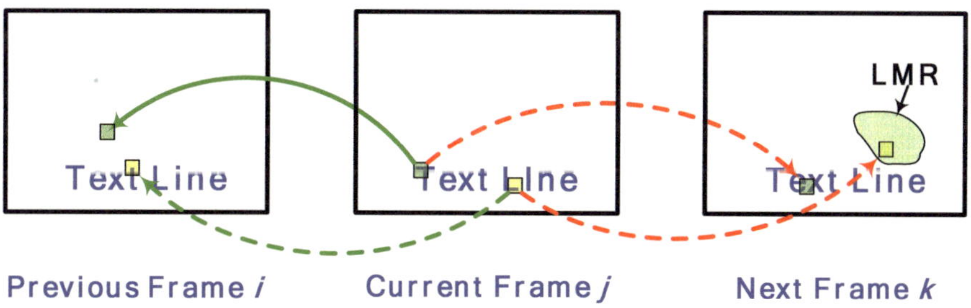

Fig. 7. Diagram of recovering a pixel in text occluded region of current frame *j* from its previous frame *i* and next frame *k*. The dash lines means the pixel cannot be recovered from its reference frames. The solid lines means the pixels can be recovered from its reference frames.

(a) video frames with detected text lines

(b) video frames after carrying out TORR

Fig. 8. GM/LM based text occluded region recovery for the three frames for the test video sequence *News1*.

(a) video frames with detected text lines

(b) video frames after carrying out TORR

Fig. 9. GM/LM based text occluded region recovery for the three frames for the test video sequence *Foxes of the Kalahari*.

1. Text detection and determining the starting/ending frames of each text line for the output video sequence. The starting and ending frames of a text line is determined by text tracking and matching. This method is with low computational costs and robust to the missing and false detections [23].
2. Video text segmentation. In the video text segmentation, text regions can be extracted by the foreground and background integrated method [23].
3. Global motion estimation. Texts are added during editing, the text regions are not undergoing global motions. So the text recovered regions can be viewed as outliers in global motion estimation.

Text occluded region recovery using GM/LM information. From the estimated global motion parameters **m** and the text occluded regions $TR = \bigcup_{i=1}^{N}(x_i, y_i)$, where N is the total pixels in the text occluded region of current frame. The corresponding diagram of a pixel in text occluded region is shown in Fig.7. TORR is carried out bi-directional and iteratively. The bi-directional approach means that a pixel in text occluded region of current frame j can be recovered by forward previous frame i and backward replacement from its next frame k (with $i<j<k$). From Fig.7 we find that the first pixel can be recovered (denoted by the solid lines) from its previous frame i and cannot recovered (denoted by the dash lines) from its next frame k. However, for the second pixel, its replacement in frame i is also in text occluded region. Moreover, its replacement in frame k is in local motion region (LMR). So the above two directional replacement are both invalid. Thus iteratively carrying out TORR is needed for the video frame. The iteration stops when all pixels in TORR are recovered. Alternatively, the replacement can be carried out by using more than one frame. It is likely that the second pixel in frame j can find correct replacement in its previous frames $i-n$ or $k+n$ (with $n>0$).

Fig.8 and Fig.9 show the subjective text occluded region recovery results. The text occluded frames in Fig.8(a) and Fig.9 (a) are from MPEG-7 test video sequences *News*1 and a documentary film of National Geography *Foxes of the Kalahari*. Fig.8 (a) and Fig.9 (a) are the video frames with detected text lines. Fig.8 (b) and Fig.9 (b) show video frames after carrying out TORR using the GM/LM based method. From the recovery results we find that the detail information of the anchorperson is kept well. This further shows the effectiveness of our GM/LM based text occluded recovery method.

6. Conclusion

In this chapter, a systematic review of the pixel domain based global motion estimation approaches is presented. With respect to its shortcomings in noise filtering and computational cost, the improvement approaches including hierarchical global motion estimation, partial pixel set based global motion estimation and compressed domain based global motion estimation are provided. Four global motion based applications including GMC/LMC in MPEG-4 video coding standard, global motion based sport video shot classification, GM/LM based error concealment and text occluded region recovery are described. The applications show the effectiveness of global motion based approaches.

7. Acknowledgement

This work is supported in part by National Natural Science Foundations of China (NSFC) No.60903121, No.61173109, and Foundation of Microsoft Research Asia.

8. Reference

[1] F. Dufaux and J. Konrad, "Efficient, robust, and fast global motion estimation for video coding", IEEE Trans. Image Processing, Vol. 9, No.3, Mar. 2000, pp.497-501.

[2] "MPEG-4 Video Verification Model version 18.0", ISO/IEC JTC1/SC29/WG11, 2001.

[3] Y. P. Su, M. T. Sun, and V. Hsu, "Global Motion Estimation From Coarsely Sampled Motion Vector Field and the Applications", IEEE Trans. Circuits Syst. Video Technol., Vol. 15, No. 2, Feb. 2005, pp. 232-242.

[4] Y. P. Su, M. T. Sun, "A Non-iterative motion vector based global motion estimation algorithm", Proc. Int. Conf. Multimedia and Expo, Taipei, Taiwan, June 27-30, 2004, pp.703-706.

[5] X. Qian, G. Liu, "Global motion estimation from randomly selected motion vector groups and GM/LM based applications", signal image and video processing, 2007, pp.179-189.

[6] Y. Keller, A. Averbuch, "Fast Gradient Methods Based on Global Motion Estimation for Video Compression", IEEE Trans. Circuits Syst. Video Technol., Vol. 13, No. 4, Apr. 2003, pp. 300-309.

[7]H. Wang, J. Wang, Q. Liu, H. Lu, Fast progressive model refinement global motion estimation algorithm with prediction, in proc. ICME 2006.

[8] H. Alzoubi, W. Pan, "very fast global motion estimation using partial data", in Proc. ICASSP 2006.

[9] H. Alzoubi, W. Pan, "efficient global motion estimation using fixed and random subsampling patterns"

[10] Y. Chen, and I. Bajic´, "Motion vector outlier rejection cascade for global motion estimation,"IEEE Signal Processing Letters, vol. 17, no. 2, 2010, pp. 197-200.

[11] M. Tok, A. Glantz, M. Arvanitidou, A. Krutz, and T. Sikora, "Compressed domain global motion estimation using the Helmholtz tradeoff estimator," in Proc. ICIP 2010,pp.777-780.

[12] Y. Chen, I. Bajic´, and P. Saeedi, "Motion region segmentation from compressed video using global motion estimation and Markov random fields," IEEE Transactions on Multimedia, vol. 13, no. 3, 2011, pp. 421-431.

[13] P. Xu, L. Xie, and S. Chang, "Algorithms and systems for segmentation and structure analysis in soccer video," in Proc. Int. Conf. Multimedia & Expo, 2001, pp. 184-187.

[14] L. Duan, M. Xu, Q. Tian, C. Xu, and J. S. Jin, "A unified framework for semantic shot classification in sports video," IEEE Trans. Multimedia, vol.7, No.6, 2005, pp.1066-1083.

[15] B. Li, J. Errico, H. Pan, and M. Sezan, "Bridging the semantic gap in sports video retrieval and summarization," J. Vis. Commun. Image R. vol.17, pp.393-424, 2004.

[16] A. Ekin, and A. Tekalp, "Generic play-break event detection for summarization and hierarchical sports video analysis," in Proc. Int. Conf. Mulmedia and Expo, vol.1, 2003, pp. 169-172.

[17] Y. Tan, D. Saur, S. Kulkarni, P. Ramadge, "Rapid estimation of camera motion from compressed video with application to video annotation," IEEE Trans. Circuits Syst. Video Techn., no.1,vol. 10, 2000,pp. 133-146.

[18] X. Qian, H. Wang, G. Liu, and X. Hou, "HMM Based Soccer Video Event Detection Using Enhanced Mid-Level Semantic", Multimedia Tools and Applications, 2011.

[19] J. Sub and Y. Ho, "Error concealment based on directional interpolation," IEEE Transactions on Consumer Electronics, vol. 43, pp. 295-302, August 1997.

[20] M. Chen, C. Chen and M. Chi, "Temporal error concealment algorithm by recursive block-matching principle", IEEE Trans. Circuits Syst. Video Technol., Vol. 15, No. 11, Nov. 2005, pp. 1385-1393.

[21] X. Qian, G. Liu, and H. Wang, "Recovering Connected Error Region Based on Adaptive Error Concealment Order Determination," IEEE Trans. Multimedia, vol.11, no.4, pp.683-695, 2009.

[22] X. Qian, and G.Liu, "An Effective GM/LM Based Video Error Concealment", Signal Image and Video Processing, 2012, vol.6,no.1, pp.9-17.

[23] X. Qian, G. Liu, H. Wang, and R. Su, "Text detection, localization and tracking in compressed videos," Signal Processing: Image Communication, vol.22 , 2007, pp.752-768.

Part 3

Quality

6

Human Attention Modelization and Data Reduction

Matei Mancas, Dominique De Beul, Nicolas Riche and Xavier Siebert
IT Department, Faculty of Engineering (FPMs),
University of Mons (UMONS), Mons
Belgium

1. Introduction

Attention is so natural and so simple: every human, every animal and even every tiny insect is perfectly able to pay attention. In reality as William James, the father of psychology said: "Everybody knows what attention is". It is precisely because everybody "knows" what attention is that few people tried to analyze it before the 19th century. Even though the study of attention was initially developed in the field of psychology, it quickly spread into new domains such as neuroscience to understand its biological mechanisms and, most recently, computer science to model attention mechanisms. There is no common definition of attention, and one can find variations depending on the domain (psychology, neuroscience, engineering, ...) or the approach which is taken into account. But, to remain general, human attention can be defined as the natural capacity to selectively focus on part of the incoming stimuli, discarding less "interesting" signals. The main purpose of the attentional process is to make best use of the parallel processing resources of our brains to identify as quickly as possible those parts of our environment that are key to our survival.

This natural tendency in data selection shows that raw data is not even used by our multi-billion cells brain which prefers to focus on restricted regions of interest instead of processing the whole data. Human attention is thus the first natural compression algorithm. Several attempts towards the definition of attention state that it is very closely related to data compression and focus resources on the less redundant, thus less compressible data. Tsotosos suggested in Itti et al. (2005) that the one core issue which justifies attention regardless the discipline, methodology or intuition is "information reduction". Schmidhuber (2009) stated that ..."we pointed out that a surprisingly simple algorithmic principle based on the notions of data compression and data compression progress informally explains fundamental aspects of attention, novelty, surprise, interestingness ...". Attention modeling in engineering and computer science domain has very wide applications such as machine vision, audio processing, HCI (Human Computer Interfaces), advertising assessment, robotics and, of course, data reduction and compression.

In section 2, an introduction to the notions of saliency and attention will be given and the main computational models working on images, video and audio signals will be presented. In section 3 the ideas which either aims at replacing or complementing classical compression algorithms are reviewed. Saliency-based techniques to reduce the spatial and/or temporal resolution of non-interesting events are listed in section 4. Finally, in section 5, a discussion on the use of attention-based methods for data compression will conclude the chapter.

2. Attention modeling: what is saliency?

In this first part of the chapter, a global view of the methods used to model attention in computer science will be presented. The details provided here will be useful to understand the next parts of the chapter which are dedicated to attention-based image and video compression.

2.1 Attention in computer science: idea and approaches

There are two main approaches to attention modeling in computer science. The first one is based on the notion of "saliency" and implies a competition between "bottom-up" and "top-down" information. The idea of saliency maps is that the sight or gaze of people will direct to areas which, in some way, stand out from the background. The eye movements can be computed from the saliency map by using winner-take-all (Itti et al. (1998)) or more dynamical algorithms (Mancas, Pirri & Pizzoli (2011)). The second approach to attention modeling is based on the notion of "visibility" which assumes that people look to locations that will lead to successful task performance. Those models are dynamic and intend to maximize the information acquired by the eye (the visibility) of eccentric regions compared to the current eye fixation to solve a given task (which can also be free viewing). In this case top-down information is naturally included in the notion of task along with the dynamic bottom-up information maximization. The eye movements are in this approach directly an output from the model and do not have to be inferred from a saliency map. The literature about attention modeling in computer science is not symmetric between those two approaches: the saliency-based methods are much more popular than the visibility models. For this reason, the following sections in this first part of the chapter will also mainly deal with saliency methods, but a review of visibility methods will be provided in the end.

2.2 Saliency approaches: bottom-up methods

Bottom-up approaches use features (most of the time low-level features but not always) extracted from the signal, such as luminance, color, orientation, texture, objects relative position or even simply neighborhoods or patches from the signal. Once those features are extracted, all the existing methods are essentially based on the same principle: looking for contrasted, rare, surprising, novel, worthy to learn, less compressible, maximizing the information areas. All those words are actually synonyms and they all amount to searching for some unusual features in a given context which can be spatial or temporal. In the following, different methods are described for still images, videos and audio signals. All those modalities are of course interesting for multimedia compression which, by definition, contains both video and audio information.

2.2.1 Still images

The literature is very active concerning still images saliency models. While some years ago only some labs in the world were working on the subject, nowadays hundreds of different models are available. Those models have various implementations and technical approaches even if initially they all derive from the same idea. It is thus very hard to find a perfect taxonomy which classifies all the methods. Some attempts of taxonomies proposed an opposition between "biologically-driven" and "mathematically-based" methods with a third class including "top-down information". This approach implies that only some methods can handle top-down information while all bottom-up methods could use top-down information more or less naturally. Another difficult point is to judge the biological plausibility which can be obvious for some methods but much less for the others. Another criterion is the computational time or the algorithmic complexity, but it is very difficult to make this comparison as all the existing models do not provide cues about their complexity. Finally a classification of methods based on center-surround contrast compared to information theory based methods do not take into account different approaches as the spectral residual one for example. Therefore, we introduce here a new taxonomy of the saliency methods which is based on the context that those methods take into account to exhibit signal novelty. In this framework, there are three classes of methods. The first one is pixel's surroundings: here a pixel or patch is compared with its surroundings at one or several scales. A second class of methods will use as a context the entire image and compare pixels or patches of pixels with other pixels or patches from other locations in the image but not necessarily in the surroundings of the initial patch. Finally, the third class will take into account a context which is based on a model of what the normality should be. This model can be described as a priori probabilities, Fourier spectrum models ... In the following sections, the main methods from those three classes are described for still images.

2.2.1.1 Context: pixel's surroundings

This approach is based on a biological motivation and dates back to the work of Koch & Ullman (1985) on attention modeling. The main principle is to initially compute visual features at several scales in parallel, then to apply center-surround inhibition, combination into conspicuity maps (one per feature) and finally to fuse them into a single saliency map. There are a lot of models derived from this approach which mainly use local center-surround contrast as a local measure of novelty. A good example of this family of approaches is the Itti's model (Figure 1) Itti et al. (1998) which is the first implementation of the Koch and Ullman model. It is composed of three main steps. First, three types of static visual features are selected (colors, intensity and orientations) at several scales. The second step is the center-surround inhibition which will provide high response in case of high contrast, and low response in case of low contrast. This step results in a set of feature maps for each scale. The third step consists in an across-scale combination, followed by normalization to form "conspicuity" maps which are single multiscale contrast maps for each feature. Finally, a linear combination is made to achieve inter-features fusion. Itti proposed several combination strategies: a simple and efficient one is to provide higher weights to conspicuity maps which have global peaks much bigger than their mean. This is an interesting step which integrates global information in addition to the local multi-scale contrast information.

This implementation proved to be the first successful approach of attention computation by providing better predictions of the human gaze than chance or simple descriptors like entropy. Following this success, most computational models of bottom-up attention use the comparison of a central patch to its surroundings as a novelty indicator. An update is obtained by adding other features to the same architecture such as symmetry Privitera & Stark (2000) or curvedness Valenti et al. (2009). Le Meur et al. (2006) refined the model by using more biological cues like contrast sensitivity functions, perceptual decomposition, visual masking, and center-surround interactions. Another popular and efficient model is the Graph Based Visual Saliency model (GVBS, Harel et al. (2007)), which is very close to Itti et al. (1998) regarding feature extraction and center-surround, but differs from it in the fusion step where GBVS computes an activation map before normalization and combination. Other models like Gao et al. (2008) also used center-surround approaches even if the rest of the computation is made in a different mathematical framework based on a Bayesian approach.

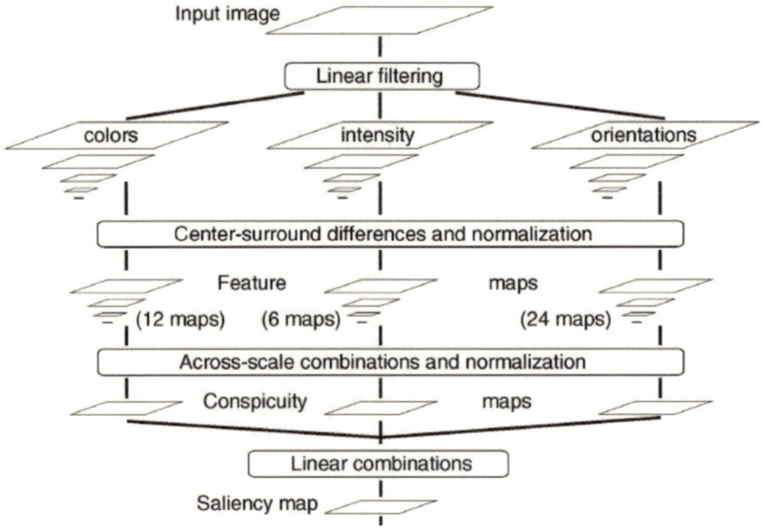

Fig. 1. Model of Itti et al. (1998). Three stages: center-surround differences, conspicuity maps, inter-feature fusion into saliency map.

2.2.1.2 Context: the whole image

In this approach, the context which is used to provide a degree of novelty or rarity to image patches is not necessarily the surroundings of the patch, but can be other patches in its neighborhood or even anywhere in the image. The idea can be divided in two steps. First, local features are computed in parallel from a given image. The second step measures the likeness of a pixel or a neighborhood of pixels to other pixels or neighborhoods within the image. This kind of visual saliency is called "self-resemblance". A good example is shown in Figure 2. The model has two parts. First it proposes to use local regression kernels as features. Second it proposes to use a nonparametric kernel density estimation for such features, which results in a saliency map consisting of local "self-resemblance" measure, indicating likelihood of saliency Seo & Milanfar (2009).

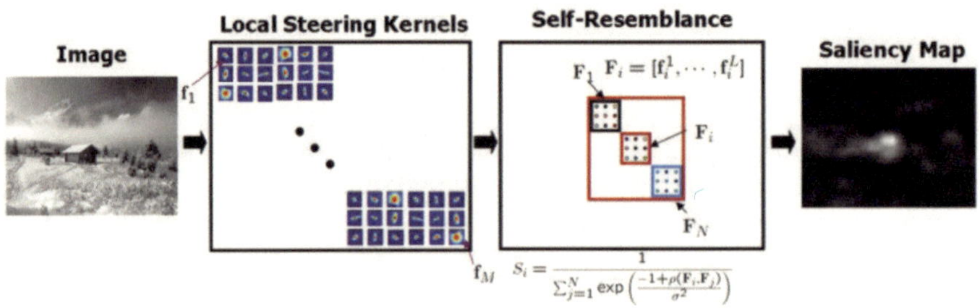

Fig. 2. Model of Seo & Milanfar (2009). Patches at different locations are compared.

A similar approach was developed in Mancas (2007) and Mancas (2009), that detects saliency in the areas which are globally rare and locally contrasted. After a feature extraction step, both local contrast and global rarity of pixels are taken into account to compute a saliency map. An example of the difference between locally contrasted features and globally rare is given in Figure 3. The leftmost image is an apple with a defect shown in red. The second image shows the fixations predicted by Itti et al. (1998) where the locally contrasted apple edges are well detected while its less contrasted but rare defect is not. The third image shows results from Mancas et al. (2007) which detected the apple edges, but also the defect. Finally the rightmost image is the mouse tracking result for more than 30 users.

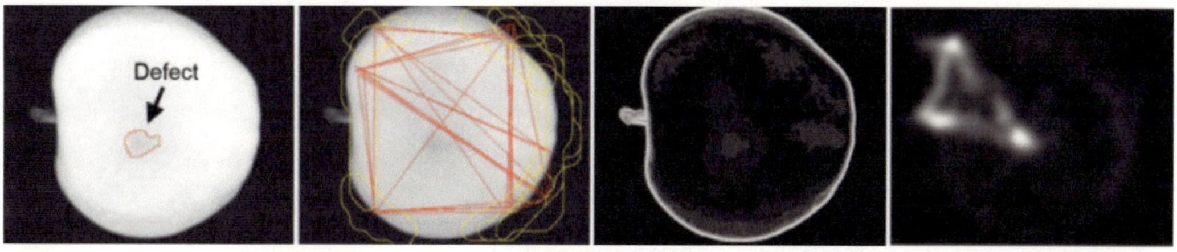

Fig. 3. Difference between locally contrasted and globally rare features. Left image: an apple with a defect in red, Second Image: Itti et al. (1998), Third image: Mancas et al. (2007), Right image: mouse tracking (ground truth).

A typical model using this context is the model of Stentiford (2001) which uses random neighborhoods and check if it is possible to find a lot of those neighborhoods or not in the rest of the image. If there are few possibilities, the patch was rare, thus salient. This model does not need feature extraction, as features remain included in the compared patches.

Oliva et al. (2003) also defined the saliency as the inverse likelihood of the features at each location. This likelihood is computed as a Gaussian probability all over the image on the features which are extracted by using a steerable pyramid. Boiman & Irani (2005) proposed a method where different patches were not only compared between them, but also their relative positions where taken into account.

A well-known model is Bruce & Tsotsos (2006). This model of bottom-up overt attention is proposed based on the principle of maximizing information sampled from a scene. The proposed operation is based on Shannon's self-information measure and is achieved in a neural circuit taking into account patches from the image projected on a new basis obtained by performing an ICA (Independent Component Analysis Hyvärinen et al. (2001)) on a large sample of 7x7 RGB patches drawn from natural images.

Recently, Goferman et al. (2010) has introduced context-aware saliency detection based on four principles. First, local low-level considerations, including factors such as contrast and color are used. Second, global considerations, which suppress frequently occurring features, while maintaining features that deviate from the norm are taken into account. Higher level information as visual organization rules, which state that visual forms may possess one or several centers of gravity about which the form is organized are then used. Finally, human faces detection are also integrated into the model. While the two first points are purely bottom-up, the two others may introduce some top-down information.

2.2.1.3 Context: a model of normality

This approach is probably less biologically-motivated in most of the implementations. The context which is used here is a model of what the image should be: if things are not like they should be, this can be surprising, thus interesting. In Achanta et al. (2009) a very simple attention model was developed. His method, first, changes the color space from RGB to Lab and finds the Euclidean distance between the Lab pixel vectors in a Gaussian filtered image with the average Lab vector for the input image. This is illustrated in the Figure 4. The mean image used is a kind of model of the image statistics and pixels which are far from those statistics are more salient.

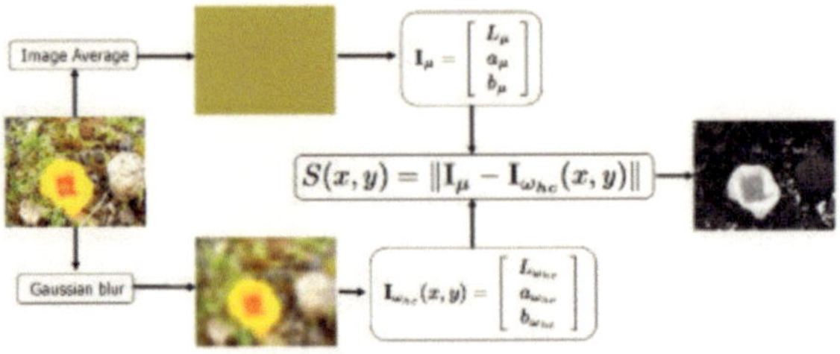

Fig. 4. Achanta et al. (2009) uses a model of the mean image.

In 2006, Itti & Baldi (2006) released the concept of surprise, central to attention. They described a formal Bayesian definition of surprise that is the only consistent formulation under minimal axiomatic assumptions. Surprise quantifies how data affects an observer, by measuring the difference between posterior and prior (model of normality) beliefs of the observer. In Hou & Zhang (2007), the authors proposed a model that is independent of any features. As it is known that natural images have a $\frac{1}{f}$ decreasing log-spectrum, the difference between this normality model obtained by low-pass filtering and the log-spectrum of the image is reconstructed into the image space and lead to the saliency map.

2.2.1.4 Attention models for still images: a comparison

It is not easy to classify attention models, for several reasons. First, there is a large variety of models. Second, some research groups (e.g., Itti's) have implemented different models, finding themselves in several categories. Also some approaches have several contexts and could be classified in more than one category, but based on the context notion, is seems possible to find this three main families of methods despite their diversity.

Figure 5 displays saliency maps computed with six models (available as Matlab codes), along with the eyestracking results to show where people really look at. For this purpose three images from the Bruce's database [1] were used. Along with the saliency maps of six models, one can find the most salient areas after automatic thresholding.

Figure 5 reveals that saliency maps can be quite different, from very fuzzy ones (Itti, Harrel or Seo) to high resolution ones (Mancas, Bruce or Achanta). It is not easy to compare those saliency maps (they should all be low-pass filtered to decrease their resolution). Nevertheless for the purpose of compression, one needs a model which is able to highlight the interesting areas but also the interesting edges as Mancas.

2.2.2 Videos

Part of the static models have been extended to video. Itti's model was generalized with the addition of motion features and flickering and in Itti & Baldi (2006) he applied another approach based on surprise to static but also dynamic images. Le Meur et al. (2007b) used motion in addition to spatial features. Gao et al. (2008) generalized his 2D square center-surround approach to 3D cubic shapes. Belardinelli et al. (2008) used an original approach of 3D Gabor filter banks to detect spatio-temporal saliency. Bruce & Tsotsos (2009)

[1] http://www-sop.inria.fr/members/Neil.Bruce/

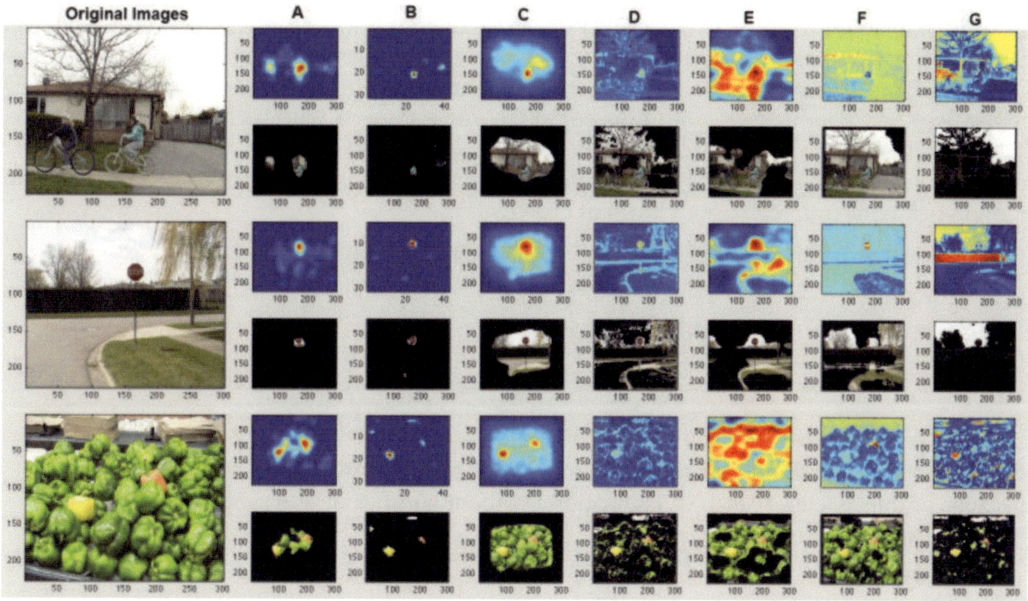

Fig. 5. For three original images (on the left), the eye-tracking results (column A) and six other saliency models maps. B = Itti and Koch (1998), C = Harrel et al. (2007); D = Mancas (2007), E = Seo and Milanfar (2009), F = Bruce and Tsotsos (2005), G = Achanta (2009). A thresholded applied on the saliency maps is shown on the images bellow.

extended his model by learning ICA not only on 2D patches but on spatio-temporal 3D patches. As shown in Figure 6, similarly to Gao, Seo & Milanfar (2009) introduced the time dimension in addition to his static model. Another model is SUN (Saliency Using Natural

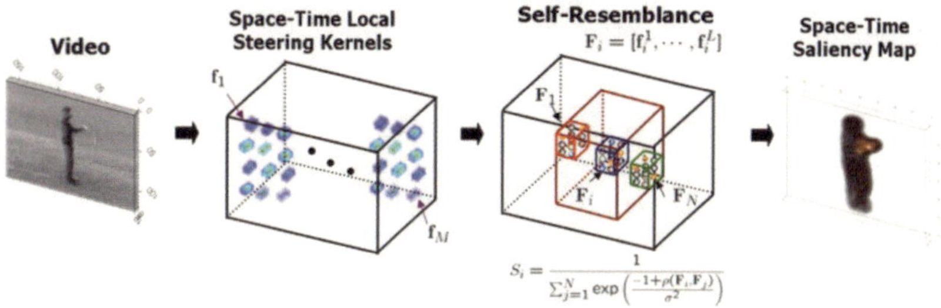

Fig. 6. Seo & Milanfar (2009) generalized to video in 2009.

statistics) from Butko et al. (2008) that propose a Bayesian framework for saliency. Two methods are implemented. First, the features are calculated as responses of biologically plausible linear filters, such as DoG (Differences of Gaussians) filters. Second, the features are calculated as the responses to filters learned from natural images using independent component analysis (ICA).

Frintrop (2006) introduces the biologically motivated computational attention system VOCUS (Visual Object detection with a Computational attention System) that detects regions of interest in images. It operates in two modes, in an exploration mode in which no task is provided, and in a search mode with a specified target. The bottom-up mode is based on an enhancement of the Itti model.

Finally, Mancas, Riche & J. Leroy (2011) has developed a bottom-up saliency map to detect abnormal motion. The proposed method is based on a multi-scale approach using features extracted from optical flow and global rarity quantification to compute bottom-up saliency maps. It shows good results from four objects to dense crowds with increasing performance. The idea here is to show that motion is most of the time salient but within motion, there might be motion which is more or less salient. Mancas model is capable of extracting different motion behavior from complex videos or crowds (Figure 7).

Fig. 7. Detection of salient motion compared to the rest of motion. Red motion is salient because of unexpected speed. Cyan motion is salient because of unexpected direction Mancas, Riche & J. Leroy (2011).

2.2.2.1 Extension to 3D

With the release of the Microsoft's Kinect sensor [2], in November 2010, 3D features have become easily accessible. In terms of computational attention this depth information is very important. For example, in all models released up to now, movement perpendicular to the plane of the camera could not be taken into account. A 3D model-based motion detection in a scene has been implemented by Riche et al. (2011). The proposed algorithm has three main steps. First, 3D motion (speed and direction) features are extracted from the RGB video and the depth map of the Kinect sensor. The second step is a spatiotemporal filtering of the features at several scales to provide multi scale statistics. Finally, the third step is the rarity-based attention computation within the video frame.

2.2.3 Audio signals

There are very few auditory attention models compared to visual attention models. However, we can classify existing models into different categories.

As shown in Figure 8, Kayser et al. (2005) computes auditory saliency maps based on Itti's visual model (1998). First, the sound wave is converted to a time-frequency representation ("intensity image"). Then three auditory features are extracted on different scales and in parallel (intensity, frequency contrast, and temporal contrast). For each feature, the maps obtained at different scales are compared using a center-surround mechanism and normalized. The center-surround maps are fused across scales achieving saliency maps for individual features. Finally, a linear combination builds the saliency map.

Another approach to compute auditory saliency map is based on following the well-established approach of Bayesian Surprise in computer vision (Itti & Baldi (2006)). An auditory surprise is introduced to detect acoustically salient events. First, a Short-Time Fourier transform (STFT) is used to calculate the spectrogram. The surprise is computed in the Bayesian framework.

[2] `http://www.xbox.com/kinect`

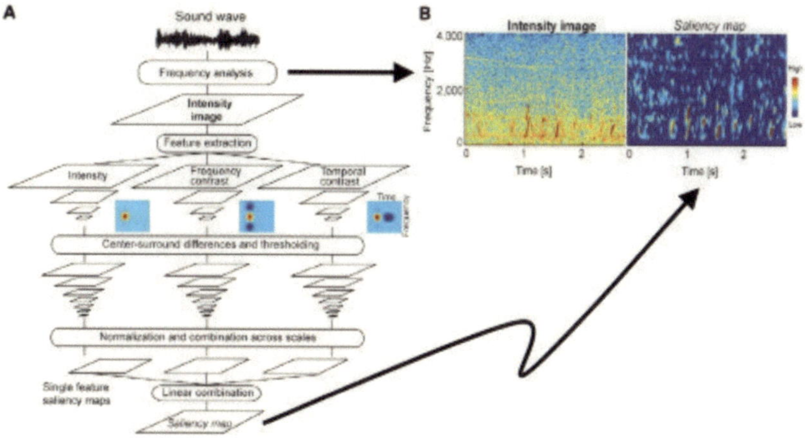

Fig. 8. Kayser et al. (2005) audio saliency model inspired from Itti.

Couvreur et al. (2007) define features that can be computed along audio signals in order to assess the level of auditory attention on a normalized scale, i.e. between 0 and 1. The proposed features are derived from a time-frequency representation of audio signals and highlight salient regions such as regions with high loudness, temporal and frequency contrasts. Normalized auditory attention levels can be used to detect sudden and unexpected changes of audio textures and to focus the attention of a surveillance operator to sound segments of interest in audio streams that are monitored.

2.3 Saliency models: including top-down information

There are two main families of top-down information which can be added to bottom-up attention. The first one mainly deals with learnt normality which can come from the experience from the current signal if it is time varying, or from previous experience (tests, databases) for still images. The second approach is about task modeling which can either use object recognition-related techniques or which can model the usual location of those objects of interest.

2.3.1 Top-down as learnt normality: attending unusual events

Concerning still images, the "normal" gaze behavior can be learnt from the "mean observer". Eye-tracking techniques can be used on several users, and the mean of their gaze on a set of natural images can be computed. This was achieved by several authors as it can be seen on Figure 9. Bruce and Judd et al. (2009) used eye-trackers while Mancas (2007) used mouse-tracking techniques to compute this mean observer. In all cases, it seems clear that, for natural images, the eye gaze is attracted by the center of the images.

This fact seems logical as natural images are acquired using cameras and the photographer will naturally tend to locate the objects of interest in the center of the picture. This observation might be interesting in the field of image compression as high quality compression seems to be required mainly in the center of the image while peripheral areas could be compressed with lower rates.

Of course, this observation for natural images is very different from more specific images which use a priori knowledge. Mancas (2009) showed using mouse tracking that gaze density

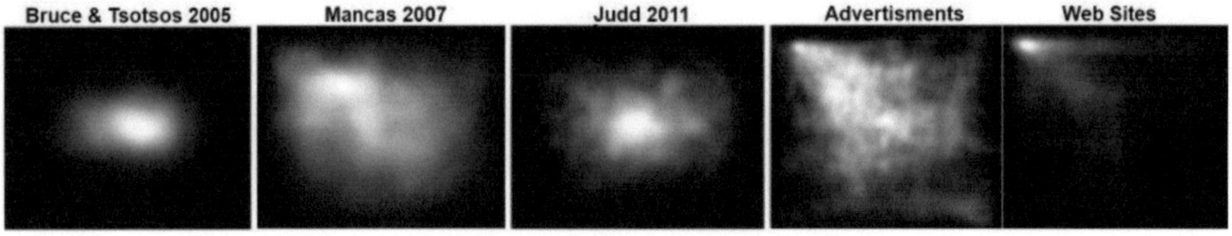

Fig. 9. Three models of the mean observer for natural images on the left. The two right images: model of the mean observer on a set of advertising and websites images.

is very different on a set of advertisements and on a set of websites as it is showed in Figure 9 on the two right images. This is partly due to a priori knowledge that people have about those images. For example, when viewing a website, the upper part has high chance to contain the logo and title, while the left part should contain the menu. During images or video viewing, the default template is the one of natural images with a high weight on the center of the image. If supplemental knowledge is known about the image, the top-down information will modify the mean behavior towards the optimized gaze density. Those top-down maps can highly influence the bottom-up saliency map but this influence is variable. In Mancas (2009) it appears that top-down information seems more important in the case of websites, than advertisements and natural images. Other kinds of models can be learnt from videos, especially if the camera is still. It is possible to accumulate motion patterns for each extracted feature which provides a model of normality. As an example, after a given period of observation, one can say: here moving objects are generally fast (first feature: speed) and going from left to right (second feature: direction). If an object, at the same location is slow and/or going from right to left, this is surprising given what was previously learnt from the scene, thus attention will be directed to this object. This kind of considerations can be found in Mancas & Gosselin (2010). It is possible to go further and to have different cyclic models in time. In a metro station, for example, normal people behavior when a train arrives in the station is different from the one during the waiting period in terms of people direction, speed, density ... In the literature (mainly in video surveillance) the variations in time of the normality models is learnt through HMMs (Hidden Markov Models) Jouneau & Carincotte (2011).

2.3.2 Top-down as a task: attending to objects or their usual position

While the previous section dealt with attention attracted by events which lead to situations which are not consistent with the knowledge acquired about the scene, here we focus on the second main top-down cue which is a visual task ("find the keys"). This task will also have a huge influence on the way the image is attended and it will imply object recognition ("recognize the keys") and object usual location ("they could be on the floor, but never on the ceiling").

2.3.2.1 Object recognition

Object recognition can be achieved through classical methods or using points of interest (like SIFT, SURF ... Bay et al. (2008)) which are somehow related to saliency. Some authors integrated the notion of object recognition into the architecture of their model like Navalpakkam & Itti (2005). They extract the same features as for the bottom-up model, from the object and learn them. This learning step will provide weight modification for the fusion of the conspicuity maps which will lead to the detection of the areas which contain the same feature combination as the learnt object.

2.3.2.2 Object location

Another approach is in providing with a higher weight the areas from the image which have a higher probability to contain the searched object. Several authors as Oliva et al. (2003) developed methods to learn objects' location. Vectors of features are extracted from the images and their dimension is reduced by using PCA (Principal Component Analysis). Those vectors are then compared to the ones from a database of images containing the given object. Figure 10 shows the potential people location that has been extracted from the image. This information, combined with bottom-up saliency lead to the selection of a person sitting down on the left part of the image.

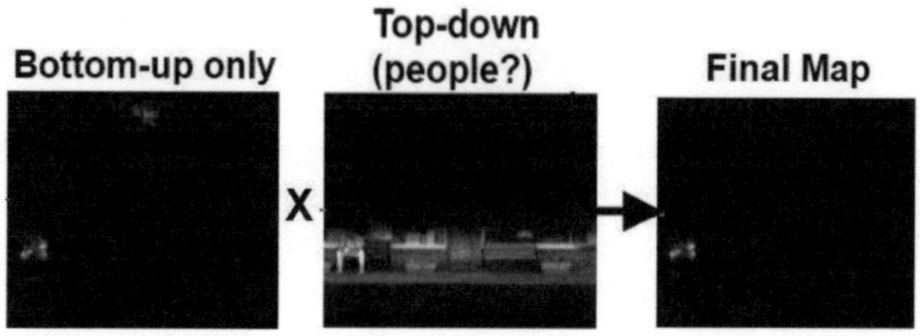

Fig. 10. Bottom-up saliency model inhibited by top-down information to select only salient people.

2.4 Visibility models

Compared to other Bayesian frameworks (e.g. Oliva et al. (2003)), these models have a main difference. The saliency map is dynamic even for static images, as it will change depending on the eye fixations and not only the signal features: of course, given the resolution drop-off from the fixation point to the periphery, it is clear that some features are well identified in some eye fixation, while less or even not visible during other eye fixations. Najemnik & Geisler (2005) found that an ideal observer based on a Bayesian framework can predict eye search patterns including the number of saccades needed to find a target, the amount of time needed as well as the saccades spatial distribution.

Other authors like Legge et al. (2002) proposed a visibility model capable to predict the eye fixations during the task of reading. In the same way, Reninger used similar approaches for the task of shape recognition. Tatler (2007) introduces a tendency of the eye gaze to stay in the middle of the scene to maximize the visibility over the image (which reminds the top-down centered preference for natural images we developed in section Top-down as learnt normality: attending unusual events.

3. Attention-based visual coding

Since the late 1990's techniques based on attention have been introduced in the field of image and video coding (e.g., Kortum & Geisler (1996); Maeder et al. (1996)). Attention can be used to compress videos or to transmit the most salient parts first during the data transfer from a server to a client. This section will first introduce general principles of video compression, then review some of the major achievements in saliency-based visual coding.

3.1 General video coding and compression

The goal of this section is to briefly introduce the concepts of video coding and compression, which tends to be used interchangeably since they are heavily related. What follows in this section is a short introduction to general video compression for which Lorente (2011) is an example of recent exhaustive review.

Video compression is the process of converting a video signal into a format that takes up less storage space or transmission bandwidth. It can be considered as a coding scheme that reduces bits of information representing the video. Nevertheless the overall visual quality has to be preserved, leading to a compromise between the level of artifacts and the bandwidth.

Two types of compression can be distinguished: lossy and lossless compression Richardson (2003). In a lossless compression system statistical redundancy is removed so that the original data can be perfectly reconstructed. Unfortunately, at the present time lossless methods only allows a modest amount of compression, insufficient for most video applications. On the other hand, lossy compression provides bigger compression ratios, at the expense of not being able to reconstruct perfectly the original signal. Lossy compression is the type of compression most commonly used for video, attention-based or not.

It is interesting to note that, even if generic compression algorithms do not explicitly use saliency, they implicitly exploit the mechanisms of human visual perception to remove redundant information Geisler & Perry (1998). For example retinal persistence of vision makes the human eye keep an instantaneous view of a scene for about one-tenth of a second at least. This allows video (theoretically a continuum of time) to be represented by a series of discrete frames (e.g., 24 frames per second) with no apparent motion distortion.

Coding standards define a representation of visual data as well as a method of decoding it to reconstruct visual information. Recent hybrid standards like H.264/AVC Wiegand et al. (2003) have led to significant progress in compression quality, allowing for instance the transmission of high definition (HD) television signals over a limited-capacity broadcast channel, and video streaming over the internet Richardson (2003).

Emerging video coding standard H.265 [3] aims at enhancing video coding efficiency using intensive spatiotemporal prediction and entropy coding. Nevertheless, this new standard only considers *objective* redundancy, as opposed to attention-based methods described below.

3.2 A review of the attention-based methods

The above mentioned compression methods tend to distribute the coding resources evenly in an image. On the contrary, attention-based methods encode visually salient regions with high priority, while treating less interesting regions with low priority (Figure 11). The aim of these methods is to achieve compression without significant degradation of perceived quality.

Saliency-based methods derive from biological properties of the human eye, that enable one to focus only on a limited region of an image at a time. It is thus a subjective notion, but a lot of research has been devoted to its modeling and quantification.

In the following there is an attempt to list the methods currently available in the literature, pointing to their strengths and weaknesses when possible. Although there is currently no

[3] `http://www.h265.net`

Fig. 11. Illustration of the distortions introduced by general compression methods (three first images on the left) compared to saliency-based compression (three last images on the right), at three different compression levels. Adapted from Yu & Lisin (2009))

unified taxonomy, we have divided the methods into interactive, indirect and direct, the latter being the most commonly studied.

3.2.1 Interactive approaches

As described above, earlier approaches for modeling the human visual system (HVS) relied on eye-tracking devices to monitor attention points (e.g., Kortum & Geisler (1996)).

With such devices, encoding continuously and efficiently follows the focus of the observer. Indeed, observers usually do not notice any degradation of the received frames. However, these techniques are neither practical (because of the use of the eye-tracking device) nor general (because they are restricted to a single viewer). A general coding scheme should be independent of the number of observers, the viewing distance, and any hardware device or user interaction.

Even in the absence of eye tracking, an interactive approach has demonstrated usefulness. Observers can for example explicitly point to priority regions with the mouse Geisler & Perry (1998). However, extending this approach to general-purpose non-interactive video compression presents severe limitations.

Attempts to automatize this approach by using attention-based methods are very complex as top-down information is very important and if clear salient objects are not present in a frame, people gaze can be very different. Despite progresses in attention modelling and even though human gaze is well modelled in the presence of salient objects, it is not possible to obtain a reliable model of human gaze in the absence of specific salient objects (as can be seen in Figure 12). Indeed, the highly dynamical process of eye movements is influenced a lot by previous gaze position if no salient objects pops out from the background.

Fig. 12. The two left images show several users eye tracking results which are spread through the image and very different, while the two images on the right showing clear regions of interest will exhibit much more correlated fixations.

3.2.2 Indirect approaches

Indirect compression consists in modifying the source image to be coded, while keeping the same coding scheme. Such methods are thus generally driven by a saliency map based methods.

The seminal model of Itti et al. (1998) was later applied to video compression in Itti (2004) by computing a saliency map for each frame of a video sequence and applying a smoothing filter to all non-salient regions. Smoothing leads to higher spatial correlation, a better prediction efficiency of the encoder, and therefore a reduced bit-rate of the encoded video.

The main advantages of this method are twofold. First, a high correlation with human eye movements on unconstrained video inputs is observed. Second a good compression rate is achieved, the average size of a compressed video being approximately half the size of the original one, for both MPEG-1 and MPEG-4 (DivX) encodings.

Another method combines both top-down and bottom-up information, using a wavelet decomposition for multiscale analysis Tsapatsoulis et al. (2007). Bit rate gain ranging from 15% to 64% for MPEG-1 videos and from 10.4% to 28.3% for MPEG-4 are reported.

Mancas et al. (2007) proposed an indirect approach based on their attention model. An anisotropic pre-filtering of the images or frames is achieved keeping highly salient regions with a good resolution, while low-pass filtering the regions with less important details (Figure 13). Depending on the method parameters, images could be compressed twice as much for standard JPEG. Nevertheless even though the quality of the important areas remain unchanged, the quality of the less important regions can dramatically decrease. It is thus not easy to compare the compression rate as the quality of the images remains subjective.

Fig. 13. Two pairs of images (original and anisotropic filtered). Adapted from Mancas et al. (2007).

The main advantage of indirect approaches is that they are easy to set up because the coding scheme remains the same. The intelligence of the algorithm is applied as a pre-processing step while standard coding algorithms are used afterwards. This fact also led people to easily quantify the gain in terms of compression as the main compression algorithm can be used directly on the image or on the saliency pre-processed image. However, one possible problem is that the degradation of less salient zones can become strong. Selective blurring can lead to artifacts and distortions in low-saliency regions Li et al. (2011).

3.2.3 Direct approaches

Recent work on modeling visual attention (Le Meur, Itti, Parkhurst, Chauvin ...) paved the way to efficient compression applications that modify the heart of the coding scheme to enhance the perceived quality. In this case some modifications to the saliency map are generally necessary to dedicate it directly to coding. The saliency maps will not only be used in the pre-processing step, but also in the entire compression algorithm.

Li et al. (2011), a recent extension of Itti (2004), uses a similar neurobiological model of visual attention to generate a saliency map, whose most salient locations are used to generate a so-called *guidance map*. The latter is used to guide the bit allocation through quantization parameter (QP) tuning by constrained global optimization. Considering its efficiency at achieving compression while preserving visual quality and the general nature of the algorithm, the authors suggest that it might be integrated in general-purpose video codecs.

Future work in this direction should include a study of possible artifacts in the low-bit rate regions of the compressed video, which may themselves become salient and attract human attention. Another possible issue pointed out in Li et al. (2011) is that the attention model does not always predict accurately where people look at. For example high speed motion increases saliency, but regions with lower motion can attract more attention (e.g., a person running on the sidewalk, while cars are going faster).

Other approaches with lower computational complexity have been investigated, and in particular two methods using the spectrum of the images: the Spectral Residual Hou & Zhang (2007) and the Phase spectrum of Quaternion Fourier Transform Guo & Zhang (2010). The goal here is to suppress spectral elements corresponding to frequently occurring features.

The Phase spectrum of Quaternion Fourier Transform (PQFT) is an extension of the phase spectrum of Fourier transform (PFT) to quaternions incorporating inter-frame motion. The latter method derives from the property of the Fourier transform, that the phase information specifies the location each of the sinusoidal components resides within the image. Thus the locations with less periodicity or less homogeneity in an image create the so-called *proto objects* in the reconstruction of the image's phase spectrum, which indicates where the object candidates are located. A multi-resolution wavelet foveation filter suppressing coefficients corresponding to background is then applied. Compression rates between 32.6% (from 8.88Mb for raw H-264 file to 5.98Mb for compressed file) and 38% (from 11.4Mb for raw MPEG-4 file to 7.07Mb for compressed file) are reported in Guo & Zhang (2010).

These Fourier-based approaches are computationally efficient, but they are less connected to the Human Visual System. They also have two main drawbacks linked to the properties of the Fourier transform. First, if an object occupied most of the image, only its boundaries will be detected, unless resampling is used (at the expense of a blurring of the boundaries). Second, an image with a smooth object in front of a textured background will lead to the background being detected (saliency reversal).

Using the bit allocation model of Li et al. (2011), a scheme for attention video compression has recently been suggested by Gupta & Chaudhury (2011). It proposes a learning-based feature integration algorithm, with a Relevance Vector Machine architecture, incorporating visual saliency propagation (using motion vectors), to save computational time. This architecture is based on thresholding of mutual information between successive frames for flagging frames requiring recomputation of saliency.

3.2.4 Enhancing the objective quality

Many encoding techniques have sought to optimize perceptual rather than objective quality: these techniques allocate more bits to the image areas where human can easily see coding distortions, and allocate fewer bits to the areas where coding distortions are less noticeable. Experimental subjective quality assessment results show that visual artifacts can be reduced through this approach. However two problems arise: first, the mechanisms of human perceptual sensitivity are still not fully understood, especially as captured by computational models; second, perceptual sensitivity may not necessarily explain people's attention.

The use of top-down information is very efficient as it is very likely to be attended. Face detection is one of the crucial features, but also text detection, skin color, motion-related events for video-surveillance, . . . (see for example Tan & Davis (2004) and references therein).

4. Image retargeting based on saliency maps

In previous sections, the compression algorithms do not modify the original spatial (frame resolution) and temporal (video length) size of the signal: an obvious idea which drastically compresses an image is of course to decrease its size. This size decrease can be brutal (zoom on a region and the rest of the image is discarded) or softer (the resolution of the context of the region of interest is decreased but not fully discarded). The first approach will of course be more efficient from a compression point of view, but it will fully discard the context of the regions of interest which can be disturbing.

The direct image cropping will be called here "perceptual zoom" while the second approach which will keep some context around the region of interest will be called "anisotropic resolution". Both approaches provide image retargeting. Retargeting is the process of resizing images while minimizing visual distortion and keeping at best the salient content.

Images can be resized (zoomed) according to two families of methods, either taking into account the relevance of the content or not. In the first case, it not only requires to preserve the content but also the structure of the original image Shamir & Sorkine (2009) so the cropping should avoid to be too restrictive.

The second case comprises methods such as letter and pillar boxing, fixed windowing cropping and scaling. These methods are fast but often give poor results. Indeed, fixed windowing cropping can leave relevant contents outside the window, while scaling can engender losses of important information which could eventually lead to an unrecognizable image Liu & Gleicher (2005). Therefore, these classical methods are not mentioned further in this section.

4.1 Spatio-temporal visual data repurposing: perceptual zoom

Human beings are naturally able to perceive interesting areas of an image, as illustrated in the previous sections of this chapter. Zooming in images should therefore focus on such regions of interest.

Images manipulation programs provide tools to manually draw these rectangles of interest, but the process can be automated with the help of attention algorithms presented above in this chapter. Interestingly, such techniques can also be used for real time spatio-temporal images broadcast Chamaret et al. (2010).

Figure 14 shows several perceptual zooms depending on a parameter which will threshold the smoothed Mancas (2009) saliency map.

In the next section, the main general retargeting methods based on content-aware cropping are presented. Then, attention-based retargeting methods are more specifically described.

4.1.1 General retargeting methods

An interactive cropping method is proposed by Santella et al. (2006), whose purpose is to create aesthetically pleasing crops without explicit interaction. The location of important content of the image is realized by segmentation and by eye-tracking. With a collection of gaze-based crops and an optimization function, the method identifies the best crops.

Another approach is to calculate automatically an "active window" with a predefined size, as presented by Tao et al. (2007). In this case the retargeted image has to satisfy two

Fig. 14. Example of images along with rectangles providing different attention-based automatic zooms. After a saliency map (Mancas (2009)) is computed and low-pass filtered, several threshold values are used to extract the bounding boxes of the more interesting areas. Depending on this threshold, the zoom is more or less precise/important.

requirements: to preserve temporal and spatial distance, and to contain useful information such as objects shapes and motions. These methods are composed of the following three steps. First, extraction of the image foreground, for example by minimizing an energy function to automatically separate foreground from background pixels. Second, optimization of the active window to fit in the target size. Third, clustering to reduce the number of parameters to be estimated in the optimization process.

4.1.2 Saliency maps based methods

Figure 15 perfectly illustrates the process of the saliency-based retargeting. From the original image, on the left, a saliency map is computed (in the middle) from which an area with higher intensity is extracted using some algorithm and its bounding-box will represent the zoom.

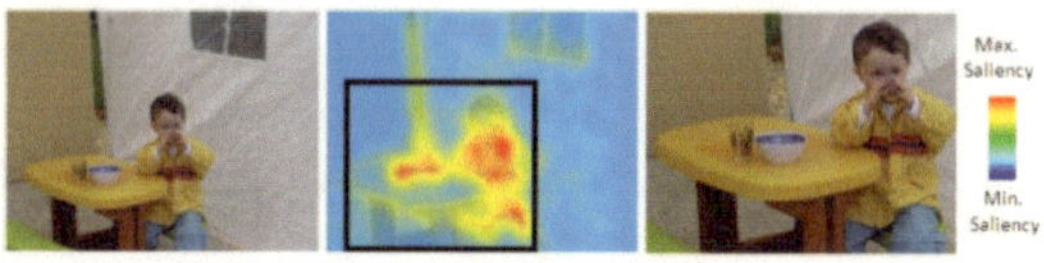

Fig. 15. Example of retargeting: left, the original picture; middle, the saliency map; right, the reframed picture. (adapted from Le Meur & Le Callet (2009))

A technique to determine automatically the "right" viewing area for spatio-temporal images is proposed in Deselaers et al. (2008). Images are first analyzed to determine relevant regions by using three strategies: the visual saliency of spatial images, optical flow for movements and the appearance of the image. A log-linear algorithm then computes the relevance for every position of the image to determine a sequence of cropping positions with a correct aspect ratio for the display device.

Suh et al. (2003) uses the Itti & Koch (2001) algorithm to compute the saliency map, that serves as a basis to automatically delineate a rectangular cropping window. A fast greedy algorithm was developed to optimize the window, that has to take into account most of the saliency while remaining sufficiently small.

The previous methods show that the perceptual zoom not only compresses the images, but it also allows better recognition during visual search!

The Self-Adaptive Image Cropping for Small Displays Ciocca et al. (2007) is based on an Itti and Koch bottom-up attention algorithm but also on top-down considerations as face detection, skin color .... According to a given threshold, the region is either kept or eliminated.

The RSVP (Rapid Serial Visual Presentation de Bruijn & Spence (2000)) method for images can also be adapted to allow in a sequential way and during a short time the visualization and browsing of the interest regions Fan et al. (2003). Here also, the bottom-up attention saliency is computed with Itti & Koch (2001) while top-down information is added: texts and faces detection. The most relevant interest regions are proposed to mobile phones as key images.

Liu et al. (2007) start by segmenting the image into several regions, for which saliency is calculated to provide a global saliency map. The regions are classified according to their attractiveness, which allows to present image regions on small size screens and to browse in big size images.

A completely automatic solution to create thumbnails according to the saliency distribution or the cover rate is presented by Le Meur et al. (2007a). The size of the thumbnail can be fixed and centered on the saliency map global maximum or adapted to certain parameters such as the saliency distribution. The gaze fixation predicted by a Winner-Take-All algorithm can thus be used and the search for the thumbnail location ends when a given percentage of the total image saliency is reached. A subset of the corners coordinates of the squares in which are predicted eye gaze centered on a local maximum of saliency is determined. The coordinates of the upper left and the lower right corners of the final zoom thumbnail are set to include a square area centered on the relevant local maximum.

4.2 Spatio-temporal resolution decrease for uninteresting regions: anisotropic resolution

Perceptual zoom does not always preserve the image structure. For example, Figure 14 shows that the smallest zoom on the left image only comprises part of the castle, which is likely to attract attention. In this case the zoom loses the structure and context of the original image. To keep the image structure when retargeting two main methods are described in this section: warping and seam carving. These methods may cause non-linear visual distortions on several regions of the image (Zhou et al. (2003)).

4.2.1 Warping

Warping is an operation that maps a position in a source image to a position in a target image by a spatial transformation. This transformation could be a simple scaling transformation Liu & Gleicher (2005). Another approach of warping is to place a grid mesh onto the image and then compute a new geometry for this mesh (Figure 16), such that the boundaries fit the new desired image sizes, and the quad faces covering important image regions remain intact at the expense of larger distortion to the other quads Wang et al. (2008).

Automatic image retargeting with fisheye-view warping Liu & Gleicher (2005) uses an "importance map" that combines salience and object information to find automatically, with a greedy algorithm, a minimal rectangular region of interest. A non-linear function is then used for warping to ensure that the distortion in the region of interest is smaller than elsewhere in the image.

Non-homogeneous content-driven video-retargeting Wolf et al. (2007) proposes a real-time retargeting algorithm for video. Spatial saliency, face detection and motion detection are computed to provide a saliency matrix. An optimized mapping is computed with a sparse linear system of equations which takes into account some constraints such as importance modeling, boundary substitutions, spatial and time continuity.

Ren et al. (2009) introduces a retargeting method based on global energy optimization. Some content-aware methods only preserve high energy pixels, which only achieve local optimization. They calculate an energy map which depends on the static saliency and face detection. The optimal new size of each pixel is computed by linear programming.

The same group proposes a retargeting approach that combines an uniform sampling and a structure-aware image representation Ren et al. (2010). The image is decomposed with a curve-edge grid, which is determined by using a carving graph such that each image pixel corresponds to a vertex in the graph. A weight is assigned to each vertex connection (only vertical direction) which depends on an energy map using saliency region and face detection. The paths with high connection weight sums in the graph are selected and the target image is generated by uniformly sampling the pixels within the grids.

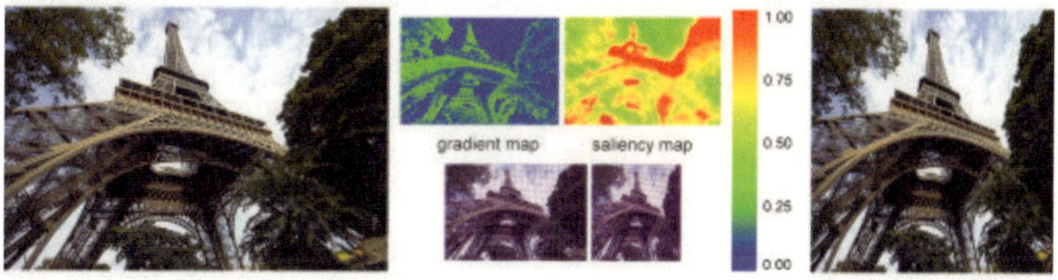

Fig. 16. The original image (left) is deformed by a grid mesh structure to be fit in the required size (right). The scaling and stretching depend on the gradient and saliency map. Source : `http://graphics.csie.ncku.edu.tw/Image_Resizing/`

Wang et al. (2008) present a warping method which uses the grid mesh of quads to retarget the images (figure 16). The method determines an optimal scaling factor for regions with high content importance as well as for regions with homogeneous content which will be distorted. A significance map is computed based on the product of the gradient and the saliency measure which characterizes the visual attractiveness of each pixel. The regions are deformed according to the significance map. A global optimizing process is used repetitively to minimize the quad deformation and grid bending.

4.2.2 Seam carving

Seam carving Avidan & Shamir (2007) allows to retarget the image thanks to an energy function which defines the pixels importance. The most classical energy function is the gradient map, but other functions can be used such as entropy, histograms of oriented gradients, or saliency maps Vaquero et al. (2010). Low-energy pixels are connected together to make a seam path. The seam paths cross vertically and horizontally the image and are removed. Dynamic programming is used to calculate the optimal seams. The image is readjusted by shifting pixels to compensate the disappeared seams. The process is repeated as often as required to reach the expected sizes.

Figure 17 shows an example of seam carving: the original images (A and B) are reduced either by discarding vertical or horizontal seams. On the top row, the classical gradient is used as the energy map, while saliency maps of Wonjun et al. (2011) are used for the bottom row. Depending on the energy map which is used distances, shapes as well as aspect ratio distortions can cause anisotropic stretching Chamaret et al. (2010). Even if saliency maps

Fig. 17. The original images (A and B) and for each one seams removal (vertical seams for A and horizontal seams for B) using gradient (top-row) and using a saliency map (bottom row). Adapted from: `http://cilabs.kaist.ac.kr`

most of the time work better than simple gradient, they are not perfect and the results can be very different depending on the method used.

For spatio-temporal images, Rubinstein et al. (2008) propose to remove 2D seam manifolds from 3D space-time volumes by replacing dynamic programming method with graph cuts optimization to find the optimal seams. A forward energy criterion is presented which improves the visual quality of the retargeted images. Indeed, the seam carving method removes the seams with the least amount of energy, and might introduce energy into the images due to previously non-adjacent neighbors becoming neighbors. The optimal seam is the one which introduces a minimum amount of energy.

Grundmann et al. (2010) proposed a saliency-based spatio-temporal seam-carving approach with much better spatio-temporal continuity than Rubinstein et al. (2008). The spatial saliency maps are computed on each frame but they are averaged over and history of frames in order to smooth the maps from a temporal point of view. Moreover, the seams proposed by the author are temporally discontinuous providing only the appearance of a continuous seam which helps in keeping both spatial and temporal coherence.

5. Discussion and perspectives

5.1 Two main approaches

In this chapter we discussed the use of saliency-based methods on two main approaches to image and video compression. The first one uses the result of the saliency maps to compress the signal but it does not modify the original spatial (frame resolution) and temporal (video length) size of the signal. The second one uses saliency maps to crop or reduce the spatio-temporal resolution of the signal. In this latter case, the compression is not obtained through signal quality reduction, but through quantity reduction. Of course, both methods can be used together and they are more or less interesting depending on the application.

5.2 Automatic human attention prediction issues

As already shown in Figure 12, different viewers' gaze can be predictable or not depending on the situation, thus a compression system should take this fact into account. If there is not a real salient object standing out from the background, the compression scheme should not take saliency into account while, this one can help if salient objects are present.

Another point to take into account is the shape of the saliency maps. As stated in section Attention models for still images: a comparison, saliency maps with a high resolution and which also highlight edges might be more convenient for compression purposes than more fuzzy approaches. Those maps preserve important details where artifacts would be clearly disturbing.

Attention-based visual coding seems to become less crucial as the bandwidth of Internet and TV continuously increase. Nevertheless, for precise applications like video-surveillance where the quality of uninteresting textures is not a problem and where the transmission bandwidth may be a problem, especially for massive HD multi-camera setups, the saliency-based approaches are very relevant. In the same way, storage of huge amount of live visual data is very resource-demanding and the best compression is needed while preserving the main events.

Concerning image and video retargeting and summarization, the perceptual zooming and smart resizing is of great importance in the context of smart mobile devices becoming common. Those devices have limited screen sizes and their bandwidth is much less easy to control in terms of quality of service and bandwidth. Intelligent and flexible methods of automatic thumbnailing, zoom, resizing and repurposing of audio-video data are crucial for a fast developing HD multimedia browsing market. Of course, in this case, a very good spatio-temporal continuity is required.

5.3 Quality evaluation and comparison issue

Coding artifacts in non-salient regions might attract attention of the viewer to these regions, thereby degrading visual quality. This problem is particularly noticeable at low bit rates as it can be seen in Figure 18: for example some repeating patterns like textures are not interesting but they become interesting (actually annoying) if they have compression artifacts or defects. Several methods have been proposed to detect and reduce such coding artifacts, to keep user's attention on the same regions that were salient before compression. It is however difficult to find appropriate criteria and quality metrics Farias (2010); Ninassi et al. (2007), and benchmark datasets (e.g.,Li et al. (2009)).

Fig. 18. First row: classical compression, Second row: attention-based compression. Adapted from http://www.svcl.ucsd.edu/projects/ROI_coding/demo.htm.

Another recurring problem encountered in writing this review is the lack of cross-comparison between the different methods. For example few authors report compression rates for an equivalent perceptual quality. The notion of "equivalent quality" itself seems difficult to define as even objective methods are not necessary perceptually relevant. This problem is particularly important for the methods in section Attention modeling: what is saliency? but it is also present in the retargeting and summarization methods from section Image retargeting based on saliency maps.

One way to fill in these data would be to provide datasets on the internet that would serve as benchmarks.

5.4 Saliency cross-modal integration: combining audio and visual attention

In a multimedia file a lot of information is included into the visual data. But also, supplemental or complementary information can be found within the audio track: audio data could confirm visual data information, help in being more selective or even bring new information that is not present in the camera field of view. Indeed, in some contexts sound might even be the only way to determine where to focus visual attention, for example if several persons are in a room but only one is talking. It seems thus that the use of both visual and audio saliency is a relevant idea.

Multimodal models of attention are unfortunately very few and they are mainly used in the field of robotics such in Ruesch et al. (2008). Another interesting idea is to localize the sound-emitting regions in a video. Recent work as Lee et al. (2010) has shown the ability to localize sounds in an image.

Given the computationally intensive nature and the real-time requirements of video compression methods and especially in the case of multimodal integration of saliency maps, some algorithms have exploited recent advances in Graphics Processing Unit (GPU) computing. In particular, a parallel implementation of a spatio-temporal visual saliency model has been proposed Rahman et al. (2011).

5.5 Saliency models and new trends in multimedia compression

Visual compression has been a very active field of research and development for over 20 years, leading to many different compression systems and to the definition of international standards. Even though video compression has become a mature field, a lot of research is still ongoing. Indeed, as the quality of the compression increases, so does users' level of expectations and their intolerance to artifacts. Exploiting saliency-based video compression is a challenging and exciting area of research and especially nowadays when saliency models include more and more top-down information and manage to better and better predict real human gaze.

Multimedia applications are a continuously evolving domain and compression algorithms must also evolve and adapt to new applications. The explosion of portable devices with less bandwidth and smaller screens, but also the future semantic TV/web and its object-based description will lead in the future to a higher importance of saliency-based algorithms for multimedia data repurposing and compression.

6. References

Achanta, R., Hemami, S., Estrada, F. & Susstrunk, S. (2009). Frequency-tuned Salient Region Detection, *IEEE International Conference on Computer Vision and Pattern Recognition (CVPR)*.

Avidan, S. & Shamir, A. (2007). Seam carving for content-aware image resizing, *ACM Trans. Graph.* 26(3): 10.

Bay, H., Ess, A., Tuytelaars, T. & Gool, L. V. (2008). Surf: Speeded up robust features, *Computer Vision and Image Understanding (CVIU)* 110(3): 346–359.

Belardinelli, A., Pirri, F. & Carbone, A. (2008). Motion saliency maps from spatiotemporal filtering, *In Proc. 5th International Workshop on Attention in Cognitive Systems - WAPCV 2008*, pp. 7–17.

Boiman, O. & Irani, M. (2005). Detecting irregularities in images and in video, *International Conference on Computer Vision (ICCV)*.

Bruce, N. D. B. & Tsotsos, J. K. (2009). Saliency, attention, and visual search: An information theoretic approach, *Journal of Vision* 9(3).

Bruce, N. & Tsotsos, J. (2006). Saliency based on information maximization, *in* Y. Weiss, B. Schölkopf & J. Platt (eds), *Advances in Neural Information Processing Systems 18*, MIT Press, Cambridge, MA, pp. 155–162.

Butko, N. J., Zhang, L., Cottrell, G. & Movellan, J. (2008). Visual saliency model for robot cameras, *IEEE Inter. Conf. on Robotics and Automation (ICRA)*, pp. 2398Ű-2403.

Chamaret, C., Le Meur, O., Guillotel, P. & Chevet, J.-C. (2010). How to measure the relevance of a retargeting approach?, *Workshop Media Retargeting ECCV 2010*, Crete, Grèce, pp. 1–14.

Ciocca, G., Cusano, C., Gasparini, F. & Schettini, R. (2007). Self-adaptive image cropping for small displays, *IEEE Transactions on Consumer Electronics* 53(4): 1622–1627.

Couvreur, L., Bettens, F., Hancq, J. & Mancas, M. (2007). Normalized auditory attention levels for automatic audio surveillance, *International Conference on Safety and Security Engineering (SAFE)*.

de Bruijn, O. & Spence, R. (2000). Rapid serial visual presentation: A space-timed trade-off in information presentation, *Advanced Visual Interfaces*, pp. 189–192.

Deselaers, T., Dreuw, P. & Ney, H. (2008). Pan, zoom, scan – time-coherent, trained automatic video cropping, *IEEE Conference on Computer Vision and Pattern Recognition*, IEEE, Anchorage, AK, USA.

Fan, X., Xie, X., Ying Ma, W., Jiang Zhang, H. & qin Zhou, H. (2003). Visual attention based image browsing on mobile devices, *Proc. of ICME 2003*, IEEE Computer Society Press, pp. 53–56.

Farias, M. C. Q. (2010). *Video Quality Metrics (in: Digital Video)*, InTech.

Frintrop, S. (2006). Vocus: A visual attention system for object detection and goal-directed search, *Thesis print*, Vol. 3899 of *Lecture Notes in Artificial Intelligence*, Springer Berlin / Heidelberg.

Gao, D., Mahadevan, V. & Vasconcelos, N. (2008). On the plausibility of the discriminant center-surround hypothesis for visual saliency., *J Vis* 8(7): 13.1–1318.

Geisler, W. S. & Perry, J. S. (1998). A real-time foveated multiresolution system for low-bandwidth video communication, *in Proc. SPIE*, pp. 294–305.

Goferman, S., Zelnik-Manor, L. & Tal, A. (2010). Context-aware saliency detection, *Proc. IEEE Conf. Computer Vision and Pattern Recognition (CVPR)*, pp. 2376–2383.

Grundmann, M., Kwatra, V., Han, M. & Essa, I. (2010). Discontinuous seam-carving for video retargeting, *Proc. IEEE Conf. Computer Vision and Pattern Recognition (CVPR)*, pp. 569–576.

Guo, C. & Zhang, L. (2010). A novel multiresolution spatiotemporal saliency detection model and its applications in image and video compression., *IEEE Trans Image Process* 19(1): 185–198.

Gupta, R. & Chaudhury, S. (2011). A scheme for attentional video compression, *Pattern Recognition and Machine Intelligence* 6744: 458–465.

Harel, J., Koch, C. & Perona, P. (2007). Graph-based visual saliency, *Advances in Neural Information Processing Systems 19*, MIT Press, pp. 545–552.

Hou, X. & Zhang, L. (2007). Saliency detection: A spectral residual approach, *Proc. IEEE Conf. Computer Vision and Pattern Recognition CVPR '07*, pp. 1–8.

Hyvärinen, A., Karhunen, J. & Oja, E. (2001). *Independent Component Analysis*, New York: Wiley.

Itti, L. (2004). Automatic foveation for video compression using a neurobiological model of visual attention, *IEEE Transactions on Image Processing* 13(10): 1304–1318.

Itti, L. & Baldi, P. F. (2006). Modeling what attracts human gaze over dynamic natural scenes, *in* L. Harris & M. Jenkin (eds), *Computational Vision in Neural and Machine Systems*, Cambridge University Press, Cambridge, MA.

Itti, L. & Koch, C. (2001). Computational modelling of visual attention, *Nature Reviews Neuroscience* 2(3): 194–203.

Itti, L., Koch, C. & Niebur, E. (1998). A model of saliency-based visual attention for rapid scene analysis, *IEEE Transactions on Pattern Analysis and Machine Intelligence* 20(11): 1254 –1259.

Itti, L., Rees, G. & Tsotsos, J. (2005). *Neurobiology of Attention*, Elsevier Academic Press.

Jouneau, E. & Carincotte, C. (2011). Particle-based tracking model for automatic anomaly detection, *IEEE Int. Conference on Image Processing (ICIP).*

Judd, T., Ehinger, K., Durand & Torralba, A. (2009). Learning to predict where humans look, *IEEE Inter. Conf. on Computer Vision (ICCV)*, pp. 2376–2383.

Kayser, C., Petkov, C., Lippert, M. & Logothetis, N. K. (2005). Mechanisms for allocating auditory attention: An auditory saliency map, *Curr. Biol.* 15: 1943–1947.

Koch, C. & Ullman, S. (1985). Shifts in selective visual attention: towards the underlying neural circuitry., *Hum Neurobiol* 4(4): 219–227.

Kortum, P. & Geisler, W. (1996). Implementation of a foveated image coding system for image bandwidth reduction, *In Human Vision and Electronic Imaging, SPIE Proceedings*, pp. 350–360.

Le Meur, O. & Le Callet, P. (2009). What we see is most likely to be what matters: visual attention and applications, *Proceedings of the 16th IEEE international conference on Image processing*, ICIP'09, IEEE Press, Piscataway, NJ, USA, pp. 3049–3052.

Le Meur, O., Le Callet, P. & Barba, D. (2007a). Construction d'images miniatures avec recadrage automatique basé sur un modéle perceptuel bio-inspiré, *Traitement du signal*, Vol. 24(5), pp. 323–335.

Le Meur, O., Le Callet, P. & Barba, D. (2007b). Predicting visual fixations on video based on low-level visual features, *Vision Research* 47: 2483–2498.

Le Meur, O., Le Callet, P., Barba, D. & Thoreau, D. (2006). A coherent computational approach to model bottom-up visual attention, *Pattern Analysis and Machine Intelligence, IEEE Transactions on* 28(5): 802 –817.

Lee, J., De Simone, F. & Ebrahimi, T. (2010). Efficient video coding based on audio-visual focus of attention, *Journal of Visual Communication and Image Representation* 22(8): 704–711.

Legge, Hooven, Klitz, Mansfield & Tjan (2002). Mr.chips 2002: new insights from an idealobserver model of reading, *Vision Research* pp. 2219–2234.

Li, J., Tian, Y., Huang, T. & Gao, W. (2009). A dataset and evaluation methodology for visual saliency in video, *Multimedia and Expo, 2009. ICME 2009. IEEE International Conference on*, pp. 442 –445.

Li, Z., Qin, S. & Itti, L. (2011). Visual attention guided bit allocation in video compression, *Image and Vision Computing* 29(1): 1 – 14.

Liu, F. & Gleicher, M. (2005). Automatic image retargeting with fisheye-view warping, *Proceedings of User Interface Software Technologies (UIST).*

Liu, H., Jiang, S., Huang, Q., Xu, C. & Gao, W. (2007). Region-based visual attention analysis with its application in image browsing on small displays, *ACM Multimedia*, pp. 305–308.

Lorente, J. D. S. (ed.) (2011). *Recent Advances on Video Coding*, InTech.

Maeder, A. J., Diederich, J. & Niebur, E. (1996). Limiting human perception for image sequences, *in* B. E. Rogowitz & J. P. Allebach (ed.), *Society of Photo-Optical Instrumentation Engineers (SPIE) Conference Series*, Vol. 2657, pp. 330–337.

Mancas, M. (2007). *Computational Attention Towards Attentive Computers*, Presses universitaires de Louvain.

Mancas, M. (2009). Relative influence of bottom-up and top-down attention, *Attention in Cognitive Systems*, Vol. 5395 of *Lecture Notes in Computer Science*, Springer Berlin / Heidelberg.

Mancas, M. & Gosselin, B. (2010). Dense crowd analysis through bottom-up and top-down attention, *Proc. of the Brain Inspired Cognitive Sytems (BICS)*.

Mancas, M., Gosselin, B. & Macq, B. (2007). Perceptual image representation, *J. Image Video Process.* 2007: 3–3.

Mancas, M., Pirri, F. & Pizzoli, M. (2011). From saliency to eye gaze: embodied visual selection for a pan-tilt-based robotic head, *Proc. of the 7th Inter. Symp. on Visual Computing (ISVC)*, Las Vegas, USA.

Mancas, M., Riche, N. & J. Leroy, B. G. (2011). Abnormal motion selection in crowds using bottom-up saliency, *IEEE ICIP*.

Najemnik, J. & Geisler, W. (2005). Optimal eye movement strategies in visual search, *Nature* pp. 387–391.

Navalpakkam, V. & Itti, L. (2005). Modeling the influence of task on attention, *Vision Research* 45(2): 205–231.

Ninassi, A., Le Meur, O., Le Callet, P. & Barbba, D. (2007). Does where you gaze on an image affect your perception of quality? applying visual attention to image quality metric, *IEEE Inter. Conf. on Image Processing (ICIP)* , Vol. 2, pp. 169–172.

Oliva, A., Torralba, A., Castelhano, M. & Henderson, J. (2003). Top-down control of visual attention in object detection, *IEEE Inter. Conf. on Image Processing (ICIP)* , Vol. 1, pp. I – 253–6 vol.1.

Privitera, C. M. & Stark, L. W. (2000). Algorithms for defining visual regions-of-interest: Comparison with eye fixations, *IEEE Trans. Pattern Anal. Mach. Intell.* 22(9): 970–982.

Rahman, A., Houzet, D., Pellerin, D., Marat, S. & Guyader, N. (2011). Parallel implementation of a spatio-temporal visual saliency model, *Journal of Real-Time Image Processing* 6: 3–14.

Ren, T., Liu, Y. & Wu, G. (2009). Image retargeting using multi-map constrained region warping, *ACM Multimedia*, pp. 853–856.

Ren, T., Liu, Y. & Wu, G. (2010). Rapid image retargeting based on curve-edge grid representation, *IEEE Inter. Conf. on Image Processing (ICIP)* , pp. 869–872.

Richardson, I. E. (2003). *H.264 and MPEG-4 Video Compression: Video Coding for Next Generation Multimedia*, 1 edn, Wiley.

Riche, N., Mancas, M. & B. Gosselin, T. D. (2011). 3d saliency for abnormal motion selection: the role of the depth map, *Proceedings of the ICVS 2011*, Lecture Notes in Computer Science, Springer Berlin / Heidelberg.

Rubinstein, M., Shamir, A. & Avidan, S. (2008). Improved seam carving for video retargeting, *ACM Transactions on Graphics (SIGGRAPH)* 27(3): 1–9.

Ruesch, J., Lopes, M., Bernardino, A., Hornstein, J., Santos-Victor, J. & Pfeifer, R. (2008). Multimodal saliency-based bottom-up attention a framework for the humanoid robot icub, *IEEE Int. Conf. on Robotics and Automation*, p. 6.

Santella, A., Agrawala, M., Decarlo, D., Salesin, D. & Cohen, M. (2006). Gaze-based interaction for semi-automatic photo cropping, *In CHI 2006*, ACM, pp. 771–780.

Schmidhuber, J. (2009). Driven by compression progress: A simple principle explains essential aspects of subjective beauty, novelty, surprise, interestingness, attention, curiosity, creativity, art, science, music, jokes, *in* G. Pezzulo, M. Butz, O. Sigaud & G. Baldassarre (eds), *Anticipatory Behavior in Adaptive Learning Systems*, Vol. 5499 of *Lecture Notes in Computer Science*, Springer Berlin / Heidelberg, pp. 48–76.

Seo, H. J. & Milanfar, P. (2009). Static and space-time visual saliency detection by self-resemblance, *Journal of Vision* 9(12).

Shamir, A. & Sorkine, O. (2009). Visual media retargeting, *ACM SIGGRAPH ASIA 2009 Courses*, SIGGRAPH ASIA '09, ACM, New York, NY, USA, pp. 11:1–11:13.

Stentiford, F. W. M. (2001). An estimator for visual attention through competitive novelty with application to image compression, *Proc. Picture Coding Symposium*, pp. 101–104.

Suh, B., Ling, H., Bederson, B. B. & Jacobs, D. W. (2003). Automatic thumbnail cropping and its effectiveness., *Proceedings of the 16th annual ACM symposium on User interface software and technology (UIST)*, pp. 95–104.

Tan, R. & Davis, J. W. (2004). Differential video coding of face and gesture events in presentation videos, *Computer Vision and Image Understanding* 96(2): 200 – 215. Special Issue on Event Detection in Video.

Tao, C., Jia, J. & Sun, H. (2007). Active window oriented dynamic video, *Workshop on Dynamical Vision at the Inter. Conf. on Comp. Vision (ICCV)*

Tatler, B. (2007). The central fixation bias in scene viewing: Selecting an optimal viewing position independently of motor biases and image feature distributions, *Journal of Vision* 7.

Tsapatsoulis, N., Rapantzikos, K. & Pattichis, C. (2007). An embedded saliency map estimator scheme: Application to video encoding, *International Journal of Neural Systems* 17(4): 1–16.

Valenti, R., Sebe, N. & Gevers, T. (2009). Image saliency by isocentric curvedness and color, *Inter. Conf. on Comp. Vision (ICCV)*.

Vaquero, D., Turk, M., Pulli, K., Tico, M. & Gelf, N. (2010). A survey of image retargeting techniques, *SPIE Applications of Digital Image Processing*.

Wang, Y.-S., Tai, C.-L., Sorkine, O. & Lee, T.-Y. (2008). Optimized scale-and-stretch for image resizing, *ACM Trans. Graph. (Proceedings of ACM SIGGRAPH ASIA)* 27(5).

Wiegand, T., Sullivan, G. J., Bjntegaard, G. & Luthra, A. (2003). Overview of the h.264/avc video coding standard., *IEEE Trans. Circuits Syst. Video Techn.* pp. 560–576.

Wolf, L., Guttmann, M. & Cohen-Or, D. (2007). Non-homogeneous content-driven video-retargeting, *Proceedings of the Eleventh IEEE International Conference on Computer Vision (ICCV-07)*.

Wonjun, K., Chanho, J. & Changick, K. (2011). Spatiotemporal saliency detection and its applications in static and dynamic scenes, *IEEE Trans. Circuits and Systems for Video Tech.* 21(4): 10.

Yu, S. X. & Lisin, D. A. (2009). Image compression based on visual saliency at individual scales., *International Symposium on Visual Computing*, pp. 157–166.

Zhou, Lu, L. & Bovik., A. (2003). Foveation scalable video coding with automatic fixation selection, *IEEE Transactions on Image Processing* 12(2): 243–254.

7

Video Quality Assessment

Juan Pedro López Velasco
Universidad Politécnica de Madrid,
Spain

1. Introduction

One of the main aspects which affects the video compression and needs to be deeply analyzed is the quality assessment. The chain of transmission of video over a determined channel of distribution, such as broadcast or a digital way of storage, is limited, and requires a process of compression, with a consequent degradation and the apparition of artifacts which are necessary to evaluate, in order to offer a suitable and appropriate quality to the final user.

The quick evolution of technology, especially referred to television and multimedia services, which has evolved from analog to digital. The constant increasement of resolution from standard television to high definition and ultrahigh-definition or the creation of advanced production of contents systems such as 3-dimensional video, make necessary new quality studies to evaluate the video characteristics to provide the observer the best viewing that could expect.

Once the change from analog to digital television has been completely developed, the next step was encoding the video in order to obtain high compression without damaging the quality contemplated by the observer. In analog television the quality systems were well-established and controlled, but in digital television it is required new metrics and procedures of measurement of the quality of video.

The quality assessment must be adapted to the human visual system, which is why researchers have performed subjective viewing experiments in order to obtain the conditions of encoding of video systems to provide the best quality to the user.

There has been a process of standardization in video encoding, the group of experts of MPEG developed techniques that assure the quality which would be improved with the evolution of the standards. MPEG-2 offered a reasonably good quality, but the evolution of the standards developed another one which was twice efficient as MPEG-2, which is called AVC/H.264, i.e. to obtain a similar quality than the first standard it was only necessary half the bitrate used in the new standard.

The quality assessment has also been force to evolve Parallel to technologies. The concept is not any more limited to the perceived quality of the video, but now there are other additives carried to this concept, making appear a new term called Quality of Experience (QoE) which is becoming more popular because it is a more complete definition, just because the user is not only observing the video, is living a real experience which depends on the content and expectatives placed on it.

In this chapter, a review of the systems that are particularly used for this important purpose will be analyzed, and spreading to the experience lived by the observer to talk in terms of QoE.

The purpose of this chapter is to provide a state of the art of vision quality assessment, analyzing models and metrics used in a variety of applications.

2. Human visual system

Visual perception is very important to human. We are constantly receiving information and processing it, in order to interact with the environment that surrounds us. That justifies the big interest existed in video and measurement of its quality, because there is a big necessity of receiving that information in our visual system as faithful as it appears in nature.

The evolution of technologies in codification has made video compression more efficient with the reduction of introduced artifacts. But the accuracy in developed vision models and quality metrics has increased when in consequence of the video content transfer from analogue to digital. The vision models are based on human perception, moving closer to the final consumer.

The human visual system is extremely complex, but analyzing its behavior, characterizing the operation of the eye. The eye is a human body organ which is sensitive to a wide range of wavelengths from the radio-electric spectrum, from 400 to 780nm approximately. A large part of our neurological resources are used in visual perception.

For all these reasons, optimizing the performance of digital imaging systems with respect to the capture, display, storage and transmission of visual information is one of the most important challenges in this domain.

Video compression schemes should reduce the visibility of the introduced artifacts, creating more effective systems to reproduce video an image: Additionally printers should use the best half-toning patterns, and so on. In all these applications, the limitations of the human visual system (HVS) can be exploited to maximize the visual quality of the output. To do this, it is necessary to build computational models of the HVS and integrate them in tools for perceptual quality assessment.

3. Quality assessment

3.1 Types

There are different kinds of developing quality assessment. The main objective of quality assessment consists in the evaluation of any equipment of codification, transmission of its conditions of work, to assure the expectations of the users that are viewing the contents.

The chain of distribution joins different processes that degrade the image on each phase. In broadcasting the phases that affects more intensively to the quality of video are commonly the contribution and the distribution in which the video suffers degradations because of the process of encoding of the signal. This degradation will be analyzed.

Fig. 1. Phases of video broadcast

The easiest way for this purpose consists in selecting a high number of observers, with a great variety of sex, age and condition, and asking them to watch a series of contents, previously and well selected to cover the range of contents which could appear on a normal TV channel. The observers will be given a questionnaire to fill with their opinions about the quality observed. Once the questionnaires are complete, the statistics will reveal a collection of consequences.

The studies must follow a protocol which is basically described in ITU-R Recommendation BT-500 about subjective assessment with variations to adapt the study to the real situation but not far from the standards. The selection of video contents and the duration of sequences are important decisions to do a proper job and to be able to compare with similar studies.

Although the subjective studies offer real results as the response of the observers is collected, that kind of studies are expensive in time and money, and they are not always so efficient, because sometimes it depends on the place to elaborate the study and its conditions of lighting or comfort of the user, being able to change a valid result because of an external condition. That is the reason for the proliferation of objective measurements which are based on mathematical algorithm using the properties of the image, which keep a higher fidelity to the subjective obtained results.

One of the main points to describe in next sections is measurement of artifacts and impairments.

All process of video encoding generates degradation on the image, with a consequent apparition of concrete defects which are called artifacts, and will affect to the perceived quality of the observer. Researchers have made studies in order to evaluate this phenomenon, artifacts such as blockiness, blurring, ringing, color bleeding or motion compensation mismatches, have been widely analyzed and a collection of metrics with or without reference have been developed in this field, which use test signals and measurement procedures to determine the level of distortion.

Finally, the theme of evolution of technologies and its influence in quality assessment will be approached, by description of the state of the art of quality measurement in stereoscopic systems. The classic methods are utilized for this purpose, but the detection of new artifacts and types of impairments, makes the necessity of developing new metrics. Additionally, the concept is not only physical, and the evolution has lead to the term Quality of Experience (QoE).

3.2 Artifacts

Artifacts are defined as visible differences due to some technical limitation that presents an image. These effects occur in the process of production of video signal, in the phases of capture, compression, transmission, reception and delivery to the final recipient, the displayed picture may differ from the original.

They appear both in analogue and digital systems, but we will focus on the artifacts derived from the digital ones, especially because of video compression in the process of encoding and decoding.

Most common artifacts are caused by three reasons:

- Artifacts due to analog and digital formats, its relationship and conversions between them (noise and blurring).
- Artifacts due to coding and compression (block distortion, blurring and ringing).
- Artifacts due to transmission channel errors (errored blocks by lost packets).
- Blocking effect

The blocking effect, also known as tiling or blockiness, refers to a block pattern in the

compressed sequence. It is due to the independent quantization of individual blocks. It appears especially on compression standards that utilises macroblocks of a certain size when performing a transform. A high impaired image presents artificial horizontal and vertical edges, clearly visible, parallel to the picture frame.

High compression, which reduces bitrate, in DCT-based encoding such as MPEG-2 or H.263 or similar, macroblocks with less information create homogeneous values in block pixels with boundaries in their edges, as a result of truncation of coefficients. Advanced codecs such as H.264 utilizes deblocking filters to reduce the visibility of this artifact. This effect is easy distinguished in next example of "Nasa" sequence and its tiling diagram.

For a given quantization level, block distortion is usually more visible in smoother areas of the picture

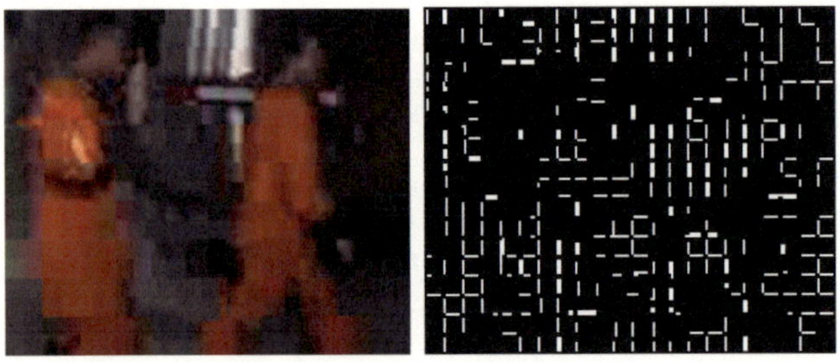

Fig. 2. Example of sequence high blocking effect

- Blur

Blur artifact is defined as a loss of energy and spatial detail as a reduction of edge sharpness, because of suppression of the high-frequency coefficients by coarse quantization. Blurring is also generated when reducing the bitrate of encoding. As this effect occurs in high frequencies, it is more visible in sequences with higher spatial complexity.

Next example of "Nasa" test sequence shows the consequences of reducing the bitrate, from the original one on the left to a high reduction seen on right image.

Fig. 3. Evolution of blurriness when reducing bitrate

- Ringing

The ringing artifact occurs when the quantization of individual DCT coefficients due to irregularities in high frequencies in the reconstruction of macroblocks. The effect is related to Gibb's phenomenon. It is more visible in high contrast edges, in areas with smooth textures. It is easily visible on next example, around the edges of the objects, apparing like duplications of their contours.

Fig. 4. Example of high ringing artifact

- Noise

Noise is defined as an uncontrolled or unpredicted pattern of intensity fluctuations that affects to the perceived quality of an image.

There are multiple types of noise impairments commonly produced by compression algorithms. Two common impairments are mosquito noise and quantization noise.

- Mosquito noise. Mosquito noise is a temporal artifact seen mainly in smoothly textured regions as luminance/chrominance fluctuations around high-contrast edges or moving objects. It is a consequence of the coding differences for the same area of a scene in consecutive frames of a sequence.
- Quantization noise. This is a type of noise produced after a severe truncation of the values of the coefficients while performing a transform such as DCT or Hadamard.

Other artifacts related are flickering, in images with high texture content, or aliasing, when the content of the scene is above the Nyquist rate, either spatially or temporally

4. Subjective quality assessment

4.1 Introduction

The user's opinion in video technologies is important. For that reason, the evaluation of a video compression codec must be developed with its help, in order to know the level of acceptance of it.

Several studies have been developed to measure the quality of new technology systems every period. In first instance, it was used to analyze the impact of digital television in the transition from analogue to digital. And in the transition from standard definition to high-definition TV, including the studies of main encoders (MPEG-2, H.264/AVC) in the adaptation to different formats and storage, last time assessment was developed for blu-ray codecs. Also for the Definition of settings or quality parameters: bitrate, resolution (e.g. in HD: 720p or 1080i) or features for a TV channel, for example.

Next generation of encoding codecs HVC (High-efficiency Video Codec) which represents the evolution of H.264 is being analyzed by subjective assessment, to measure the impact on users and the necessity of its establishment.

So, it is clear that subjective quality evaluation is still important and it will always be together with the objective one. Methods and technologies change, but the purpose of video quality is still the same.

In this section, the most frequent techniques to develop a subjective quality study, in order to evaluate a determined system. There is a great variety of subjective testing methods, depending on the way of presenting the video sequences to the observers.

Then, there are single or double stimulus experiments, depending on if the original image is presented or only the degraded one.

The problem with this kind of studies is the requirement for a large number of observers viewing a limited amount of video contents, because if the time of contents viewed is extended for two long, the tiredness and fatigue of the observers will affect to the wished measurement. But it is still very used nowadays and will be necessary to introduce the objective assessment to explain in next section.

4.2 Description of requirements

Once the decision of developing subjective quality assessment made, requirements to complete a suitable subjective study must be consider. Before developing the study the conditions must be established to facilitate the repetition of it or the comparison with similar studies. Requirements will be listed in this section.

- Viewing conditions.

  There are different viewing conditions in case of referring to a laboratory environment than the ones used in home environment. Assuring the best conditions is a basic aim in order to allow a meaningful evaluation to be made derived from the assessment. The distance to the screen of the observers depends on the size of the screen. This is a very important aim to obtain suitable results.

The screen must be arranged in contrast and brightness and the angle of observation must not exceed 30º.

- Conditioning of the room.

  The room must be conditioned in lighting, with seat comfort and no reflections on screen. Because the viewers will spend a considerable time and this must not affect to their scores.

- Observers

  The minimum number of participants in the study, for the sample to be enough is 15, but it is recommended to find as many observers as possible, 60 or more. The viewers are preferred to be non-professional, possessing no trained-eyes. Professional viewers tend to search for the impairment and their opinion is not always so impartial.

  There must be a representative variety of age and sex in viewers. The observers must make a previous training to understand the objective of the test.

- Materials / Test sequences.

  There must be a selection of sufficient test material, including different type of contents emitted by a conventional TV channel (sports, movies, news, documentary, etc.), and with different settings of spatial (more or less level of detail and high frequencies) and temporal (faster or slower contents) complexity.

  Each sequence must have a duration of between 10 and 20 seconds due to human memory and perception, to assure a correct viewing, neither too short than the viewers do not have time to observe the image in detail, nor too long to avoid causing fatigue in the observer.

  A number of organizations have developed test still pictures and sequences, whose use is recommended for the assessment.

- Presentation of results

  The results must be presented in detail. All information is necessary to validate the study and verify its good performance. Data given must include: details of the test configuration and materials, type of source and displays, number of subjects or observers that participated, reference system used and its specific variations, scores and mean scores adjusted to 95% confidence interval.

  Logistic curve-fitting and logarithmic axis will allow a straight line representation, which is the preferred form of presentation, as legible as possible.

- Sound.

  Audio quality assessment is preferably developed independently of the video assessment. In fact, it is recommended not to use sound or audio in video studies, in order to avoid distractions in the observer, modifying their opinion, off target.

  Furthermore, in case of using it, selection of the accompanying audio material should be considered at the same level of importance as the selection of video material.

Additionally, it is important that the sound be synchronized with the video. This is most noticeable for speech and lip synchronization, for which time lags of more than approximately 100 ms are considered very annoying.

4.3 Methods

Definition of settings of methods

A collection of settings can be varied, depending on the type of desirable results to obtain at the end of the quality study. In this section, some of the most important are described.

- Single or Double Stimulus methods

In double stimulus methods, viewers are shown each pair of video sequences, the reference and the impaired one. Whereas, in single stimulus methods, viewers are shown only the impaired sequence.

The number of stimulus defines the possibility of comparison to a reference, which allow the observer to detect the artifacts and impairments more easily on the image than without any original signal.

In real conditions the user does not have a reference to compare, so a single stimulus method is considered more realistic. But, a double stimulus avoids more efficiently the errors occurred by context effects. Context effects occur when subjective ratings are influenced by the severity and ordering of impairments within the test session.

In double stimulus there are two different kinds of presenting each pair of sequences, depending on the number of screens used on the study. With two screens every pair can be presented simultaneously, allowing the user to compare at the same time detecting the variation of quality.

The comparison scale is only available in double stimulus methods.

- With or without repetition methods

One of the main problems and context effect affecting to the results of subjective assessment is the fatigue of the observers. The observer has a limited time in which its scores are effective.

Long sessions produce high fatigue and exhaustion, which distort the results and invalidates the assessment. For that reason, the time of each session must be reduced to less than half an hour with extended breaks.

Depending on the accuracy of the study, each pair can be presented twice, with one or more repetitions. If the variety of parameters to measure in sequences is wide, it is possible to reduce the time for sessions, presenting each pair of sequences only once, i.e. without repetition. The objective is saving time, expanding the quality parameters (QP) under evaluation, avoiding the fatigue of observers.

- Absolute or Comparison methods

Depending on the objective of the study, it is possible to define the expected results obtained. Absolute results are related to single stimulus methods, whereas, comparison methods are more related to double stimulus methods, although it is possible to obtain absolute measurements with full reference.

First type of methods utilizes indistinctly the quality or the impairment scale, while the second type utilizes a scale called "comparison scale", which assigns the relation between the members of each pair of sequences.

- Continuous or discrete (non-continuous) evaluation methods

There are different options of combining video in a continuous war: one program or a series of sequences of different or the same type of content. These programs may include one or various quality parameters under evaluation (e.g. bitrate). Each program should have duration of at least 5 minutes

The time of response of the viewer must be fast to identify the impairment observed. Nevertheless, the varying delay may influence the assessment results if only the average over a program segment is calculated. Studies are being carried out to evaluate the impact of the response time of different viewers on the resulting quality grade.

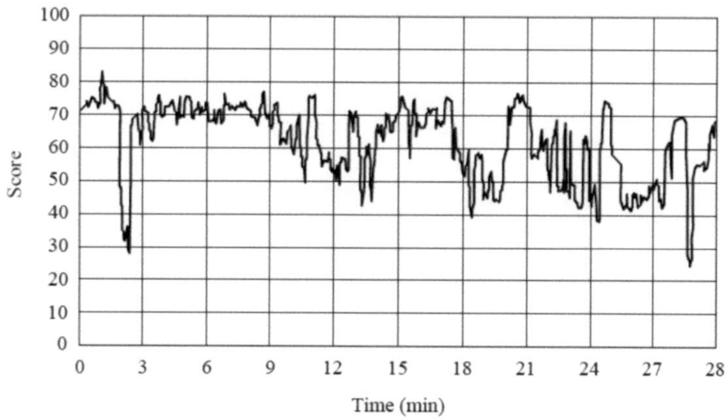

Fig. 5. Example of data from a continuous assessment

- Type of scale

  There are different types of scale, depending on desirable results that the researcher expects to obtain from the study. The four most representatives appear below.

  1. Quality Scale (QS)

     This scale is used in different methods to evaluate in absolute the perceived quality of a video sequence. There are variations with different number of grades.

5	Excellent
4	Good
3	Fair
2	Poor
1	Bad

2. Impairment Scale (IS)

   Unlike the QS, IS scale tries to extract the effect over the human perception of an artifact or other impairment.

5	Imperceptible
4	Perceptible, but not annoying
3	Slightly annoying
2	Annoying
1	Very annoying

3. Comparison Scale (CS)

   This scale is not allowed for single stimulus methods. The objective is to establish a relative judgment between a pair of sequences to evaluate impairment or degradation in image. It is a 7-grade scale, as follows.

+3	Much worse
+2	Worse
+1	Slightly worse
0	The same
-1	Slightly better
-2	Better
-3	Much better

4. Numerical Scale (NS)

   The numerical scale uses numbers to obtain the opinion of the observers. The scale depends on the number of grades on the scale

   The most frequent scale used in numerical terms is known as Mean Opinion Score (MOS), normalized as the five-grade scale in range from 1 to 5. Other scales are the 10-grade scale from 1 to 10, or 8-grade scale from 1 to 8, but sometimes it is difficult to find equivalent adjectives for each grade. Other different numbers scales are, for example, "compare scale", which utilizes 7 grades including zero to indicate no perceptible variation.

   Zero is rarely used because of its negative connotations.

Most frequent methods

Combining the different settings to develop a subjective evaluation method, it is possible to define the most common methods. Even so, there are other combinations, also acceptable, that do not appear on the next list of the most representatives.

- The double-stimulus impairment scale (DSIS) method.

This is the method used by the European Broadcasting Union (EBU), in order to measure the robustness of systems (i.e. failure characteristics).

The reference and the test sequence are shown only once. Subjects rate the amount of impairment in the test sequence comparing one to the other.

Fig. 6. Scheme of a DSIS system

- The double-stimulus continuous quality-scale (DSCQS) method

The main purpose of DSCQS method is to measure the quality of systems relative to a reference. Viewers are shown pairs of video sequences (the reference sequence and the impaired sequence) in a randomized order. It is widely accepted as an accurate test method with little sensitivity to context effects, as viewers are shown the sequence twice. Viewers are asked to rate the quality of each sequence in the pair after the second showing. It is also used to measure the quality of stereoscopic image coding

Since standard double stimulus methods like DSCQS provide only a single quality score for a given video sequence, where a typical video sequence might be 10 seconds long, questions have been raised as to the applicability of these testing methods for evaluating the performance of objective real-time video quality monitoring systems.

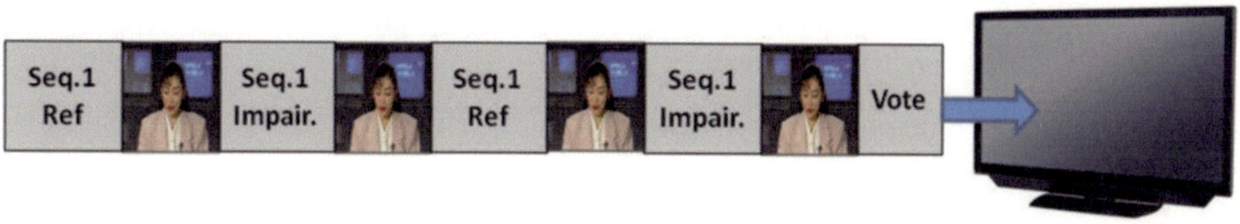

Fig. 7. Scheme of a DSCQS system

- Single-stimulus (SS) methods

The purpose of this method is to quantify the quality of systems (when no reference is available).

The method of this type called Absolute Category Rating (ACR) utilizes a single stimulus. Viewers only see the video under test, without the reference. They give one rating for its overall quality using a discrete five-level scale from 'bad' to 'excellent'. The fact that the reference is not shown with every test clip makes ACR a very efficient method compared to DSIS or DSCQS, which take almost 2 or 4 times as long, respectively.

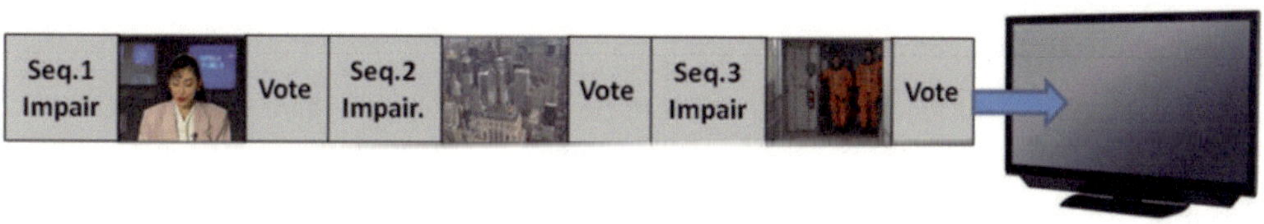

Fig. 8. Scheme of a SS system

- Stimulus-comparison (SC) or Pair-Comparison (PC) methods

For this method, test clips from the same scene but different conditions (quality parameter under evaluation) are paired in all possible combinations, and viewers make a preference judgment for each pair. This allows very fine quality discrimination between clips.

This method uses a comparison scale.

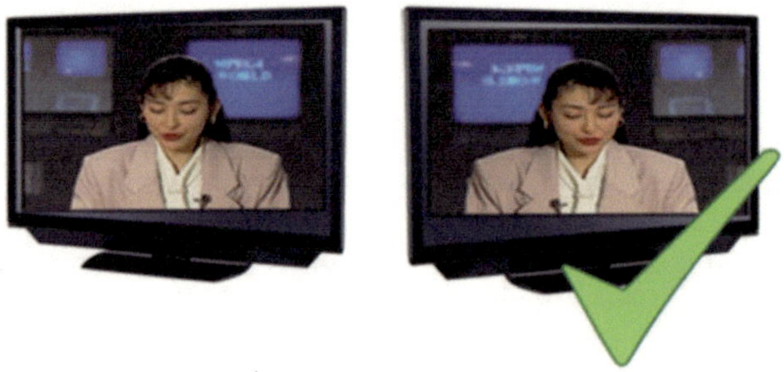

Fig. 9. Scheme of a SC system

- Single stimulus continuous quality evaluation (SSCQE)

Instead of seeing separate short sequence pairs, viewers watch a program of typically 20–30 minutes' duration which has been processed by the system under test; the reference is not shown. Using a slider, the subjects continuously rate the instantaneously perceived quality on the DSCQS scale from 'bad' to 'excellent'.

The purpose of this type of study is to assess not only the basic quality of the images but also the fidelity of the information transmitted.

Fig. 10. Scheme of a SSCQE system

- Simultaneous double stimulus for continuous evaluation (SDSCE) method

Two screens are necessary for this method of evaluation, which are parallel placed in front of the user. The left screen plays the reference sequence, while the right one plays the impaired sequence that viewers must score.

The main purpose of this method is to measure the fidelity between two video sequences. It is also used to compare different error resilience tools.

Each video pair is shown once or twice. The duration of the test session is shorter, and allows to evaluate a higher amount of quality parameters.

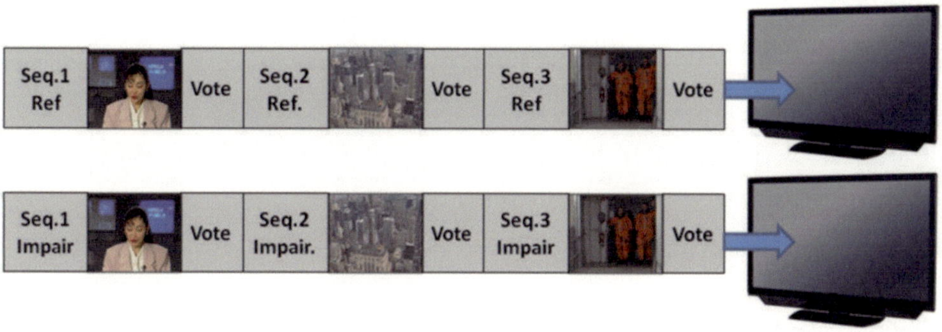

Fig. 11. Scheme of a SDSCE system

5. Objective quality assessment

In this section, the most important metrics are described to make to offer an overview of the techniques that develop this type of quality assessment.

There are three types of objective quality assessment depending on the presence and availability of a reference image or any of its features to develop the study: Full-Reference (FR), Reduced-Reference (RR) and No-Reference).

Old metrics designed for digital imaging systems, such as MSE (Mean Sqaured Error) and PSNR (Peak Signal-to-Noise Ratio), which are still very used to develop quality assessment, are defined in this section. They are still adequate for evaluating error measures

The analysis of measurement of artifacts such as tiling or blurring, especially introduced by video compression algorithms, will be interesting to offer the reader a perspective of evolution of metrics.

5.1 Objective quality metrics

Depending on the presence of a video reference, three kinds of analysis are defined:

- Full Reference (FR) metrics, when the original image is present and can be used to compare it to the degraded image in order to obtain the reduction of quality because of the process of encoding and decoding.

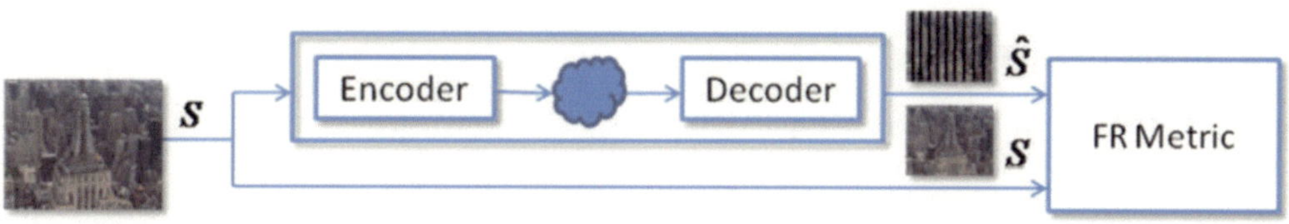

Fig. 12. Full Reference (FR) metric diagram

- Reduced Reference (RR) metrics. The original image is not available for the study but there are some properties and characteristics of it which can be used to obtain quality results.
- No-Reference (NR) metrics. There is no original image or properties of it, in this case the degraded image and its affection to the human visual system is the only tool to conclude with the quality of an image. This kind of metrics are more complicated but

are of vital importance in environments which are difficult to provide any reference, such as mobile or internet multimedia services.

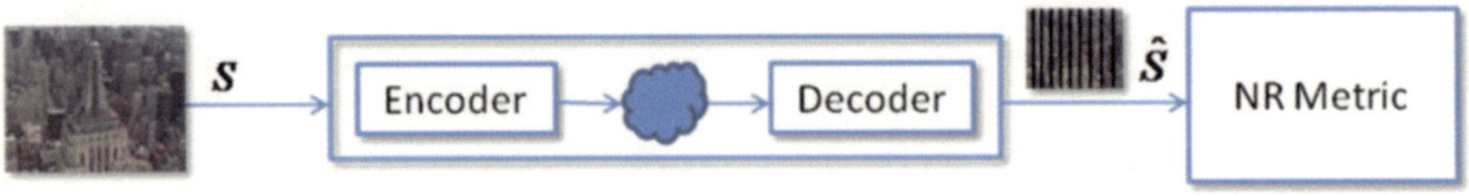

Fig. 13. No Reference (NR) metric diagram

5.2 Full-reference metrics

In this section, the most representative FR metrics are defined, classified in four different groups of metrics: based on statistics and pixel difference, based on structural similarity, based on artifact detection, and based on vision models.

- Pixel-based metrics

Most of the quality metrics are full-reference, especially the pixel-based (or statistics-based) metrics, focused on comparing pixel-by-pixel the difference between the original image used as a reference and the impaired image.

These metrics offer a good estimation of the global quality measured objectively, but are widely criticized for not correlating well with the perceived quality measurement obtained by subjective methods, that incorporates human vision models.

The most important are among others: MSE, SNR and PSNR.

MSE (Mean Square Error)

The mean squared error (MSE) is one the most popular difference metrics in image and video processing. The MSE is the mean of the squared differences between the luminance level values of pixels between two images (X and Y), normally the original frame used as a reference and an impaired image, obtained by processing of the first image. M and N are the horizontal and vertical dimensions of each frame of the sequence.

$$MSE = \frac{1}{M \cdot N} \sum_{i=0,j=0}^{M-1,N-1} (X_i - Y_i)^2$$

SNR (Single-To-Noise Ratio)

Also based on pixel by pixel comparison, this metric measures the relation between the original image and the degraded image, in order to evaluate the degradation on image.

SNR was widely substituted by its evolution PSNR, because it offers a higher efficiency than SNR, and a global extension more easy to compare in studies with different signals.

$$PSNR = 10\log_{10}\left(\frac{\sum_{i=0,j=0}^{M-1,N-1} |X_i|^2}{\sum_{i=0,j=0}^{M-1,N-1} (X_i - Y_i)^2} \right) \text{ [dB]}$$

PSNR (Peak Single-To-Noise Ratio)

As SNR used the same signal to compare with, it is more difficult to export the conclusion from one study to another, that is why the original signal was changed by the peak value (255 in a RGB channel, or 240 in luminance, for example) to obtain more general results, with a more efficient method.

$$PSNR = 10\log_{10}\left(\frac{\sum_{i=0,j=0}^{M-1,N-1} Max^2}{\sum_{i=0,j=0}^{M-1,N-1} (X_i - Y_i)^2} \right) \text{ [dB]}$$

- Based on artifacts

A collection of metrics attempt to assess the effects of artifacts described on section 0, instead of offering a global idea of quality, as with pixel-based metrics. Some examples of most representative metrics are introduced next.

Blockiness or tiling

The metric defined by MSU Graphics & Media Lab measures subjective blocking effect in video sequence, based on energy calculation and gradients. In contrast areas of the frame blocking is not appreciable, but in smooth areas these edges are conspicuous.

Other metrics are based on the structure of the pixelized image. The model included in Lee et al. research, first extracts edge pixels and computes horizontal (H(t,i, j)) and vertical (V (t,i, j)) gradient component of the edge pixels. The gradient is calculated using the Sobel operators. From the horizontal and vertical gradient images, the magnitude (R) and angle (θ) are extracted:

$$R(t,i,j) = \sqrt{H(t,i,j)^2 + V(t,i,j)^2}$$

$$\theta(t,i,j) = \tan^{-1}\left[\frac{V(t,i,j)}{H(t,i,j)}\right]$$

Analyzing the angles of the gradient, the pixels with gradient parallel to the picture frame are considered as belonging to blocking region, if they have a determined magnitude. Comparing to the original image, errors are avoided due to real edge pixels.

Other interesting metric on this field are the ones by Winkler et al., 2001 and Wang et al., 2002.

Blurring

Blurring metrics are based on the analysis of energy in high frequencies and analysis of edges and their spread. As it proposes Marziliano et al. in 2004. The reduction of edge energy between the original and the impaired image shows the loss of quality due to blurring artifact.

Other metrics, such as proposed in Lee et al. Research, utilizes the gradient calculated in every pixel of the image to detect the blur artifact by analyzing the diminution of this magnitude between the original and the impaired image. SI is the root mean square of the spatial gradient (SG), so blurring is computed as follows:

$$BL(x) = \frac{1}{\sqrt{FxC}}\left(\sqrt{\sum_{i=0}^{F-1}\sum_{j=0}^{C-1} SG_{ref}^2(i,j)} - \sqrt{\sum_{i=0}^{F-1}\sum_{j=0}^{C-1} SG_{impaired}^2}\right)$$

Ringing

Ringing artifacts are fundamentally related to the Gibb's phenomenon, when quantization of individual coefficients results in high-frequency irregularities of the reconstructed block. Yu et al. offers a segmentation algorithm to identify regions with ringing artifacts, which is more evident along high contrasts in regions with smooth texture and complex texture. The original and the processed video sequences are input into the metric and decomposed respectively by the spatial-temporal filter banks

- Based on structural similarity

The methods traditionally for quality assessment attempted to quantify the visibility of differences between pairs of images, a distorted image and ist corresponding reference image using a variety of known properties of the human visual system. Under the assumption that human visual perception is highly adapted for extracting structural information from a scene, some researchers introduce alternative studies for quality assessment based on the degradation of structural information.

SSIM

The most representative metric based on Structural Similarity is SSIM. The metric proposed by Wang et al. is based on the combination of three properties of the image luminance, contrast and structure, by comparison between the original and the impaired image, three conditions must be met: symmetry, boundedness and being unique maximum.

$$SSIM(x,y) = [l(x,y)]^{\alpha} \cdot [c(x,y)]^{\beta} \cdot [s(x,y)]^{\gamma}$$

VQM

Xiao, F. proposed a modified DCT-based video quality metric (VQM) based on Watson's proposal, which exploits the properties of visual perception, using the existing DCT coefficients, so it only incurs slightly more computation overhead.

- Based on vision models

There are a wide range of systems which utilizes models that attempt to reproduce similarities with the Human Visual System. In this section, four of them are introduced.

- Just Noticeable Differences (JND). The Sarnoff Model also known as Visual Discrimination Model (VDM) was copyrighted by Tektronix Company and commercialized in their PQA600 Picture Analyzer. The model works in spatial domain. Its acceptable conclusions are obtained as a result of its high fidelity in comparison with HVS, due to its complexity.
- Visual Differences Predictor (VDP). Unlike JND, VDP works in frequency domain, and it is very popular in prediction of encoding errors thanks to the labour of S.

Daly. The model is based on the comparison of two images after creating a diagram of disparity, to detect the image variation.

- Moving Picture Quality Metric (MPQM). As PSNR does not take the visual masking phenomenon into consideration, every single pixel error contributes to the decrease of the PSNR, even if this error is not perceived. This method includes characteristics of Human Visual System intensively studied: contrast sensitivity and masking.
- Perceptual Distortion Metric (PDM). This model of vision was developed by Winkler, S. Based on the HVS, allowing the system to find similarities with the human eye. The structure of the model is based on the fact of finding the optimus components of the model, modifying both the reference and impaired image.

5.3 No-reference metrics

When the reference is not available to design the objective quality method, for example in environments such as internet or video mobile, then it is necessary to utilize no-reference metrics to evaluate the degradation.

Most of the times, these kind of studies are focus on analyzing impairments due to artifacts, that degrade the perception of the user. So, the no-reference metrics are distributed in groups, depending on the artifact characterized.

Blocking Effect or Blockiness

Most existing no-reference metrics focus on estimating blockiness, which is still relatively easy to detect due to its regular structure, although in practice that is not so easy due to the use of deblocking filters in H.246 and other encoders.

Different techniques are used, such as Wu and Yuen whose research in developing a NR metric based on measuring the horizontal and vertical differences between rows and columns at block boundaries, offers interesting results. Means and standard deviations of the blocks adjacent to each boundary determined masking effect pondering.

On the other hand, Wang et al. model the blocky image as a non-blocky image an then appear the interference with a pure blocky signal. The level of blockiness artifact is detected by evaluating the blocky signal.

Other alternatives are the approach proposed by Baroncini and Pierotti, with the use of multiple filters which extract significant vertical and horizontal edge segments due to blockiness, and also Vlachos proposed an algorithm based on the cross-correlation of subsampled images, and Tan and Ghanbari a metric for blocking detection based in videos compressed in MPEG-2.

Blur

Another typical artifact defined for no-reference metrics is blurring. It appears in almost all processing phases in communications chain of production. Blurring manifests as a loss of spatial detail in moderate to high spatial activity regions of images. Blurring is directly related to the suppression of the higher order AC DCT coefficients through coarse quantization.

Marziliano et al. worked on blurriness metric. Other metrics have been developed to achieve results while working with other kind of artifacts. Marziliano et al. worked on blurriness metric. As object boundaries are represented by sharp edges, the spreading of significant edges in the image gives a nice approach of blurring. Blurriness and ringing metrics have been developed to evaluate JPEG2000 coding as well.

Other metrics carry out the measure by working with DCT coefficients directly. Coudoux et al. detected the vertical block edges and combined them with several masking models applied in the DCT domain.

Ringing

Ringing is a shimmering effect around high contrast edges. Ringing is not necessarily correlated with blocking as the amount of ringing depends in the amount and strength of edges in the image. A visible ringing measure (VRM) based on the average local variance has been developed in [5]. It is relation to the Gibbs effect.

Marziliano et al. present a ringing metric based on their blur metric describe on previous section, which utilizes the carachteristics from JPEG2000 video encoding to obtain suitable results, but the metric does not extend to other compression standard, but it means a good approximation.

Other metrics

There are other studies in metrics based on noise, or other artifacts related to determined video compression standards such as MPEG-2 or JPEG-2000.

Finally, it is important to mention the systems based on the combination of various individual metrics, weighted to properties of the image and their spatial and temporal complexity.

6. Quality in emerging technologies: 3D

One of the most important achievements related to digital video developed in last years has been the next generation 3D stereoscopic contents. Their development is based on the search for illusion of depth perception. After some vain attempts due to a first of generation of 3D developed by anaglyph movies, finally acceptable results have been achieved as seen in the success among users.

3D video offers a new experience to the user, but the acceptance of this experience must be evaluated, in order to draw conclusions about the generation of video contents. That is the reason why quality assessment in 3D systems is more related to the concept of Quality of Experience (QoE) of the user, because it is not just an enhancement of the quality, but a fundamental change in the character of the image.

6.1 Binocular disparity

The concept of binocular disparity is defined as the fact that the brain extracts depth information from the left and the right eye views, receiving a slightly horizontally shifted perspective of the same scene. As a result, the observer perceives the objects in image positioned in three-dimensional space, creating an illusion of depth perception, positioning them in front of or behind the viewing screen. Binocular disparity refers to the difference captured by two cameras in computer stereovision. The disparity of an object in a scene depends both on camera baseline and on the distance between the object and the camera. There are different techniques to realize this, such as color or polarization filters, whose intention is to separate the left and right eye views, and orient them to each eye, to produce that illusion.

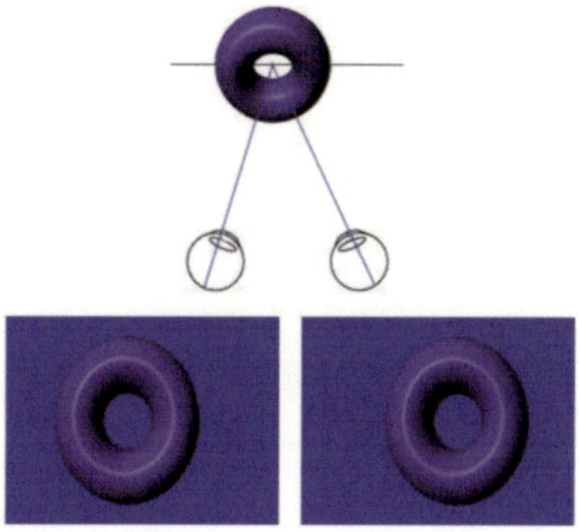

Fig. 14. Description of binocular disparity

The complexity of developing perfect binocular disparity is the cause of introducing impairments and defects on image. We pay our attention to three main factors, namely: scene content, camera baseline and screen size

6.2 3D quality systems

3D stereoscopic dimension carries all the 2-D quality assessment, but in addition some other specific factors must be analyzed to assure the QoE of the final consumer. In this chapter some general aspects to understand 3D video are described in order to justify the alternatives used in quality assessment and their differences with 2-D video.

The term 3D denotes stereoscopy, i.e. two-view system used for visualization. Due to the difficulty of creating this type of contents by the use of dual cameras, still a high percentage of stereoscopic video is obtained by the conversion of video from 2D to 3D based on the extraction of depth information from monoscopic images.

The quality is improving with this method, but it is necessary to evaluate the results in depth calculation and the experience of the final user. This aim is of vital importance in 3D quality assessment, at least until the production of all the contests are in real 3D.

Formats and Encoding 3D

Another feature to consider is the different ways of encoding the views, left and right. As both views are correlated, and present similar content with small differences between them, the techniques for compression take advantage of this feature to reduce the amount of data generated, because it is much higher the amount of data required for broadcasting, and new systems of encoding are necessary to develop its features. It is also important the synchronism, i. e. the methods used in compression are recommendable to assure that both views are seen at the same time with each eye. For this purpose, a series of systems appeared in two groups:

- Frame Compatible Service (FSC). In FSC, both views are content in the same frame. The disadvantage of this system is the reduction of resolution of the complete image (this fact affects to the global quality) but the synchronism is assured.
  There are different versions of these services: side-by-side, up-down, line-by-line and checkboard, depending on the way of distributing both views in the frame.
- Service compatible (SC). MVC (Multiview Video Coding) is the main standard for this type of services. This standard is an amendment to H.264/MPEG-4 AVC video compression standard that enables efficient encoding of sequences captured simultaneously from multiple cameras using a single video stream. MVC is the standard used in Blu-ray 3D releases, because allows older devices and software to decode stereoscopic video streams, ignoring additional information for the second view.

Also, depending on the type of 3D display, the method of assessment is different, according to the settings of each technique used. The groups of technologies according to its displaying technique are:

- With glasses:
  - Passive glasses (normally with circular or linear polarization). In FSC, both views are content in every frame. The glasses help the eyes to separate the views and redirect them to the corresponding eye.
  - Active glasses. The image is presented to each eye alternating from one view to other every frame. The system must assure the synchronism between display and glasses.
- Without glasses: Autostereoscopic. Different techniques, such as parallax barriers or lenticular displays, are used for this purpose, but there is still a lot of work in this field. Serious quality studies are developed.

6.3 Classic video methods of quality assessment

Further analysis suggested that visible 2D artifacts detract from stereo quality even more than they do in the conventional 2D (non-stereo) image.

As any type of video, sterescopic video is acceptable to be evaluated by classic methods of quality assessment, including subjective and objective (FR or NR).

These video sequences admit metrics such as PSNR or blocking and blurring measurement, because they have also be processed using same techniques as 2-D video (i.e. H.264, MPEG-2; VC-1).

But stereoscopic video has the advantage of disposing two views (left and right) well-correlated. This fact could benefit the assessment, since for normal (without excesive parallax) 3-D captures, one view could be used to predict the second one.

6.4 Visual comfort and fatigue

The visual comfort of stereoscopic images is certainly one of the most critical problems in stereoscopic research. The term visual discomfort is generally used to refer to the subjective sensation of discomfort often associated with the viewing of stereoscopic images. Sources of visual discomfort may include excessive binocular disparities, conflicts between accommodation and vergence (the simultaneous movement of both eyes in opposite directions), appearance of specific artifacts such as crosstalk or boundaries and imperfections in 3D rendering.

A large number of studies have been developed in order to predict the response of the user to this parameter, analyzing the maximum exposure time to avoid the fatigue and the main reasons of visual discomfort, in order to avoid it in the future and obtain better quality of experience. M. Lambooij reviews the principle conclusions in this field.

6.5 Parallax and depth adjustment

The parallax is the corresponding distance on the plane of the image to the inter-ocular distance when visualizing a determined object. The effect over the objects differs in the capture of the images modifying the distance between the pair of cameras used to take the stereoscopic images.

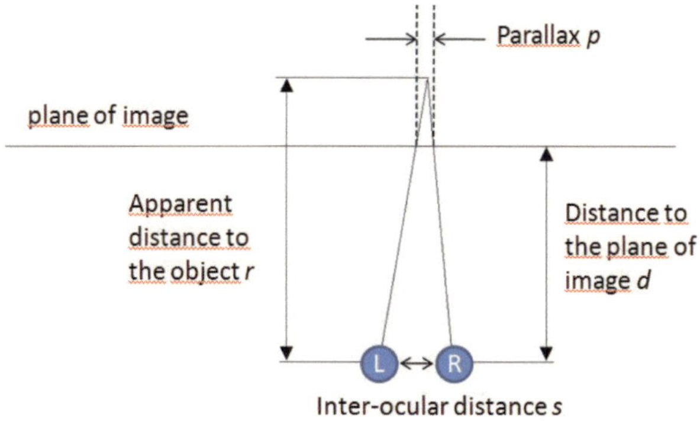

Fig. 15. Scheme of parallax distance

Hyper-stereoscopy is a very characteristic effect in 3D images in which the observer appreciates the volume of the objects much closer to them. This effect is a consequence of modifying the parallax on the image. When separating the pair of cameras a distance higher than the average of the distances between human eyes. So, it could be a reality that the hyper-stereoscopy increases the quality of experience in users who are viewing this kind of images, but it is necessary to define a limit in which this effect stops being satisfying to the users.

The quality of experience increases but it is necessary to develop new studies to determine the limits of parallax in order to develop recommendations for contents creators and broadcasters.

6.6 Artifacts related to stereoscopic systems

Crosstalk (Ghosting)

Crosstalk, also known as ghosting, is the artifact defined as the leakage of one eye's image into the image of the other eye, i.e. imperfect image separation.

Recent experiments by Tsirlin et al. describe the effect of crosstalk on the perceived magnitude of depth from disparity and from monocular occlusions.

Boundaries

Due to imperfect depth maps, a degradation artifact is particularly notably around object boundaries. This is derived from a texture-depth misalignment whose apparition is consequence of techniques of capture and processing of 3D-images and must be supressed as much as possible.

Y. Zhao proposes a novel solution of suppression of misalignment and alignment enforcement between texture and depth to reduce background noises and foreground erosion, respectively, among different types of boundary artifacts.

Puppet- theatre and cardboard effects

The puppet-theatre effect is a size distortion characteristic of 3-D images, revealed as an annoying miniaturization that make people and other objects look like animated puppets Spatial distortion prediction system for stereoscopic images.

As a result appears the cardboard effect which is a distortion resulting in an unnatural depth percept, where objects appear distributed in the image as if they were in different discrete depth planes, showing little volume.

Both effects affect to the sensation of reality, spoiling it. The puppet-theatre effect is therefore not perceived as an artifact, physically measurable; rather, but should be subjectively evaluated, as it decreases the quality of the 3D experience.

Studies from the NHK (Japan Broadcasting Corporation) research these phenomena by variation of position of the objects, and shooting, display and viewing conditions to predict the level of distortion introduced by this effect.

7. Conclusions

The large amount of studies developed for this purpose related to quality assessment gives a general idea about the importance of this theme in video compression. The evolution of metrics and techniques is constant, finding the best ways of evaluating the quality of video sequences.

A complete state of the art in quality assessment has been developed, describing techniques of subjective and objective assessment, with the most common artifacts and impairments derived from compression and transmission. In objective research,

8. Acknowledgment

This research has been developed by a member of the research group G@TV (Group of Application of Visual Telecommunications) in Polytechnic University of Madrid (Universidad Politécnica de Madrid).

The work presented on this chapter is a result of multiple studies developed through years in the field of video quality assessment, including a software implementation based on full-reference and no-reference metrics. Additionally, multiple quality studies have been developed for a wide range of purposes and projects, such as ADI, Palco HD, ACTIVA, Furia and Buscamedia were financed by Spanish Ministry of Industry

In the environment of project ADI (Interactive High Definition) subjective assessment that analyzes the impact on users of High Definition TV (HDTV) as an evolution of Standard Definition (SDTV). Besides, objective quality assessment was developed. Palco HD project led by satellite communications company Hispasat and in collaboration with TSA (Telefónica Audiovisual Services) and RTVE (Spanish Radio and Television). Activa project led by cable company ONO and Buscamedia led by communications company Indra.

Also privately funded projects in collaboration with companies such as Telefónica I+D for developing no-reference objective quality assessment in video mobile environment or with platform Impulsa TDT, developing subjective assessment in order to define video settings in High Definition TDT (Terrestrial Digital Television).

Finally, thanks to David Jiménez for introducing me in the field of video quality assessment.

9. References

Abraham, J. G.: "Sarnoff Vision Optimized MPEG-2 Encoder", University of Texas at Arlington.

Ahumada, A. J., J. & Null, C. (1993). Image quality: a multimensional problem, Digital Images and Human Vision pp. 141–148.

Alpert, Th. (CCETT), Evain, J.-P. (EBU). "Subjective quality evaluation - The SSCQE and DSCQE methodologies". EBU Technical Review, 1997.

Baroncini, V. and Pierotti, A. Single-ended objective quality assessment of DTV. Proc. SPIE 3845, 244 (1999)

Coudoux, F.X., Gazalet, M.G. , Derviaux, C. and Corlay, P. "Picture quality measurement based on block visibility in discrete cosine transform coded video sequences".

Daly, S., Held, R. T. and Hoffman, D. M.. "Perceptual Issues in Stereoscopic Signal Processing". IEEE TRANSACTIONS ON BROADCASTING, VOL. 57, NO. 2, JUNE 2011

Daly, S.. The Visible Differences Predictor: An algorithm for the assessment of image fidelity. In A. Watson, editor, Digital Image and Human Vision, pages 179.206. Cambridge, MA: MIT Press, 1993.

Farias, M. Q., "No-Reference and Reduced Referenced Video Quality Metrics: New Contributions". September, 2004. Department of Electrical & Computer Engineering, University of California, Santa Barbara, CA.

Feng, X. DCT-based Video Quality Evaluation. Final Project for EE392J, Winter 2000.

ITU Recommendation P.930, "Principles of a reference impairment system for video", 1996

Jarvenpaa, T. and Salmimaa, M., "Optical characterization of autostereoscopic 3-D displays," .J. Soc. Inf. Display, vol. 16, pp. 825–833, 2008.

Jorke, H. and Fritz, M., Stereo projection using interference filters, p.60550G, 2006.

Kooi, F. and Toet, A. "Visual confort of binocular and 3D displays," Displays, vol. 25, pp. 99–108, 2004

Lambooij, M. and IJsselsteijn, W. A. "Visual discomfort and visual fatigue of stereoscopic displays: a review," J. Imaging Sci. Technol., vol. 53, pp. 030201-1–030201-14, 2009.

Lambooij, M., IJsselsteijn, W., Bouwhuis, D.G., and Heynderickx, I. Evaluation of Stereoscopic Images: Beyond 2D Quality, IEEE TRANSACTIONS ON BROADCASTING, VOL. 57, NO. 2, JUNE 2011.

Lambooij, M.; Fortuin, M. F.; IJsselsteijn, W. A. and Heynderickx, I. "Visual discomfort associated with 3D displays," in 5th Int. Workshop Video Process. Quality Metrics for Consum. Electron., 2010.

Lee, C., Lee, J., Lee, S., Lee, K. , Choi, H., Seo, G. and Park, J.. Full Reference Video Quality Assessment for Multimedia Applications. Dept. Of Electrical and Electronic Eng., Yonsei University, Seoul, South Korea

Liu, K., Xu, Y., Loncar, M. "Reduced slab boundary artifact in multi-slab 3D fast spin-echo imaging". Editorial Wiley.

Liu, S. and Bovik, A. C.: "Efficient DCT-Domain Blind Measurement and Reduction of Blocking Artifacts. IEEE Transactions on Circuits and Systems for Video Technology, vol. 12, nº.12, diciembre 2002.

López, J.P., Díaz, M., Jiménez, D. and Menéndez, J. M. "Tiling effect in quality assessment in high definition digital television". 12th IEEE International Symposium on Consumer Electronics- ISCE2008, ISBN: 978-1-4244-2422-1, Vilamoura, April 2008

López, J.P., Jiménez, D., Díaz, M. and Menéndez, J. M. "Metrics for the objective quality assessment in high definition digital video". IASTED International Conference on Signal Processing, Pattern Recognition and Applications (SPPRA) 2008.

Masaoka K. et al., "Spatial distortion prediction system for stereoscopic images," J. Electron. Imaging, vol. 15, no. 1, p. 013002, 2006.

Moorthy, A.K. and Bovik, A.C. "Visual Quality Assessment Algorithms: What Does the Future Hold?", International Journal of Multimedia Tools and Applications, Special Issue on Survey Papers in Multimedia by World Experts, Vol: 51 No: 2, Page(s): 675-696, February 2011.

MSU Graphics & Media Lab (Video Group). "MSU Quality Measurement Tool: Metrics information". http://compression.ru/video/quality_measure/info_en.html

Pala, S. , Stevens, R. and Surman, R. "Optical crosstalk and visual comfort of a stereoscopic display used in a real-time application," in Stereoscopic Displays and Virtual Reality Syst. XIV, 2007, pp. 649011.1–649011.12.

Pan, C. C. , Lee, Y. R. , Huang, K. F. and Huang, T. C. "Crosstalk evaluation of shutter-type stereoscopic 3D display," in Soci. for Inf. Display, 10 2010, pp. 128–131.

Pinson, M. and Wolf, S. Comparing subjective video quality testing methodologies. Institute for Telecommunication Sciences (ITS), National Telecommunications and Information Administration (NTIA), U.S. Department of Commerce.

Punchihewa, A. and Bailey, D. G. "Artifacts in Image and Video Systems: Classification and Mitigation". Institute of Information Sciences & Technology, Massey University

Recommendation ITU-R BT.500-11. "Methodology for the subjective assessment of the quality of television pictures".

Salmimaa, M. and Jarvenpaa, T. "3-D crosstalk and luminance uniformity from angular luminance profiles of multiview autostereoscopic 3-D displays," Journal of Society for Information Display, vol. 16, pp. 1033–1040, 2008.

Schor, C. M. and Wood, I. "Disparity range for local as a function of luminance spatial frequency," Vision Res., vol. 23, pp. 1649–1654, 1983.

Seuntiens, P. J. H., Meesters, L. M. J. and Ijsselsteijn, W. A. "Perceptual attributes of crosstalk in 3D images," Displays, vol. 26, pp. 177–183, 2005.

Tam, W. J., Speranza, F., Yano, S., Shimono, K. and Ono, H. "Stereoscopic 3D-TV: Visual Comfort". IEEE TRANSACTIONS ON BROADCASTING, VOL. 57, NO. 2, 2011

Tan, K.T. and Ghanbari, M. "Blockiness detection for MPEG-2 coded video", IEEE Signal Processing Letters, vol. 7, no. 8, pp. 213-215, 2000.

Tsirlin, I., Laurie M. Wilcox, and Robert S. Allison. "The Effect of Crosstalk on the Perceived Depth From Disparity and Monocular Occlusions", IEEE TRANSACTIONS ON BROADCASTING, VOL. 57, NO. 2, JUNE 2011

Video Quality Experts Group (VQEG). Final report from the video quality experts group on the validation of objective quality metrics for video quality assessment phase I. http://www.its.bldrdoc.gov/vqeg/projects/frtv phaseI, 2000.

Vlachos, T. Detection of blocking artifacts in compressed video. Centre for Vision, Speech & Signal Process., Surrey Univ., Guilford.

Wang, Z., Bovik A.C., Sheikh, H.R. and Simoncelli, E. P. Image Quality Assessment: From Error Visibility to Structural Similarity.

Wang, Z., Bovik, A.C. and Evans, B., "Blind measurement of blocking artifacts in images" IEEE International Conference on Image Processing, 2000.

Wang, Z., Lu, L. and Bovik, A.C.. "Video Quality Assessment Based on Structural Distorsion Measurement". Signal Processing: Image Communication, Vol. 19, No. 1, January 2004.

Wedi, T., Kashiwagi Y.. "Subjective quality evaluation of H.264/AVC FRExt for HD movie". Joint Video Team (JVT) of ISO/IEC MPEG & ITU-T

Wilcox, L. M. and Stewart, J. A. D., "Determinants of perceived image quality: Ghosting vs. brightness," in Stereoscopic Displays and Virtual Reality Syst. X, 2003.

Winkler, S. Digital Video Quality: Vision models and metrics. John Wiley & Sons, Ltd. 2005

Winkler, S. "A perceptual distortion metric for digital color video." in Proc. SPIE, vol. 3644, pp. 175–184, San Jose, CA, 1999.

Winkler, S.: "Issues in vision modeling for perceptual video quality assessment." Signal Processing 78(2): 231–252, 1999.

Winkler, S.: "The Evolution of Video Quality Measurement: From PSNR to Hybrid Metrics". IEEE Trans. Boradcasting Vol. 54, No. 3, September 2008.

Winkler, S.: "Video Quality and Beyond", European Signal Processing Conference (Eusipco 2007), 2007.

Woods A. J. and Tan, S. S. L. "Characterising sources of ghosting in time-sequential stereoscopic video displays," in Stereoscopic Displays and Virtual Reality Syst. IX, 2002.

Woods, A. J. "Understanding crosstalk in stereoscopic displays," in Three-Dimensional Syst, Appl., 2010.

Woods, A. J. and Harris, C. R. "Comparing levels of crosstalk with red/cyan, blue/yellow, and green/magenta anaglyph 3D glasses," in Stereoscopic displays and applications XXI, 2010, pp. 0Q1–0Q12.

Woods, A. J. and Rourke, T. "Ghosting in anaglyphic stereoscopic images,"in Stereoscopic Displays and Virtual Reality Syst. XI, 2004.

Yamanoue H., M. Okui, and F. Okano, "Geometrical analysis of puppet-theatre and cardboard effects in stereoscopic HDTV images,"IEEE Trans. Circuits Syst. Video Technol., vol. 16, no. 6, pp. 744–752, 2006.

Yu, Z.,Wu, H. R., Chen, T. (2000). A perceptual measure of ringing artifact for hybrid MC/ DPCM/DCT coded video. In Proc. IASTED International Conference on Signal and Image Processing, pp. 94–99, Las Vegas, NV.

Zhao, Yin, Ce. Zhu, Zhenzhong Chen, Dong Tian, and Lu Yu. Boundary Artifact Reduction in View Synthesis of 3D Video: From Perspective of Texture-Depth Alignment, IEEE TRANSACTIONS ON BROADCASTING, VOL. 57, NO. 2, JUNE 2011.